Books should be returned or renewed by the last date
above. Renew by phone **08458 247 200** or online
www.kent.gov.uk/libs

796.35865

Libraries & Archives

CUSTOMER SERVICE EXCELLENCE
UK
The Government Standard

Kent
County
Council

made minced meat-based lunches.

Phil Tufnell played 42 Test matches and 20 One-Day Internationals for England between 1990 and 1997. In a 17-year first class career, he took more than 1,000 wickets with his left-arm spin. Following retirement in 2002, Tufnell became a hugely popular TV personality. He was the winner of I'm a Celebrity, Get Me Out of Here! in 2003, and enjoyed a long run in Strictly Come Dancing in 2009. Current broadcasting commitments include being team captain on A Question of Sport and regular features on The One Show. Since 2003 he has been a star turn of Test Match Special. In 2011, he was awarded an honorary doctorate from Middlesex University.

Justyn Barnes, who collaborated with Phil Tufnell on the writing of this book, is the editor and author of more than 40 books, including The Reduced History of Cricket, Freddie Flintoff: England's Hero and Four More Weeks: Diary of a Stand-in Captain with Mark Ramprakash. A Tavare-esque 36 not out in 30 overs for London Schools Under-15s represented the height of his cricketing achievements and his strike rate deteriorated thereafter. He bonded with Phil over their shared interests in quirky human behaviour, fine wines and home-

TUFFERS'

ALTERNATIVE GUIDE TO THE ASHES

PHIL TUFNELL

with Justyn Barnes

headline

First published in 2013 by
HEADLINE PUBLISHING GROUP

First published in paperback in 2014 by
HEADLINE PUBLISHING GROUP

1

Cataloguing in Publication Data is available from the British Library

Paperback ISBN 978 0 7553 6295 0

Typeset in Minion by Avon DataSet Ltd,
Bidford-on-Avon, Warwickshire

Printed and bound in Great Britain by Clays Ltd, St Ives plc

Headline's policy is to use papers that are natural, renewable and recyclable
products and made from wood grown in sustainable forests. The logging
and manufacturing processes are expected to conform to the environmental
regulations of the country of origin.

HEADLINE PUBLISHING GROUP
An Hachette UK Company
338 Euston Road
London NW1 3BH

www.headline.co.uk
www.hachette.co.uk

To all the English and Aussie cricketers who've made
Ashes history, from the legends to the leg ends.

ACKNOWLEDGEMENTS

Justyn Barnes – for your exceptionally hard work and for creating a fun atmosphere in which to produce this book.

Neil Robinson, his assistants Zoe English, Linda Gordon, Andrew Trigg and all the team at the MCC Library, Lord's – your kind cooperation and access given to your amazing archive of cricket books was invaluable.

My Twitter followers – for contributing hundreds of brilliant (and bizarre) #tuffersashes tales that summed up just why the Ashes means so much to so many people.

John English – for your sharp eye and editing skills.

Benj Moorhead – for doing everything possible to ensure I've got my Ashes facts straight.

Jonathan Taylor, Holly Harris and all at Headline – for backing 'the difficult second book' all the way.

Mike Martin – for taking care of business.

My Dawnie – for your love and support as always.

CONTENTS

INTRODUCTION

I inherited my passion for the Ashes from my dad, who used to bunk over the fence at Lord's and The Oval as a boy to watch the matches. He occasionally talked to me about the West Indies and other teams, but it was really all about the Aussies for him. He would tell me, 'I saw Don Bradman play', 'I saw Keith Miller'. Miller was his ultimate cricketing hero – a handsome fella, former fighter pilot and a daredevil cricketer who played like a man who'd cheated death and enjoyed himself whether he was playing or pulling an all-nighter.

Growing up in the seventies, Australia just seemed to be the place to be for cricket. Cricket in England was still quite reserved and the game in Australia appeared to be more exciting. There was the World Series, day–night floodlit cricket, the coloured kits. Although Kerry Packer's breakaway World Series ruined the Ashes – and Test cricket – for a while, his innovations did change the game and revive it as an entertainment.

Playing in Australia was very sexy. It was like the Indian Premier League is these days. Everyone wanted to go there.

That feeling only got stronger for me when I started making my way at Middlesex Cricket Club in the eighties. I remember our West Indian fast bowler, Wayne Daniel, telling me: 'Tuffers, it's the only place to go. Australia, that's where it is. All the guurrls. Everything's big, man.'

All our senior pros who'd played for England – Mike Gatting, John Emburey, Paul Downton, Norman Cowans, etc. – said the same. Ask them the best ground they've ever played at?

'Sydney' or 'The MCG'.

What's the best country you've ever toured?

'Australia.'

Every time.

Lovely to get picked for India or Sri Lanka, but Australia was the ultimate.

First, they said that's where you made your reputation as a cricketer. Second, you had a brilliant time doing it.

I was so lucky that my introduction to Test cricket was to go on an Ashes tour, and it exceeded my expectations. In many ways, I fitted in better in Australia than in England.

I was never one for mixing with opposition players, but I fell in love with the Aussie people in general. I liked their upfront attitude. And they were cricket-mad, enjoyed a beer, having a party – I was thinking, 'Crikey, this is the way to live.'

England was all rather buttoned up and I felt a bit of an outsider. I was the oik who played at the poshest club in England. I think that's how the Aussies saw me – they have always had a culture where they've needed a bit of fight to kick back against the establishment and when they see someone doing well in spite of being a bit rebellious, they're like, 'Good on ya.'

The amount of people who came up to me and said, 'Eh, Tuffers, you shoulda been an Aussie, mate. You're one of us.' Someone like Mike Atherton was a tough, nuggety cricketer in the mould of an Australian player, but their fans didn't see that 'larrikin' side to him. There is a free-spirited side to me that the Aussie people seemed to relate to.

Having said all that, as an English cricketer, there's no country I wanted to beat more than Australia. The feeling was mutual for the Aussie boys. 'As an Australian, it's bred into us at an early age that we can accept defeat from anyone except England,' said Merv Hughes.

That all goes back to the history between the two countries, and the fact that Australia did not become a separate country from England until 1901, and it's this 'Empire v Colony' tradition which helps to give the Ashes series a unique edge. There's a huge amount of patriotic pride and passion involved and that can spill over.

Take Ian Botham and Ian Chappell. Both great players and competitors and quite similar personalities in many ways, but they can't be in the same room together. Their feud started with an altercation in a Melbourne bar back in 1977, the details of which depend on which side you listen to, but included 21-year-old Beefy pushing or punching Chappell off his bar stool. More than three decades later, in 2010, a chance crossing of paths in the car park of the Adelaide Oval cricket ground ended up with another dust-up between the two old warriors. Just goes to show the depth of feeling the Ashes rivalry can arouse.

Generally, though, the battles are confined to hard-fought cricket contests. There was a short exchange between Colin Cowdrey and Jeff Thomson during the Perth Test in 1974 that sums up the competitive spirit of the Ashes for me.

Forty-something Cowdrey had come out as a replacement for the injured John Edrich, a victim of Thomson's harum-scarum bowling. But Cowdrey was a fine and brave player of fast bowling, moving into line against Thommo's frighteningly quick deliveries.

Thommo was a long-haired young tearaway. Cowdrey was the quintessential English gentleman-type cricketer as Thomson's fellow bowler, Max Walker, recalled: 'Colin arrived in Perth, about 43 degrees, pear-shaped man, wearing a pin-striped suit, three-piecer . . . the only thing missing was the bowler hat.'

The contrast between the two men could not have been greater and yet at a drinks break, Cowdrey went up to Thomson, offered his hand and said: 'How do you do, I'm Colin Cowdrey.'

'G'day, I'm Jeff Thomson.'

The polite introductions done and drinks consumed, Thommo then resumed trying to knock Cowdrey's block off. I say, pitch the odd one up, old boy!

This is just one of hundreds of Ashes stories I've discovered during the making of this book. The project has been a huge eye-opener for me. Even though I played in five England–Australia Test series and now have the pleasure of commentating on the Ashes for BBC *Test Match Special*, I've realised I didn't know very much at all about its rich 131-year history.

By digging into my own Ashes memories and comparing to the anecdotes of other participants from both England and Australia, I've tried to give you an insight into every aspect of the ultimate cricket experience: squad selection, team tactics, odd rituals, outrageous antics, magic performances, red-faced cock-ups, turning points on the pitch, barmy nights off it, funny sledges, behind-the-scenes bust-ups . . . and everything else in between. Along the way, I'll offer my own sideways slant on famous – and infamous – incidents and introduce you to some incredible characters and obscure Ashes tales you may never have heard before.

For me, the Ashes has always been the most exciting sporting event in the world. What I've learnt on my time-travelling journey back and forth between eras has confirmed just why it is so special and will only increase my enjoyment of series to come. I hope this book does the same for you too.

Phil Tufnell, March 2013

CHAPTER I

SQUAD SELECTION

GO FOR THE BURN

In the run-up to an Ashes series, one of the favourite pastimes of cricket fans, journalists, ex-players and pundits is speculating who will be picked for the squad. It's a nerve-racking time for players in contention for a place, with their destiny resting in the hearts and minds of selectors. And there is a long and proud history of English and Aussie selectors making, to be polite, eccentric choices. I mean, I was informed that my selection for my first Ashes series might depend on losing the ponytail I was sporting at the time. Sounds ridiculous but, strangely enough, it was soon after Mike Gatting frogmarched me to the barber's to get it chopped off during a Middlesex game that I received my Test call-up.

One of my favourite selection stories occurred way back in

1890 when the Australia touring side included a Tasmanian fella called E. J. K. Burn. He was a half-decent batsman, but for some reason the selectors chose him as wicketkeeper for the 1890 series. It was only during the voyage to England that they discovered that he'd never kept wicket in his life. If I'd been in Burn's shoes, with the prospect of an all-expenses paid trip to the other side of the world, I'd probably have kept my head down too until my contract was signed and the ship a long way out of port. I can just imagine their first practice session on the ship.

'Where's your gloves, Burn?'

'Er . . .'

Luckily for Australia, they also had John 'Black Jack' Blackham aboard. Black Jack had been regarded as the finest wicketkeeper in the world over the previous decade. He was known for keeping closer to the wicket than anyone else and unlike many at that time, rarely bothered with a long-stop fielder to pace bowlers to back him up.

Even though he was knocking on a bit, 36 years old by 1890, he showed he'd lost none of his sharpness on the tour and luckily for Australia, Burn's wicketkeeping services were not required.

HOW MANY SELECTORS DO YOU NEED TO WIN THE ASHES?

The England selectors were in vintage form for the 1950/51 series. After the team got battered by Bradman's boys on his last tour in 1948, a selection committee was formed in 1949 to give them two years instead of the usual one to prepare for the return in Australia.

The committee included no fewer than five MCC selectors and four Test selectors so there was plenty of manpower. Between them they managed to do the sum total of bugger all until a couple of months before the series, at which point they thought they better find themselves a skipper. So they asked Yorkshire captain Norman Yardley if he fancied the job and he told them he wasn't available to tour. They then tried George Mann, who also said no because he was busy with his family's brewery business.

Does anyone want to captain England?

In the end, they leapt on all-rounder Freddie Brown after he smashed a quickfire century for the Gentlemen v Players at Lord's. Freddie had had a chance at captaining England before but without success, and he certainly wasn't expecting the offer – he was actually booked to go on a slightly less prestigious cricket tour with a Northamptonshire engineering works team.

Instead, aged 38, and despite modest averages with bat and ball in his previous nine Tests, he found himself not only on an England tour again for the first time in 18 years, but in charge.

With Freddie added to the selection committee, there was a grand total of 11 selectors (the non-touring England captain of that season was also on board), a team in itself to choose the 17-man squad ... and one of the 17 was Freddie. The Aussies had a mere three selectors in comparison. If nothing else we were going into the series beating Ozzie on sheer weight of selectors.

But making decisions by massive committee proved to be, well, bizarre.

Amazingly, Bill Edrich, England's leading batsman on the previous Ashes tour and an ace slip fielder to boot, was omitted. Young Frank Lowson, who'd scored 2,000 runs during 1950 in only his second season for Yorkshire, was also left behind. His fielding was thought too weak, apparently. But a place was given to bowler John Warr, who in the words of the acclaimed author and journalist E. M. Wellings 'had not begun to learn to field'.

And ahead of Lowson, the selectors also went for three Cambridge University students.

Jack Hobbs predicted: 'We shall get a towsing in Australia.' And a press critic said West Indies should be taking on Australia instead as he couldn't see the point of sending another inadequate England side over to get stuffed again. Quite an achievement to choose a squad so weak that it made people think the Ashes contest should be completely scrapped.

As it happened, led by big-hearted Freddie, England acquitted themselves reasonably well in the series despite being outclassed. They bowled bravely, but minus Edrich their batting line-up was fatally weakened. And the less said about the Cambridge Uni toffs the better. After losing the first four Tests, England did manage to win the final rubber, breaking Australia's 25-match unbeaten run. The victory must have delighted England's Selector XI. Maybe if we'd have had 55 selectors we would have whitewashed the Aussies?

WHEN SYDNEY WENT TO SYDNEY

One of the joys of the Ashes, though, is when what appears to be the oddest selection for a squad proves to be inspired. And none has looked much madder or proved more inspired than that of dynamite bowler Sydney Francis Barnes for the 1901/02 tour.

S. F. Barnes wouldn't even have been considered but for Lord Hawke – an England selector who was notorious for putting his adopted club, Yorkshire, before country – refusing to let premier Yorkshire bowlers Wilfred Rhodes and George Hirst go on the tour. Hawke claimed they were too tired, but the real reason was a 'Battle of the Roses' clash of egos between Hawke and the Lancashire and England captain Archie MacLaren.

So Archie was bowler-lite and 28-year-old Barnes, who had little first-class experience, made the right impression at the right time. Making a rare appearance for Lancashire's first XI against Leicestershire in August 1901, Barnes impressed, taking six wickets.

'That man is a fine bowler. I'm going to ask him to join my team to Australia,' MacLaren reportedly told senior players afterwards.

Barnes assumed it was a joke when Lancashire batsman Albert Ward asked him if MacLaren had said anything about going to Australia. When he received a telegram during a Lancashire League game a few days later inviting him to tour, Barnes still thought it was a dressing-room prank. It was only when his Burnley captain ordered him off the pitch to accept the offer that he knew it was for real.

MacLaren was pilloried by the London press for selecting the untried Barnes to try and regain the Ashes – one paper suggested he be put in a lunatic asylum. But there was method in his supposed madness. Okay, Barnes had never even seen a Test match, but MacLaren, who'd toured Australia twice before (and averaged 40 with the bat) had a hunch that his style would be suited to the conditions and his unusual ability to bowl kind of medium-pace spinners would bamboozle the Aussies. He was right. Very right.

Fittingly, Sydney took his first Ashes wicket in Sydney, a casual one-handed caught-and-bowled of Victor Trumper, one of the world's best batsmen. He bowled a whopping 131.2 overs in the first two Tests, taking 19 wickets at just under 16 runs apiece, including three five-fers, before limping out of the Third Test. The score was 1–1. Without Sydney for the rest of the series, England went down 4–1.

In the space of just two Tests, he'd established himself as a world-class bowler. He went on to become England's most successful bowler in Australia of all time, taking a further 58 Test wickets on two further tours. And if it hadn't been for Lord Hawke being a bit of an egotistical sod, it might never have happened for Sydney.

DON'T LISTEN TO THE OPPO

When the Aussies arrived in England for the 1989 series, they actually tried to encourage the selectors to pick Ian Botham by making public 'Bring on Botham!'-type comments. Captain

Allan Border said later it was because they wanted to beat an England side with him in it and also because they didn't think he was still capable of performing to the superhuman standards of 1981 any more.

Whether the Australians' tub-thumping had any influence or not, Botham was brought in for the Third Test that summer with England already 2–0 down. And sure enough at the age of 33, while he had all the fighting spirit of old he wasn't able to turn the tide. A miserable Ashes summer for Beefy was complete when he dislocated a finger trying to take a sharp chance in the slips in the Fifth Test, ruling him out of the final game at The Oval.

HOW DO YOU SOLVE A PROBLEM LIKE PHILIPPE?

As S. F. Barnes proved, just because you're an excellent player doesn't necessarily mean you are the easiest character to deal with. For instance, by all accounts, my predecessor for Middlesex and England, Philippe-Henri Edmonds, was a tricky bloke to manage. A very educated chap, Phil didn't particularly like to be told what to do and, like Mrs Merton, enjoyed a heated debate – he was one of the few people I saw argue with Mike Brearley when he was captain at Middlesex. But he also happened to be the best left-arm spinner in the country for many years.

When Bob Willis was Phil's England skipper in the early eighties, he lost patience with him. Breaking point came when he asked Phil to keep things tight and instead he bowled a bouncer that flew straight over wickie's head for four byes – quite an achievement for a spinner!

Concluding that Phil was more trouble than he was worth, Bob didn't pick him on the next tour of Oz in the winter of 1982/83, taking Eddie Hemmings, Vic Marks and Geoff Miller instead, which judged on pure playing ability was ridiculous. Bob later admitted he made a mistake: 'He was probably a better bowler than the guys we took. Leaving him out was me being weak.' Alec Stewart said a similar thing after omitting Andy Caddick and me from the 1998/99 series.

When you are on those long tours, you do need good tourists, so I can understand why a captain may think I don't need someone like this fella giving me grief for three or four months. But, equally, it's dangerous to leave your best players at home.

I think Gatt had the right attitude when it came to whether or not to select supposedly awkward players for an Ashes series, which was basically, bring them on and I'll manage them. He didn't hesitate to pick Phil Edmonds for the 1986/87 tour, and it worked out brilliantly. Having captained Phil at Middlesex, he'd discovered he didn't have nearly as many arguments with him as Brearley did, mainly because in Gatt's words, 'I wasn't as educated as Brears, so a lot of it went over my head. Phil could be an idiot, but on that tour he was tremendous.'

IF YOU'RE NOT IN THE SQUAD, STAY CLOSE

For those in contention to be selected for an Ashes tour, not making the final squad is a terrible disappointment. But it needn't be the end of the road. In my day, if you didn't make the cut, you'd always try to go and play some club cricket in Australia while the series was on because there was half a chance you'd get a call-up. Given an injury or two, the selectors might look around and go, 'Oh, Chris Lewis is playing down the road. Ask him to come along – saves flying someone out.'

On my second tour of Oz in 1994/95 just about everyone seemed to be getting injured. Our vice-captain Alec Stewart broke his index finger, recovered in time for the First Test in Brisbane, broke it again in the Second Test and missed the rest of the series. Shaun Udal broke a finger in the first match of the tour at Lilac Hill. Joey Benjamin and Devon Malcolm got chickenpox. Phil 'Daffy' DeFreitas did his groin getting out the shower. Darren Gough, Graeme Hick, Craig White and Martin McCague all got sent home. Neil Fairbrother was brought out as a replacement and got injured himself. Things got so ridiculous that our physio Dave Roberts was called up as an emergency fielder for a game in Bendigo – he promptly broke his index finger in fielding practice so he couldn't do massages.

Hilariously, the only players who were fit and available for every match were Goochy and Gatt, at 41 and 37 respectively, the oldest boys in the squad, wicketkeeper Steve 'Bumpy' Rhodes and me!

This was the tour when chairman of selectors Ray

Illingworth had announced we were going to 'fight fire with fire', choosing the inexperienced Benjamin and Northern Ireland-born, Aussie-bred fast bowler McCague (or 'the rat who joined the sinking ship' as a Sydney newspaper famously labelled him) and controversially leaving out Angus Fraser. Instead, we found ourselves fighting fire with a load of crocked bowlers, and Gus, who'd shrewdly chosen to play club cricket in Sydney, was fit and ready for the call. It came sooner than he can ever have imagined – he was drafted into the squad before the series even began when Dev went down with chickenpox 48 hours prior to the First Test. Then McCague had a shocker in the first innings, ate a dodgy oyster at an official reception and cried off the second innings with a stomach upset before a stress fracture in his back ended his tour. By the Third Test, with us getting smashed out of sight, Illingworth had to eat humble pie and put Gus into the starting eleven. He ended up playing in the last three matches, taking plenty of wickets and showing why he should have been in the squad in the first place.

So, in conclusion, squad selection is not an exact science. And sometimes in the past, it's not what you know, it's who you know . . . and sometimes, even, where you choose to take your holidays.

CHAPTER 2

PRE-TOUR PREPARATION

LET'S GET PHYSICAL AT LILLESHALL

Before central contracts, the training the England squad did as a unit before tours was pretty limited. I remember doing a bit of pre-Ashes training at the National Sports Centre in Lilleshall for a week or ten days, but it was basically just our physio Laurie Brown taking physical jerks (I'm talking about the exercises, not us players . . .).

We all dragged our lazy arses to this place in the middle of Shropshire. You were given a cell of a room, got up at the crack of dawn for a breakfast of greasy egg and bacon or some muesli, then went out in the freezing cold for a run round the AstroTurf. Touch your toes, then go and have a net.

The net sessions could last two-and-a-half hours. Just bowling on a slab of concrete.

Everyone had new balls which would be pinging around. It was all right for the batters who could go in for 25 minutes and they were done, but there were no net bowlers, so we'd just have to bowl and bowl and then bowl a bit more. By the end, my arm was hanging off. Then maybe we'd have a swim because someone had decided swimming was really good for you.

Occasionally, a sports psychologist or someone like that would come in to talk to us. And we'd all sit there sweating and knackered, not really listening because we'd been training for about six hours. There didn't seem to be any real science to it, it was just a matter of getting it done.

As you can tell, I loved it. But I much preferred the so-called 'warm-weather training' trips to Vale do Lobo in Portugal we did in pre-season with my club, Middlesex. There the main priority was a golfing break in the sunshine. The resort didn't even have a cricket pitch.

'Why have we come here, Gatt?'

'Why do you think . . . shut up!'

They put down 22 yards of concrete for us with a mat on it on a bit of old scrub at the back. We were trying to do fielding practice and balls were bouncing up all over the place, hitting us on the head.

'Oh, this is a bit dangerous . . . anyway, what time are we teeing off?'

Highly professional.

BOOT-CAMPING HELL

I thought Lilleshall was bad, but thank God I retired before the trend for pre-Ashes boot camps kicked in.

Going into the 2006/07 series, the Australians were desperate for revenge. They were confident – Brett Lee was signing souvenir cricket balls 'Aust–Eng 2006/07 – 5–0' long before the series started and coach John Buchanan was willing to do whatever it took to make sure the players were ready so that the defeat of 2005 in England would not be repeated. Not that the players were too happy that he was going to eat into their downtime by making them do a boot camp in the Outback (which in Australia, so I understand, is any-where that is not a town) before they headed off to play in the Champions Trophy, the Ashes and then the World Cup. Pity there wasn't a DVD of the camp, though: sadistic England fans would have enjoyed watching Ponting, Warne, McGrath and co. suffer as special forces-type commandos barked orders at them, called them by numbers instead of names, didn't allow them to speak and deprived them of sleep, food and water. The players had to lug 20-litre jerry cans filled with water up a hill, drop to do 20 press-ups whenever they disobeyed instructions, abseil face-first down a cliff and hike 5 miles in the middle of the night after being woken up by the sound of explosions near their mosquito-ridden camp.

The idea was to push the players (and the support staff who had to do it as well) to breaking point and the only way to get through it was to help each other out. Apparently, the Aussie cricketers did a lot better than the Brisbane Broncos rugby league team had the previous year and their teamwork showed when they destroyed Freddie Flintoff's team in the series.

Four years later, at the end of an extended international cricket summer, the England boys were looking forward to some time off with their families (or in the case of Stuart Broad and Graeme Swann, trips to Las Vegas). So they were not thrilled at the prospect of a pre-Ashes 'bonding' trip.

Things were looking up when they arrived at Gatwick Airport early one morning, though, as it was revealed they were heading to Munich, raising hopes of going on a massive Oktoberfest bender. Instead, on landing in Germany, they were driven to a field in the middle of nowhere by members of the Australian police force for four days of hiking, log-carrying and sleep deprivation.

Captain Andrew Strauss recalled day one where they trekked 25 miles and did about 1,000 press-ups. They weren't allowed to speak. Worst of all, they had to walk and run carrying bricks in each hand for three hours, stopping only to do press-ups or shoulder presses with bricks. 'It was the most painful thing I've ever done,' he said.

In Graeme Swann's words: 'It was easily the worst four days of my life . . . For someone like me who absolutely detests authority, being frogmarched around and told what to do was purgatory.'

If anyone swore, the whole group had to drop and do 50 press-ups. With rules like that, if I'd been there, we would all have ended up with shoulders like Vitali Klitschko. Which would have been handy because the trip concluded with the boys pairing up for a boxing session during which big Chris

Tremlett threw a body punch at Jimmy Anderson and cracked one of his ribs.

Ideal preparation for a fast bowler – not. Or is that just me?

It sounds like hell, but they did go on to retain the Ashes. And looking back, Andrew Strauss credited the trip with creating a close-knit squad that had no cliques. Aside from the physical pain, the upside was sitting round a bonfire at night talking to each other about their lives away from cricket – 'It all makes you richer as a person and tighter as a group,' claimed Strauss.

Personally, I would suggest that if you really want to know Monty Panesar's life story, a nice evening sitting round a log fire in a country pub would do the job just as well.

LEST WE FORGET . . .

I think I would have been more inspired by the trip the England squad made before the 2009 series. They travelled to Flanders, Belgium, to visit the First World War battlefields to commemorate the English cricketers who lost their lives there. During a special ceremony, Stuart Broad laid a tribute of a stone cricket ball next to the memorial for Colin Blythe, a left-arm spinner who made his debut in the 1901 Ashes series and went on to take exactly 100 wickets for England before the Great War.

That evening, the team had dinner at a local restaurant in Ypres lubricated by a few bottles of wine. This led to many strong Belgian beers being sunk at the bar next door with squaddies from the local barracks till 4.30 in the morning.

Consequently, quite a number of players were nursing monumental hangovers as they staggered aboard the coach a few hours later for their second visit to the battlefield. Freddie Flintoff didn't make it, and the first sighting of him was on their return to the hotel after the sobering experience of exploring the trenches.

As Graeme Swann recalled: 'As we passed down the corridor, he opened his door and, stark naked, with an eye open above his mischievous grin, asked: "All right, lads? Have I missed owt?"'

Fred had missed out. He later apologised to the team and was told off by the management, although a few of his hungover team-mates who had only just made the coach were grateful that he took all the flak.

Back in 2001, the Aussie team went on a similar journey. On their way to England, they stopped off at the Anzac Cove in Turkey where the Australian and New Zealand army landed and were based during the Gallipoli campaign in 1915. The idea to go there had come from a conversation between Steve Waugh and the head of the Australian army the previous year, where they'd discussed the similarities between the military and what you need to build a great cricket team – discipline, camaraderie, planning, etc.

Waugh and his team went to see where their countrymen fought trench warfare and suffered brutal conditions.

'I pondered the fate of those who died and those who froze in the trenches fighting for eight months,' wrote Waugh in his 2001 tour diary. 'I didn't have much to complain about.'

While they were there, the Aussie boys also recreated a

famous cricket game that the Anzac soldiers staged to distract the local Turks while men were being evacuated onto ships. The whole experience had a big impact on them.

'To me the Anzac spirit means being together, fighting together and looking after your mates,' said Waugh. 'These are Australian values which I want the Australian team to always carry.'

But for me, more than that, trips like these show that even though playing in the Ashes sometimes feels like going to war, it certainly isn't. Seeing first-hand what war really is puts everything into perspective. Thanks to all those brave people who fought and died, we are able to have a game of bat and ball.

'TOP OF OFF STUMP' AND OTHER TACTICAL MASTERPLANS

At Lilleshall, before the Ashes, we did talk a little about tactics and the players we'd be up against in Australia, but those discussions mainly took place in the bar with the senior players. When it came to how to bowl at the opposition batters, the conclusion reached was usually the same: top of off stump.

'Okay, he likes to hook, he's very strong through the offside, he's quite good off his legs . . . how shall we bowl to him? Top of off stump?'

'Yeah, top of off stump.'

'He's a little bit shorter, and strong on the cut shot. Where do you reckon?'

'Top of off stump?'

'Yeah, top of off stump . . . another round of beers?'

We had no special tactics whatsoever. It was like, 'You're the batsman, you got yourself picked, go and make a hundred.' As for the bowlers, most of your field placings were sorted out off the cuff on the pitch.

'Shall we put in another slip?'

'Oh, go on then.'

'Phil, do you want a short leg?'

'I don't know – what do you reckon? Oh, go on then . . .'

It makes me laugh nowadays when you hear them say, you've got to have a Plan A, B and C. We didn't even have a Plan B, and Plan A was just to get our kit on and go out and play.

Mind you, when Shane Warne arrived on the scene I do remember earwigging some comical discussions among our batters on the best way to play him. One would say: 'You've got to play with the face of the bat closed, because then if it turns, you miss it.'

'No, I think you've got to open the face . . .'

'You've got to keep your head offside of the ball . . .'

'Clear your left leg . . .'

So hang on, you've got to open the face, close the face, get your head to the offside and clear your left leg . . . it was like Twister.

Before the 1994/95 series, the coach Keith Fletcher did analyse Warne extensively on video and discussed ways of combating his flipper with the batsmen. So what happened? First Test in Brisbane, opener Alec Stewart misread the flipper straight away and got bowled, Warne took 11 wickets and Australia went one up.

Basically, no one had a clue how to play Warney.

Of course, there have been some slightly more cunning plans hatched in advance of Ashes series. None more so or more infamous than Douglas Jardine's 'Leg Theory' or 'Bodyline' tactics. However, according to members of Jardine's team, far from being a masterplan the ideas were only sketchy in his head until the 1932/33 tour actually got underway. It was only when England had success experimenting with it in Oz that it became his main bowling strategy.

Jardine's greatest concern was how to curb the great Don Bradman, who had a superhuman ability to score quickly without playing a risky shot. It appears that Jardine first got the idea that Bradman was vulnerable to short-pitched bowling directed at the body from his double-century in the final Test of the 1930 series at The Oval. It was Bradman's fourth century-plus innings (including two doubles and a triple) in his first-ever Ashes series in England – not a bad effort, and even I can understand why you might want to think of a Plan B when someone bursts onto the scene like that. But there was a short period when the pitch was damp during which Harold Larwood gave him trouble with fast rib-ticklers. England's wicketkeeper that day, George Duckworth, mentioned Bradman's discomfort to Jardine (who wasn't playing in the series) and when Jardine saw film of the innings, he is said to have exclaimed: 'I've got it . . . he's yellow!' He then started to think how they could exploit this chink in The Don's armour.

What I didn't realise was that the leg-theory tactics he developed were not brand new. Former England skipper Pelham 'Plum' Warner had set the wheels in motion a couple of decades before, in the 1911/12 series Down Under. Faced with the problem of how to stop Australia's ace attacking batsman, Victor Trumper, and the other gifted stroke-players in the Australia line-up, Plum got England's quick bowlers to aim outside leg stump and bounce the ball up around the batsman's torso. The bowling may not have carried the venom of Larwood in his prime, but the tactics succeeded in cramping the style of Trumper and co. and England stormed to a 4–1 success.

After Bradman hit 334 at Leeds in 1930, it was Plum who suggested: 'We must, if possible, evolve a new type of bowler and develop fresh ideas on strategy and tactics to curb his almost uncanny skill.' It was fitting that Plum would be appointed manager of the England touring team in 1932/33.

It's not clear whether Jardine took personal advice from Plum at this stage though. He did speak to Percy Fender, the Surrey skipper, and Nottinghamshire captain Arthur Carr. Like Jardine, Carr was public-school educated (well, until Eton expelled him, that is) and he shared Jardine's professional approach to cricket even though they were both amateurs. Carr thought it was high time England played cricket with the same tough approach as the Australians and was all for sticking it to them.

In summer 1932, Jardine asked Carr to dinner in the Grill Room at the Piccadilly Hotel along with his fast bowlers Larwood and Bill Voce, who had both been selected for the tour. That was where Jardine, over brandy and cigars, first revealed his plan to bowl fast leg theory against Bradman to the people who would actually have to do it.

Next, Jardine contacted Frank Foster, a former England fast bowler who had bowled Plum's version of leg theory back in 1911/12, to find out what field placings he used.

The weird thing was that after that, Jardine appeared to tell no one else. His vice-captain Bob Wyatt claims he didn't hear anything about it until well after they arrived in Australia. And England's other seam bowlers Gubby Allen and Bill Bowes swear that neither of them heard a word about it on the ship down to Australia.

More on Bodyline later . . .

A year before the 2005 series, England captain Michael Vaughan and coach Duncan Fletcher had worked out that they needed to match Australia's average scoring rate of 3.7 an over, reasoning that if England only scored at three an over, they'd have to bat for 30 more overs than Oz just to get the same score. Against McGrath, Warne and Lee, that was not going to happen. They knew they needed to be aggressive.

There was a big debate about whether to pick Graham Thorpe or Kevin Pietersen at number five for the Tests. Thorpey had all the experience, battling qualities and had got England out of many sticky situations over the years, but new boy KP had already shown his ability to demolish international attacks in one-dayers, averaging 150 against South Africa and also cracking a 91 against the Aussies. Vaughanie went for the bold option to fit in with his overall tactics.

Before that same Ashes, Australian coach John Buchanan

gave each player in their squad a booklet called *ASHES 2005 (. . . AND BEYOND),* which started with the following words:

WE WILL CROSS OFF EACH SERIES AS WE MARCH TOWARDS WC2007. OUR AIM IS TO NOT ONLY WIN EACH SERIES BUT ALSO TO KNOW THAT INDIVIDUALLY AND AS A TEAM, WE ARE IMPROVING OUR TOTAL PERFORMANCE.

THE VISION IS TO ARRIVE AT WC2007 THE BEST SKILLED TEAM THE WORLD HAS SEEN – TECHNICALLY, PHYSICALLY, MENTALLY, TACTICALLY & 'TEAM, THE ASCENT CONTINUES WITH THE ASHES!!'

Or not.

CHAPTER 3

GETTING THERE

NAME ON THE COFFIN

I'll never forget the excitement of going on my first Ashes tour in 1990. We met up at a hotel near Heathrow Airport the night before the flight Down Under and the England players, officials and media had virtually taken over the whole place.

The night before and the morning of departure it was a hive of activity, full on. I could feel the buzz. Drinks and nibbles were laid on in the lounge. The representatives from the different bat manufacturers were there, talking to 'their boys'. Of course, no company had recognised my unique batting talents by that point – I just had a couple of free pairs of Quasar boots – so I was sitting on my tod watching all of this.

I saw the big names coming in – Ian Botham, Allan Lamb,

David Gower, all my heroes right there in front of me.

Bloody hell – this is real. This is it. I'm actually going halfway round the world with these fellas.

There was a room where all the players went to collect their gear for the trip. Rails of blazers and trousers from Austin Reed in zip-up suit covers. Shirts and ties. Brogue shoes. Training gear, trainers, new sunglasses. Best of all, we were each given a personalised cricket bag – 'Phil Tufnell England v Australia 1990/91'. I was so proud to get that. Previously, I used to womble into the Middlesex dressing room carting my anonymous Slazenger 'coffin' and I'd look enviously at our many England players – John Emburey, Paul Downton, Mike Gatting, Norman Cowans and co. – sitting with their lovely coffins in the England colours with the Three Lions. After my first Ashes series, the Slazenger bag would be out the window and I'd take my England coffin everywhere. When I walked into away county games, people would do a double take. It was a badge that said you'd arrived. Your New Zealand, Sri Lanka tour coffins ended up in the shed, but the Ashes coffin was special.

Then you'd go back to the bar and get your gear and someone else would want you.

Press people were everywhere and occasionally players would be pulled away to speak to them.

'Phil, we need you to do an interview.'

The next thing I knew there were a dozen journalists poking Dictaphones under my nose – something I wasn't used to at all. The nearest I'd got to that was a bloke at Middlesex interviewing me for the match programme and the odd little chat with a local journalist. They were asking me for my thoughts about the Ashes series ahead and I think I managed to string a few sentences together.

I have to admit I was perhaps not as focused on the task in hand as I might have been, though. Sun, beaches, barbecues and crumpet . . . that was what was going through my mind, not whether the Sydney pitch would turn. The selectors usually pick a couple of young players to give them some experience and I fitted into that category. I wasn't expecting to play too many games, and there weren't any great expectations on me as there were on the established players. I felt like I was about to go on the best holiday ever, and my cricket heroes were coming along with me. Brilliant. I was thinking, 'What a great 18–30 holiday this will be.' Actually, that was pretty much the age range of the players and, as it turned out, I wasn't far wrong in my prediction.

'You're giving me smart clothes . . .', 'Oh, you're giving me free drinks . . .', 'Everyone wants to come and talk to me . . .'. I was very, very proud to be representing my country, but I didn't have any real concept of what that actually involved and I got a bit distracted by this new world opening up to me.

In the evening I walked into the bar and there was Ian Botham and Allan Lamb sitting there having a drink. I sidled over nervously and said hello.

They turned round and looked at me blankly. Then their eyes dropped down to the George and Dragon patch on my blazer . . .

'Oh, are you coming with us?' said Botham.

'Yeah, 'fraid so. I'm Phil Tufnell.'

'Ah, pull up a chair and have a drink, then.'

There was a bit of small talk with me mostly listening, nodding and laughing in the right places. Then, about ten minutes in, Lamby says: 'So what exactly do you do, Phil?'

'I'm a left-arm spinner.'

'That's handy, we could do with one of them. Another beer?'

And that's how it all began.

At the airport the following day, people were clapping and shouting encouragement as we walked through check-in. Another new experience for me – it was the first time I'd been part of a team that stopped the traffic – and gave me a taste of how much the Ashes means to the English people. Just as it always has. When 'Plum' Warner led the England touring side in 1903/04, he'd expected a few friends to turn up to see the team off. Instead, when they gathered at London St Pancras station to start the long journey to Australia it was packed with well-wishers.

'I was simply amazed at the sight that greeted me,' he wrote later. 'Every class in the community was represented, from the Lord Chief Justice of England, President of the MCC, to "Master Bones, the butcher's boy", who on Saturday afternoon plays for the third Eleven of the Pinner Peripatetics!'

At the airport in 1990, I was the butcher's boy – well, the silversmith's son anyway – but I wasn't there just to wave the star players off, I was going with them.

FROM THE RAJAH OF BHONG TO EEYORE

The first challenge of an Ashes tour is the journey to get there. It's a long enough flight, but back in the days before people flew to Oz, it would take anything between three and eight weeks to get there by boat.

Mind you, that could have been fun. To get Down Under in 1946 to play the first Ashes series after the Second World War, the England team travelled on a Ministry of War troop ship, the *Stirling Castle*. The only other passengers aboard were 600 war brides. Seventeen cricketers; six hundred women; a month-long voyage. I can't even begin to imagine how much trouble I might have got into in my younger, friskier days with such temptation so close to my cabin door. The journey back from that tour sounded all right too, with stops in places like Cairo and the Raffles Hotel in Singapore.

So how did the players pass the weeks on the ocean wave? According to 'Plum' Warner, captain of the team which regained the Ashes in 1903/04, the lads spent most of their days aboard the *Orontes* reading or playing bridge, then after dinner there was usually a dance or concert. Plum himself won first prize in the fancy-dress ball, dolled up as 'The Rajah of Bhong'.

Fancy-dress parties were always popular, and extrovert wicketkeeper Godfrey Evans might just have been the most fancily dressed in Ashes cruising history. Aboard the *Orsova* in 1954, 'Godders' rocked up for the Ball dressed as South American samba-singing superstar Carmen Miranda, in clinging corset, floral dress, and with a wig and mountain of tropical fruits perched on his head. Admiring team-mate Frank 'Typhoon' Tyson recalled: 'He rumba-ed into the saloon to the accompaniment of the ship's orchestra, playing *Aye, Aye, Aye, I Love You Very Much.* How he kept his Covent Garden headgear balanced as he danced to the rhythm of the castanets, I shall never know!'

On that cruise, dynamite young fast bowler Tyson kept himself in tip-top condition by doing laps round the decks before breakfast. No doubt, if I'd been on that ship I would have been joining Frank every morning. For breakfast.

Young Richie Benaud heading to England for the first time in 1953 also saw the voyage as a chance to get fit. He worked out a daily regime with his mate Neil Harvey. They started gently with a late breakfast followed by an autograph-signing session (the players had to sign 15,000 sheets during the 21-day journey to give out around the country). Then they went up on deck to relax before a game of over-the-net tennis with circular quoits ('This game resembled a combination of squash, tennis and badminton,' he said). After lunch, another quiet hour on deck then two more hours of deck tennis, before a sea bath or shower, dinner, more relaxing on deck then bed.

No cricket then, but all very civilised and, as Richie noted, it gave them three hours' solid exercise per day.

'When we arrived in Tilbury on 13 April, I had never been fitter,' he wrote.

Back in 1903, 'Plum' Warner's boys would practise cricket on deck for a couple of hours every afternoon. 'Capital exercise with the thermometer standing at 90 degrees in the shade,' reckoned Plum.

The low roof where they played caused a few problems, though. Apparently, 'if the bowler hit it delivering the ball', it was declared a no-ball. I'm assuming that means the ball hitting the ceiling after it was released. If the bowlers were scraping their knuckles on the ceiling as they bowled, Plum would have been desperately short of bowlers by the time they landed in Oz.

Sometimes passengers on the boat teamed up and challenged Plum's boys to a game of deck cricket. And in what must be the biggest shock in the history of Ashes warm-up matches, a team of female passengers inflicted the first defeat of the tour, winning by three runs despite the handicap of wearing huge, billowy dresses and wide-brimmed hats!

On such a long journey, you need people who are going to pitch in and try and keep team spirits high. Sydney Barnes, who I talked about in Chapter 1 (see pages 11–12) and who turned out to be one of England's greatest-ever Ashes bowlers, was not one of those people. He was a scowling, brooding fella, and after spending a couple of weeks with him on Syd's first cruise Down Under in 1901, captain Archie MacLaren was starting to regret his decision to select him.

The oriental steamer *Omrah* carrying Archie and the boys started rocking and rolling when it hit stormy waters in the Bay of Biscay. When the ship's captain warned of another storm ahead, the young lads who'd never travelled abroad by ship before were petrified, but Archie had some words of comfort. 'If we go down,' he said, 'at least that bugger Barnes will go down with us!'

In his diary of the 1897/98 tour, the legendary England

batsman (and Indian Prince) Ranjitsinhji told a happier story of their voyage on the *Ormuz* from Tilbury Docks to the port in Albany, Australia, via Naples, Port Said and Colombo.

During the journey, a sports committee was formed to arrange on-deck games for all the passengers. 'Wainwright soon became an expert at deck billiards,' reported Ranji. 'Stoddart [the England captain] was undoubtedly champion at quoits, and Hirst and Briggs were both excellent performers at "bull board".' Bull board? No, me neither.

The division between 'gentlemen' amateur cricketers and professional 'players' was very strong in Ranji's day, and that was evident in the evenings when the downtrodden pros got together on deck and sang 'plantation songs' for the passengers.

Between bull-boarding and singing, Stoddart's team also fitted in some cricket. Ranji declared that deck cricket was 'very good training for the muscles used in actual cricket. The ball comes straight and true, but occasionally comes back with the roll of the ship.' Bit like bowling on the slope at Lord's, then.

By the time they began the last leg of their voyage from Colombo to Albany the monotony of life at sea was getting to the boys. To keep themselves entertained they started arranging cricket matches for the ladies on board. Some of the women proved to be handy in the field and 'a Melbourne lady, married to a retired captain of the Dragoon Guards, developed into an excellent fast underhand bowler,' according to Ranji. He added: 'The members of our team assisted them greatly in carrying the details of the matches.' Yes, I'm sure they did . . .

Monty Noble, the Australian captain almost continuously

from 1903 to 1909, was equally chivalrous during a voyage to England once. As their boat made its way through the Suez Canal, he didn't take kindly to a dockside vendor making filthy gestures at female passengers. So noble-by-nature Monty picked up an apple, threw it and struck the offensive chap on the bonce from about 80 yards. Well in, Monty!

Like an *X Factor* contestant, my own journey to Oz was emotional. Being a nervous flier this longest of long-haul trips was never going to be a breeze.

I told the physio Laurie Brown about my flying phobia and he gave me a green pill and a pink pill to help calm me down.

'Whatever you do, don't have any alcohol with those, though, Phil.'

Yes, Laurie.

When we boarded the plane, I turned left for the first time and the first thing I did when I sat down was order myself a Rusty Nail – Drambuie and whisky. Never had one before.

Thus began a mile-high 24 hours zombified in a haze of alcohol, Temazepam and Valium.

As a young urchin, I'd never heard of Ranji, 'Plum' Warner or Monty Noble, but I was well aware of the stunning achievement of Australian batsman David Boon just a year-and-a-half before. On the flight to England for the 1989 Ashes, Boon downed 52 cans of beer on the flight over, smashing the previous record of 46 set by another stocky, mustachioed Aussie, Rod Marsh in 1985.

Marsh had set the stiff target with the assistance of his mate Dennis Lillee who had generously acted as pacemaker, matching him beer for beer from Melbourne to Honolulu.

'Then others helped out on the last two stretches as I enjoyed a good sleep,' recalled Lillee. 'When we got to London, Graeme Wood and I were fresh enough to help him off the plane.'

Pint-sized Boon modestly denies that his record-breaking mile-high bender ever happened, but former team-mate Dean Jones (who was sitting next to him) and flight attendants (who were keeping count of the tinnies consumed) have officially confirmed his feat of drinking endurance. By the time the plane left Singapore Airport, Boon was slurping can number 23 and in steady rhythm. Eight hours later, the pilot announced the new record over the tannoy to cheers from his team-mates and fury of their coach Bob Simpson.

Unlike Marsh, who had to be carried off the plane after his effort, Jones recalls that Boon 'kinda managed to walk'. Not only that, he got through a press conference and a sponsor's cocktail party, where he had another three pints, before retiring to bed.

The binge caused Boon to sleep for two days and miss a couple of training sessions. He also got fined A$5,000 and was nearly sent home by Simpson. I'm sure the coach is relieved he didn't though, because the 'Keg on Legs' went on to score over 400 runs in that Ashes series at an average of 55.

It made me laugh to hear that Dean Jones sat next to Boon on the flight because his dad had told him to, the idea being to get as much advice as possible from an experienced pro. I think the selectors had a similar idea when they put me next to Wayne 'Ned' Larkins on the plane in 1990 and made him my first international room-mate. True, Ned was a senior player, but like Jones with Boonie, the only thing I learnt from him on the flight over was that he had an enormous capacity for alcohol. Just about the only thing I heard him say during the flight was 'Chablis' each time a stewardess came past.

So instead of discussing what to expect in my first Ashes series, I thought I'd give David Boon's beer-drinking record a crack. The memories of what followed are vague, but I think I got into the late thirties on tinnies drunk.

The combination of tranquillisers and alcohol had some strange hallucinatory side-effects. At one point, I felt like I was in a barn, sitting on hay, and was eeyore-ing like a donkey. Then, not long before we were coming in to land, I was refused a final drink by the stewardess. In my addled state, I didn't take this news too well. The next thing I knew the captain had come back from the cockpit to tell me that they would have to restrain me to the seat if I didn't calm down.

Captain Graham Gooch and coach Micky Stewart, sitting across the aisle, must have been thinking: 'What the hell have we got here?' I got told off, but some of the senior players weren't much less drunk than me, so I got off fairly lightly. Maybe it wasn't seen as a huge problem, because the previous Ashes series in Australia had been won with the same boys-on-tour mentality. People who went on that 1986/87 tour have told me it was absolute carnage.

Clearly, I wasn't in the best state when I shambled off the plane in Perth. I don't think such shenanigans would be tolerated these days. Before the boys flew to Oz for the 2006/07 series, the England and Wales Cricket Board were issuing directives about how the players should look and behave after a day in the sky. They were told to make sure they were smartly dressed (suits, ties done up straight) and walk out as a team through the airport rather than in dribs and drabs. The idea was to make a strong first impression that this was a team ready to do business.

Clearly, the sight of England's team looking spry and dapper after 30-odd hours' travel frightened the life out of the Aussies. They whitewashed us.

The away team's arrival in the airport also offers the natives an early chance to get a dig in. When Mark Taylor, who was struggling with his batting going into the 1997 series, made his way through passport control at Heathrow, the official examined his passport, looked up and said: 'Mark Taylor, eh? The Australian captain . . . But for how long?'

That's all you need and it was just the start. Before Taylor shoved the critics' words down their throats with a century in the First Test, the *Daily Mirror* stalked him trying to get him to pose with a metre-wide bat.

England medium-pace bowler John Warr was greeted off the boat at Sydney in 1950 by a docker shouting: 'Hey, Warr, you've got as much chance of taking a Test wicket on this tour as I have of pushing a pound of butter up a parrot's arse with a hot needle.' Warr proved his dissenter wrong, but only just, taking one wicket in 73 eight-ball overs in the two Tests he was selected for. For the parrot's sake, I hope the docker didn't prove himself wrong too.

Personally, I was treated to a simple, traditional welcome at Perth Airport on my first Ashes trip. As I was wobbling through the concourse, a passer-by caught my bleary eye and hailed me with a cheery 'G'day, you Pommie bastard!'

CHAPTER 4

THE BUILD-UP

PREDICTIONS, PRAWNS AND CHARMING LEN

The weeks leading up to the start of an Ashes series give players and pundits plenty of opportunities to say something daft in the media that will wind up the opposition. Before the 2005 series, former Australian bowler Terry Alderman wrote that 'anyone who got dismissed by Ashley Giles should go hang themselves', which was a little extreme. In return, Matthew Hoggard offered his opinion that legendary Aussie seamer Glenn McGrath was over the hill. Meanwhile, McGrath was predicting a wide winning scoreline for his team. 'I was saying 3–0 or 4–0 about 12 months ago, thinking there might be a bit of rain around. But with the weather as it is at the moment, I have to say 5–0.'

As it turned out all of them were wrong – Gilo took ten

wickets in the series and none of his victims committed suicide, McGrath was as brilliant as ever (when he wasn't tripping over cricket balls, that is) and Australia lost 2–1.

The defeat didn't stop McGrath predicting Aussie white-washes again in 2006/07, which proved correct, and in 2009 and 2010/11 after his retirement, which in each case proved quite wrong.

I was on the wrong end of a bit of pre-series verbals from Mark Waugh before the 1997 series. He stated in a newspaper interview that he didn't really rate me, saying that he wished I bowled more positively and had a go bowling to him round the wicket. We'd had a few battles before this, ever since he had relentlessly used the slog-sweep against me on his way to a century on his Test debut at Adelaide. He always tried to attack my bowling because he reckoned that was the best way to get on top of me.

I wasn't actually selected for the first five Tests so I didn't get a chance to prove him wrong until the final game at The Oval. There I gave Mark exactly what he wanted by bowling round the wicket to him, but he might have wished he'd kept his mouth shut because he wasn't in the best form and the ball was spinning all over the place. I got him out in the first and second innings for not many. Which was nice.

When it comes to the Ashes, the tabloid press don't bother too much about impartiality either. In 2001 the *Daily Mirror* welcomed the Aussies with the headline: 'Let's Throw A Few Prawns On The Barbie . . . And Watch England Clean Up The Ashes' with a picture of Waugh, Warne and McGrath's heads superimposed on some grilling prawns. When a journo pulled the paper out to show Steve Waugh at the first press conference of the tour, he had a good comeback: 'They don't look like Aussie prawns, they're not big enough.' And as it turned out, we certainly weren't good enough to batter Waugh's prawns.

Aussie skipper Allan Border had a less light-hearted attitude back in 1993, saying: 'I'm not talking to anyone in the British media. They're all pricks.'

At the other end of the charm scale was Yorkshireman Len Hutton who led England's team Down Under in 1954/55. Never one to make a bold statement when asked a provocative question by the Aussie press, he'd just sit there smiling, often not answering for up to 30 seconds. When he first did this, England's team manager Geoffrey Howard, sitting with him at the top table, looked round to check he hadn't fallen asleep. Eventually, he'd speak and usually come up with a dry, witty line.

And you wouldn't have thought England had any chance listening to Len.

'Noo, we 'aven't got mooch bowling,' he said. 'Got a chap called Tyson, but you won't have 'eard of him because he's 'ardly ever played . . . Batsmen? Well, we 'aven't got any batsmen really. We've got these youngsters, May and Cowdrey, but we haven't got any batsmen . . . When it comes to it, we're starting all over again. We have a lot to learn from you.'

He would also go off at massive tangents, but he did so with such charm that the spellbound Aussie reporters lapped it up. Colin Cowdrey recalled an occasion when Len was asked what he thought about Australia's star batsman Arthur Morris: 'He answered after an immense silence: "'Ave they got any sightscreens down at the bottom end at Brisbane?" Another huge silence. "Saw Arthur Morris make 196 once when the sightscreen had blown down." Then he'd lean forward, almost confidentially, to one of the reporters and say: "Remember that, Bill, the day the sightscreens blew down?'"

Under Hutton, the England team without 'mooch bowling' or any batsmen won the series 3–1. Perhaps Len's anti-hype style is the way forward for the Ashes players of today?

RENT A CAR WITH GLENN McGRATH

One thing that struck me in the build-up to Ashes series in Australia was that every time I flicked on the TV, I'd see their players in advertisements. It'd be, 'G'day, I'm Dean Jones and I do my shopping at . . .' And when we were driving around we'd see giant billboards by the road with their faces looking out at us – 'Rent a car with Glenn McGrath', that sort of thing. You'd also get the Pommie-baiting stuff – on his Ashes debut tour, the first advertising hoarding Phil DeFreitas saw was a kangaroo punching a lion.

Every other advertisement, there was an Australian Test cricketer or an Aussie Rules footballer involved – they were all national stars.

Even when they came to England, you'd see as many adverts featuring Aussie players as English players. Before the 1989 series, they did an ad for Castlemaine XXXX lager which ended up along the side of London buses. It was a picture of them all wearing the baggy green caps looking stern except for an innocent smiling Merv Hughes with beer froth on his moustache with the tagline: 'Tests prove Australians couldn't give a XXXX for anything else'.

It was a funny ad for beer-drinkers but their captain Allan Border reckoned it also sent a message to the England team that they were here to win for the baggy green and nothing else mattered.

In the eighties and nineties in England, Ian Botham was probably the only cricketer who had the individual level of celebrity to match that of the Australian Test players in their own country. Throughout my career I certainly never felt like a big star in England, even though I was seen as one of the top couple of spinners for a few years. At cricket grounds, we got the attention, but I wasn't doing adverts for Sainsbury's. I just felt like cricket was a bigger deal in Australia, that they were bigger stars who transcended the sport. Cricket hadn't opened up in that way over here at that time and it did make you feel somewhat second-class in comparison.

Nowadays, the likes of Kevin Pietersen, Alastair Cook and the boys get asked to endorse all sorts of products outside the game itself and I think there are a number of reasons for that. One is Vaughanie's boys winning the Ashes in 2005, and the English general public's reaction to that great series, and the success that has continued under Andrew Strauss and Alastair Cook. In my view things also changed a bit when I won *I'm A Celebrity . . . Get Me Out Of Here!* in 2003 – since then other cricketers have appeared on popular reality TV shows and found a wider audience.

Also, very importantly, since central contracts were introduced, the guys who play for England are actually seen as

England cricketers. We always felt like a load of county cricketers thrown together under the banner of 'England', rather than the 'Team England' of today. That feeling was heightened by the selection policies in those days, which meant that five or six places seemed to be permanently up for grabs. It was a merry-go-round, so most of us weren't seen as England players in the same way as the boys today.

Having said all that, I managed to become a TV celebrity in Australia pretty soon after arriving on my first tour. Okay, it was only because they were taking the piss out of me, but still. It all began on New Year's Day, 1991, when I made an absolute Horlicks of what should have been an easy run-out of Steve Waugh in a one-dayer at the SCG. It was the only time in my career I felt like crying on the pitch, and the Aussies didn't let me forget about it for the rest of the tour. The next few days the incident was replayed over and over on Channel 9, and one time I switched on the telly and they were talking about me on whatever their equivalent was of *The Graham Norton Show*. The next match at Adelaide, spectators unfurled a huge 'Phil Tufnell Fielding Academy' banner and my fielding just went from bad to worse under the scrutiny. As the ex-Aussie captain Ian Chappell noted, 'The other advantage England have got when Phil Tufnell is bowling is that he isn't fielding.'

I did get my own back with a bit of guerrilla advertising before the Second Test of the 2009 Ashes. A 15-metre-high image of me naked, apart from a strategically placed pot of Marmite to cover my assets, was projected onto the side of a hotel where the Aussie team were staying. Must have put them off their Vegemite, because England won the match. Well, you either love it or you hate it.

FUNCTIONAL FUN

Visiting players on an Ashes tour have always been required to attend a number of official functions in the run-up to the series. In Oz, we'd always go to a High Commission do. And in every state we went to, there'd always be a dinner.

At first, I generally found these Ashes functions to be a bit of a bore. I didn't twig until I got older that they were the best dos of the lot. These were the events where we were given the best wine and grub, and instead of just sitting with my mates I started talking to people, having a laugh with them. The posh Aussie ladies seemed to warm to my larrikin humour – 'Oh, Tuffers, you're such a laaaaff.' We had some great nights and I remember at one event, we all ended up jumping in a swimming pool.

All good fun, but the most significant official dinner in Ashes history occurred in Melbourne in 1882. It was there that Hon. Ivo Bligh (later Lord Darnley) became the first England captain to mention the 'Ashes' in a public speech. 'We have come to beard the kangaroo in his den – and try to recover those Ashes,' he said.

Most of those present at the bash wouldn't have had a clue what Bligh was on about. He was referring to the joke obituary to English cricket printed in *The Sporting Times* after England had lost to Australia at The Oval earlier that year, which lamented the 'death of English cricket . . . the body will be cremated and the ashes taken to Australia'. That article would not have been seen Down Under, but the Ashes idea soon caught on following Bligh's speech.

Sir William Clarke, president of Melbourne Cricket Club, had travelled on the same boat as the England team to Australia and he regularly invited them to his family estate in Victoria during the trip. It was there during a Christmas party that Clarke's wife Janet and the family's music teacher Florence Morphy presented Bligh with a tiny terracotta urn containing ashes. (Theories on what the ashes are the remains of have ranged from the outer casing of a cricket ball to a woman's veil, but it is most likely to be the ashes of a cricket bail.) It was just a fun gift, but the Australian press picked up on it and that's how it all began.

Bligh was so charmed by Florence Morphy, too, that they ended up getting hitched. Lord and Lady Darnley kept the urn as an ornament on the mantelpiece at their home, Cobham Hall, until the Lord's death 43 years later in 1927. His widow then gave the urn to the MCC who put it on display in the Long Room and later the Lord's Museum when that was set up in the 1950s.

While I grew to enjoy these functions around Oz, over the years their entertainment value has been variable. Back in 1950/51, the MCC squad attended a New South Wales Cricket Association reception in Sydney during which the officials of the Association and MCC stood at one end of the room, giving random speeches every now and then. The audience scattered around the room didn't listen, continuing loud conversations of their own. And it was only when the MCC captain Freddie

Brown rose to speak that people paid a blind bit of notice.

'Players were often inclined to sleep during the formal receptions,' recalled E. M. Wellings who covered the tour.

A British Sportsman's Club lunch at the Savoy in 1953 for the touring Australians sounded more entertaining. Guest speaker Sir Alan Herbert, an MP and *Punch* columnist, made the Aussies laugh, at one point reminding their fast bowlers Ray Lindwall and Keith Miller: 'When you rub the ball on your groin or belly, remember how it looks on telly.'

And in 1948, according to the legendary BBC cricket commentator Rex Alston, Don Bradman kept his audience at the Cricket Writers' Club and millions of radio listeners amused with his after-dinner speech. It was due to get 20 minutes of coverage on the old BBC Light Programme radio station (which later became Radio 2), but The Don's speech went on twice as long as expected, and the programme was allowed to run over – Bradman was 'news'.

In his speech, he suggested that England pick HRH Duke of Edinburgh, who apparently was a useful right-hand off-spin bowler.

He also referred to a false story that had just appeared in the press. The article had claimed Bradman had written a letter to a small boy who had asked for his autograph, and invited him to dinner when he played in Worcester.

'I have a letter here,' he continued, 'from a Leeds girl who says she has read the story and is looking forward to seeing me play at Headingley. She says that girls are just as keen supporters of cricket as boys, and that as a sportsman I will see fair play to the other sex and dine with her in Leeds.'

After laughter died down, Bradman concluded: 'Of course, I am not eligible, but will ask for volunteers from those members of my team who are.'

The possibility of meeting big-name cricketers attracts wealthy punters willing to pay top dollar to come to these events. Consequently, a charity auction is often part of the evening's entertainment to try and make some money for a good cause. Before the 2001 series, the Australian Cricketers' Association and Australian Cricket Board jointly hosted a function in Manchester where the first auction lot offered the chance to join in a practice session with the Aussies.

The room hadn't warmed up yet though, and the bidding stalled after a couple of bids at £275. In an effort to get the bids flowing again, Steve Waugh stuck his hand up: 'Three hundred pounds.'

Shane Warne then weighed in with a bid of £350.

Unfortunately, no one else in the room took the hint, so soon two of the greats of Aussie cricket were bidding against each other.

In the end Waugh's £500 was enough to secure him the, um, unique opportunity to train with his own team-mates.

PUNTER'S TRAUMA AND TWO-SCOOP LINDSAY

Aside from the official events, the free evenings in the run-up to an Ashes series can give players plenty of chances to enjoy themselves. In 2005, for instance, Australia's Andrew Symonds enjoyed himself a little too much on a night out in Cardiff to celebrate team-mate Shane Watson's birthday. When Symo rolled up at the ground the next morning for a one-dayer against Bangladesh, he was still merry, to say the least.

The Australians split into two groups – batsmen and bowlers – for the warm-up, and all-rounder Symonds started with the batsmen, before perhaps realising that he might be better off keeping his distance from captain Ricky Ponting. But Ponting had clocked him, and was watching as Symonds stationed himself on the edge of the bowlers' group, leant on a wheelie bin and promptly fell over.

When Ponting interrogated him, Symonds claimed he'd got back to the hotel at 'about 1.30', hard to believe given the fact that he still appeared to be a couple of sheets to the wind.

But the thing that destroyed his case was when coach John Buchanan recalled that he'd seen Symonds at breakfast at 7 a.m. An early riser, Buchanan had been surprised to see Symonds, who he'd coached at Queensland and knew he liked his sleep. Later, Ponting also remembered how Michael Clarke, usually a punctual type on match days, had run on to the team bus clutching a bacon sandwich. Turned out he'd been late because he'd had to get a spare key from reception to get into Symonds's room, who was in a deep sleep after his early breakfast, and drag him out of bed ready for departure for the ground.

A furious Ponting was forced to drop Symonds, who'd already been announced as playing, and then, to buy some time, lied to the media about the real reason. He said that Symonds hadn't fully recovered from a cold, which came as some surprise to the journalists who'd been out in the same bars as Symonds earlier that morning.

Then Australia, minus Symo, lost to Bangladesh, a side that had never come close to beating them before. Punter concluded: 'It was the most embarrassing and traumatic day of my international career.'

The skipper of the 1953 Australian side, Lindsay Hassett, was not so easily embarrassed. During their first week in England, the Aussies were dining at London's Park Lane Hotel. Captain Hassett ordered a double-scoop ice-cream for dessert, and the waiter accidentally dropped a scoop into his lap rather than into his bowl.

Rather than take up the waiter's offer to retrieve the ball of ice-cream from his groin, Hassett stood up, took off his trousers and handed them to the waiter saying, 'Have them cleaned and returned in time for coffee. Oh, and another double ice-cream please.'

TUFFERS' TEN ASHES TWEAKERS

As a member of the union, one of the pleasures of digging into the history of the Ashes has been to discover some remarkable tales of fellow spinners I knew little about before. Here's ten whose stories particularly grabbed me:

Jack Iverson

Aussie Jack made his Ashes debut for Australia in 1950/51 and he stood out for a number of reasons. For a start, he was a big fella, weighing in at around 16 stone. And while he was already 35 years old when he got his call-up, he'd only been playing first-class cricket for a year. But the thing that made Jack unique and left English batters bamboozled on that tour was his freakish grip. He held the ball between his thumb and forefinger, with his double-jointed middle finger tucked flat behind the ball against his palm. Hence the nickname, 'Wrong Grip Jake'.

The story goes that he developed his wrong grip flicking ping-pong balls and golf balls during his time serving in the Australian Defence Force in the Second World War (in school I was more of a flicking bogeys kind of lad . . .). With a cricket ball in his hand, he worked out that by flicking his middle finger in one direction or the other at the moment of release he could apply extra spin allowing him to bowl off-spin, leg-spin and fizzing top-spinners at will. So, basically, he got batsmen out by giving them the finger.

Wrong Grip Jake was the ultimate mystery spinner, and his Ashes captain and proud fellow Victorian, Lindsay Hassett, was keen to maintain his secrets. And not just from the English players but also players from New South Wales, Victoria's arch-rivals, on his own Australian team. Hassett wouldn't let Jack bowl to New South Wales players in net practice, and when Jack came on to bowl in the Ashes matches, Hassett would actually move star New South Wales all-rounder Keith Miller from his position in the slips to mid-on so he couldn't see his hand action!

For a batsman to 'pick' Jack, they had to look at his thumb, which pointed in the direction the ball was going to spin. So if the thumb was pointing towards the offside you were getting a leg-spinner, towards the legside meant a wrong 'un, and the top-spinner was bowled with the thumb aimed right at you. In the 1950/51 series, few English batsmen had a clue what Jack was going to bowl though, and he took 21 wickets at around 15 runs apiece helping Oz to a 4–1 demolition.

Incredibly for someone of his talent, those five matches were the start and end of his Test career (indeed, he only played 30-odd first-class matches in total), as family and business commitments took priority.

His Ashes experience might have been brief, but, no matter, Wrong Grip Jake will go down in history as one of its greatest bowling innovators.

Bernard Bosanquet

When 'Plum' Warner picked his Oxford Uni and Middlesex team-mate B. J. T. Bosanquet for the 1903/04 Ashes tour, he was taking a gamble that the new delivery Bosie had invented – later named the 'googly' – would baffle the Aussie batters. Bosie had come up with the off-break-that-looks-like-a-leg-break while playing a parlour game called 'Twisti-Twosti' where the aim was to bounce a tennis ball across a table so your opponent opposite couldn't get to it.

From all reports, Bosie didn't have much control over his newfangled delivery. Indeed, he would often mistime it so badly that the ball would bounce two, three or even four times before reaching the batsman.

But as Bosie didn't know what he was going to bowl, neither did the Aussies, which made him very dangerous. And when he did get his length right on the hard Australian pitches he could be devastating, as he was in the second innings of the Fourth Test in Sydney where he took six wickets in less than an hour to clinch the Ashes.

Doug Wright

This Kent and England leg-spinner toured Oz in 1946/47 and 1950/51. Doug had a high arm action and bowled at a much higher speed than other leggies of his era. This meant he could be very erratic and expensive, but when he got it right he was virtually unplayable.

On his first Ashes tour, when he was comfortably the highest wicket-taker on either side with 23 wickets, he even gave Don Bradman all sorts of trouble – Bradman said Doug was 'the best leg-spinner to tour Australia since Sydney Barnes'.

People who saw him bowl reckoned he was also one of the unluckiest bowlers in Ashes history. A handful of times in 1946/47, Doug appeared to have Bradman plumb lbw, but didn't get the decision. If only there had been the Decision Review System then . . .

Doug also made an impression due to his funky run-up, which Australian crowds used to rip the piss out of him for. 'He waves his arms widely, and rocks on his legs like a small ship pitching and tossing in a fairly heavy sea', was how the great former Aussie spinner Bill O'Reilly memorably described Doug's approach to the wicket. Others compared his skippy, stiff-legged run-up to a kangaroo.

A kangaroo skittling out the Aussies? How ironic.

Arthur Mailey

Leg-spinner Arthur's googlies were a key factor in Australia's 1920/21 Ashes whitewash, when he took a whopping 36 wickets. His bowling figures of 9 for 121 in the Fourth Test at Melbourne still stand as an Ashes record for an Aussie.

Although he was a small chap, Arthur had unusually big hands, which allowed him to give the ball a rip and he focused purely on trying to take wickets without caring how many runs they cost. It was said that he bowled like a millionaire.

As someone who enjoys art, I was interested to find out that Arthur was a very talented cartoonist too and he published many fantastic books of cricket cartoons.

Bobby Peel

A heavy-drinking, match-winning English left-arm spinner with a deadly quicker ball, Bobby Peel made a huge impact in Ashes Tests of the late nineteenth century. He took 24 wickets at under 8 runs apiece in the three-Test series of 1888 and ended up taking a total of 101 Ashes wickets in his career.

Bobby played a key role in the classic 1894/95 series Down Under, won 3–2 by England. At Sydney, after England followed on, Australia went into the sixth and final day needing just 64 to win with 8 wickets remaining. Thinking their chances of winning had gone, the England boys had had a few drinks the night before. Bobby, naturally, was in the thick of the action and had to be put under a shower in the morning just to sober up. His world-class ability to play through a raking hangover came to the fore, though, as he bagged four quick wickets and six in all as England clinched a crucial and unlikely victory by 10 runs.

Bobby could also bat a bit, once scoring a double-century for Yorkshire, but on that 1894/95 tour he became the first Test cricketer to be dismissed four times in a row for a duck.

In 1896, in the third and final Test, Australia needed just Nelson (111) in their second innings to win the match and the series at The Oval. Bobby showed his class again, taking six cheap wickets as Australia collapsed to 44 all out.

His brilliant career stumbled to a fittingly drunken end when he turned up for a Yorkshire game in 1897 totally spangled and, allegedly, had a wee on the pitch. Lord Hawke was not amused. He personally escorted Bobby from the ground and, in Bobby's own words, 'out of first-class cricket – what a gentleman!'

Chuck Fleetwood-Smith

I think I would have got on well with Chuck, who must be one of the barmiest players to play in the Ashes. He appeared for Australia against England in the late thirties and was blessed with a unique bowling talent. He was also a law unto himself, couldn't be bothered with batting or fielding and enjoyed a night out . . . hmm, remind you of anyone?

Chuck was ambidextrous and bowled with both hands as a

kid (not at the same time, I assume – that would be something special). It was typical of him that he eventually chose to bowl in the most unconventional style of all – left-arm wrist spin. Powerfully built, he generated serious revs on the ball and bowled his variations with no obvious change in his action. With such unusual skill, he should have played more for his country, but his inconsistency meant he could be expensive and the selectors tended to go for more reliable options.

On his day, Chuck was a match-winner, though, and he will always be remembered for the wonder ball which got Wally Hammond out in the final innings of the Adelaide Test in 1937. With England three down, and needing another 250-odd to win, the match was in the balance as long as Wally was at the wicket. At the start of the sixth day, Aussie skipper Don Bradman lobbed Chuck the ball. Before Hammond could add to his overnight score of 39, Chuck bowled him an early contender for 'Ball of the Century', drifting away to off in the air before biting viciously and bowling Hammond between bat and pad. Bradman later said that the Test match was decided by that one brilliant delivery. It was crucial to the outcome of the series too, bringing the score level at 2–2, and paving the way for Australia to complete a 3–2 win from 2–0 down.

But the great thing about Chuck was that even when he wasn't bowling rippers, there was never a dull moment. On the field, he could often be heard singing, making bird noises and pretending to catch butterflies. And he always had time for a chat with spectators, not worrying about small details like an Ashes match going on behind him. Well played, Chuck.

Bill O'Reilly

Leggie 'Tiger' O'Reilly was one of the greatest bowlers ever to play the game – Bradman said he actually was the best he ever faced. In the Ashes series of 1934 and 1936/37, Bill took a total of 53 wickets for Australia and with The Don plundering runs for fun it made them an irresistible force.

I liked to bowl with the aggression of a pace bowler, and Bill was the same, bowling with plenty of attitude. In his case though, he also bowled exceptionally fast for a spinner, spearing down medium-paced leg-breaks, googlies and top-spinners with a windmill action.

Bill was from the New South Wales countryside and although he was pretty much self-taught, he did have his brother Jack to thank for helping him to learn how to bowl the googly as a teenager. Jack was living in Sydney at the time and examined Arthur Mailey bowling googlies in the nets there, before sending his brother a letter explaining the technique. He must have been a good writer, because within a couple of days Bill reckoned he'd perfected it.

John Gleeson

John Gleeson wasn't the greatest Ashes leg-spinner, but Richie Benaud rated him as one of the most innovative and he was top wicket-taker for Australia in the 1970/71 series. Reviving the 'mystery bowler' skills of Jack Iverson, John experimented with various methods, but settled on bowling with a similar two-fingered grip to Jack's. Brought up on a dairy farm in New South Wales, John reckoned all those early mornings milking cows by hand gave him the finger power to bowl with the ball wedged between a bent middle finger and thumb. Udderly amazing. (Sorry.)

Johnny Briggs

It's sad to note that some of the great spinners highlighted here suffered very tough times after their playing career. Jack Iverson contracted a brain disease in his fifties which caused him to suffer depression and ultimately commit suicide by shooting himself. Chuck Fleetwood-Smith's drinking got way out of control, he became an alcoholic and spent years sleeping rough on the streets near the MCG where he'd once entertained the fans. The story of Johnny Briggs, a brilliant slow left-armer who was the first bowler in Test cricket to take 100 wickets, also had a tragic ending.

Standing under five feet four, Johnny was a little fella but played a huge part in England's 3–0 whitewash of the Aussies in 1886, taking 17 wickets, including exceptional match figures of 11 for 74 in the Lord's Test. After that, he competed with Bobby Peel for the left-arm spinner's slot in the England side through the 1880s and '90s and enjoyed great success, taking an Ashes hat-trick along the way. But on the evening of the first day of the Headingley Ashes Test in 1899, he suffered an epileptic fit and was admitted to a mental hospital. He came back for a while in 1900, but he never fully recovered, dying in an asylum just two years later.

Shane Warne

This bloke played for the Aussies in the 1990s and 2000s and apparently took quite a lot of Ashes wickets. Not much has been written about him, but after some in-depth research I have discovered that he is probably the only spinner in Ashes history to become slimmer since retiring.

CHAPTER 5

TOUR MATCHES

BICYCLING IN BOWRAL

With such a crowded international cricket schedule nowadays, there are fewer Ashes tour matches outside the Test/ODI/T20 series than there used to be – in 1990/91, we played 15, whereas Straussy's mob played roughly a third of that number in 2010/11. But the trips 'up country' to play first-class matches in out-of-the-way places are a great part of the Ashes touring experience for England players.

In my day, it was like a roadshow and we had some great times – mostly off the pitch. We'd rock up in some little town and stay in a very nice hotel. In the evening we'd head to one of the two local pubs in the place. There might be only 30-odd people in there, but the country girls always seemed pleased to see us and we'd just party. Come last orders, we'd be like, 'Right, everyone back to ours?'

'Wahey!'

The next thing people are running round corridors, jumping in swimming pools and swigging wine in the Jacuzzi. Then I'd flake out about two, three o'clock. Wake up at eight o'clock and go out and have a bowl . . . or hopefully we'd have a bat and I'd have a snooze.

One night in Bowral, I ended up going off-piste though. There was a fantastic girl who was working behind the bar at our hotel and I'd got chatting to her. Everyone had gone to bed, so I was sitting there hanging on trying to stay awake until she'd finished her shift. When she finished work, she kindly invited me back to her place, which turned out to be quite far away.

Just before dawn, I said to her, 'I've got to get back, how can I get back?'

'Well, there's a bike in the garage you can use . . .'

I pulled on my England tracksuit and went out to the garage and found this old bicycle, it was like that 1970s classic, the Grifter.

So I got on and started pedalling along. I wasn't sure exactly where I was going but I knew the rough direction towards town. And as the sun rose, it was rather a pleasant ride even though I was cream-crackered.

When I finally made it back to Bowral, it soon became clear that I had no idea where the hotel was. I was cycling round cluelessly trying to find our hotel, when I saw a local.

'Oh, excuse me, do you know where the England cricket team are staying?'

Unfazed by the sight of an England cricketer pedalling

around on a Grifter in the early hours, he replied: 'Oh yeah, Tuffers, it's down there, turn left, second right, you can't miss it, mate.'

With my well-known reputation for physical fitness, he probably thought I was out doing extra training . . .

LINE-DANCING IN GERALDTON

In those up-country games, I don't know if our captain's choice of what to do when he won the toss was ever influenced by the state of the players from the night before. But we used to come into the dressing room and compare notes on what had gone on, the women we'd, erm, 'met', etc.

Sometimes, I'd see a raised eyebrow or two from the management and realise it was not the time, but it wasn't like it was a secret. The thing I found out very quickly was that when you were going well on the pitch, it didn't matter what you did off it. When things weren't going so well, keep your nut down.

A couple of times, it got a bit too boisterous, and you could get in trouble if you accidentally went to the wrong kind of place. I can remember a time in Geraldton when a few of us ended up in this nightclub – well, I say nightclub, more of a corrugated shed with metal chairs dotted about, but people were in there having a good time. We were sitting there sinking plenty. By the time the locals started a line dance, I was absolutely hammered and decided to get involved. Sadly, in my inebriated attempt to keep up with the steps, I kept on going the wrong way, bumping into people.

The next thing I knew, I felt a clonk on the back of my head, and turned round to see a sizeable and angry-looking Aussie bloke:

'You flash Pommie ****. What are you doing over here?'

When he said 'flash' I can only assume he was referring to me wearing a collared shirt and trousers, as opposed to his outfit of a string vest, shorts and work boots (he'd made a real effort).

'Sorry, mate. Didn't mean to knock you,' I replied, all the while looking round, thinking, 'Where's Devon? Where's Judgey [Robin Smith – we called him 'Judge' because his hair looked like a judge's wig]?'

Thankfully, the big lads were nearby to bail me out: 'Time to go home, Philip . . .'

Although the level of media scrutiny on the players was nothing like as intense as it is today, you still had to be a bit wary who you mixed with out in the sticks. Gladstone Small tells a story about his first Ashes tour of 1986/87 when they were staying in Queensland sugar cane-growing territory. One evening after play, the players were relaxing by the hotel pool, when two gorgeous girls appeared flashing smiles at them.

Just as some of the chaps were bracing themselves to make their approach, David Gower piped up: 'Guys, where are we? We're in the middle of nowhere. Where have these two girls appeared from? Did they just wander out of the sugar cane?'

Turned out the girls had been planted there by a tabloid back home. How the boys found that out is not clear, but if either of the pretty ladies succumbed to the players' charms they didn't tell the newspaper that sent them.

FUN AND GAMES

So in my experience, expeditions up country were brilliant. The only slight inconvenience was that we had to play cricket as well. It was a case of up-country game, hope I don't get picked . . . Oh, bloody hell, I'm in the team, that's a pain in the arse.

Don't get me wrong, there was a lovely atmosphere at the games. Tidy grounds with picket fences, nice little pavilion, temporary stands put up specially for the occasion. It was a bit like playing at Southgate, only warmer. Three or four thousand people from the local towns and villages would come along to see us play against a Country XI or whoever, and you'd see the classic Aussie ockers with the vest and cork hat on. I would sit outside, occasionally doing a lap to chat to people and sign autographs. An ambassador for my country. Lovely.

No, the problem was that it didn't matter whether you were playing against a Prime Minister's XI or South Australia, they always put out a decent side and quite often they kicked our arses (our record in 1990/91 was won six, lost five, drew four).

There'd be a couple of local quickies with handlebar moustaches who looked like they'd just broken a sheep's neck straining at the leash to knock your block off. Then you'd have your young up-and-comers – players of the quality of Michael Bevan and Darren Lehmann – looking to make an impression.

Maybe a couple of established Test players like Greg Matthews or Dean Jones. Then there were your old legends who still had an appetite to stick it up the Poms. Dennis Lillee opened the bowling against us in the traditional tour game at Lilac Hill and Dougie Walters, who must have been about 65, bowled against us at Bowral.

Basically, the tourists' team has always been on a hiding to nothing in these games – they are expected to win when really the main object of the exercise is for each player to prepare for the Ashes. In Mark Butcher's case, it was a physical hiding – he got more stitches in his face than runs – ten stitches, nine runs – in his three first-class warm-up matches on the 1998/99 tour. But then Butch went out and scored 116 in the First Test in Brisbane, showing what poor form-guides the tour games can be.

Gatt's team went into the 1986/87 series Down Under having lost three series in a row, eight defeats in eleven Tests. Then they lost to Queensland and were outplayed in a draw with Western Australia in warm-up matches. Ashes score? 2–1 England.

Back at the end of the nineteenth century, Ranji declared himself a bit miffed at how home supporters up country claimed they'd won two-day matches based on the scores of the first innings. 'We have been told at several places where we have been headed by the local players in the first innings score, how pleased they were for beating us in a match!' he wrote. 'It is quite funny inasmuch as the order is invariably drawn from a hat, "change" bowlers begin our attack, and the batsmen indulge in free-hitting more than in anything else.'

Incidentally, Ranji also recalled a match in Hamilton, Victoria, during the 1897/98 tour, where the umpires forgot to put the bails on at the start of the innings of their opponents, Western Districts.

These warm-up games can be rather a dull spectacle in comparison to the thrills of an Ashes encounter. On their visits to England in 1977, 1981 and 1985, the Aussies played 42 first-class matches outside the Tests and drew 31. Not exactly thrilling. However, even in that tepid era there was the occasional classic like when they took on Ian Botham's Somerset team at Taunton on the '85 tour. With Jeff Thomson pinging down rapid deliveries and Botham trying to dispatch them into the car park, over 500 runs were scored on an electric first day.

Another high-scoring game, on England's 1903/04 tour, saw a bit of on-pitch gambling. England were playing a Northern Districts XVIII (yes, eighteen) of New South Wales and batsman Johnny Tyldesley scored 101 in their first innings. But later in the innings the Northern Districts wicketkeeper bet a sovereign that England numbers seven and eight, Bernard Bosanquet and Dick Lilley, who were also filling their boots, would beat Tyldesley's score.

He could be heard behind the stumps muttering, 'that must be 60', or 'that's about 80', as the pair each piled on the runs. When Bosanquet was run out for 99, he was kicking the ground, only to be delighted a few deliveries later when Lilley ended the innings 102 not out. History doesn't show whether Lilley happened to be dropped by the wicketkeeper along the way.

International stars also need to be careful what they say about the lesser lights they come up against in tour matches in case their words come back and haunt them. For instance, in his book about the 1997 Ashes tour of England, Steve Waugh had written that Worcester's part-time medium-pace bowler David Leatherdale 'wouldn't even get a bowl in a Chinese restaurant'. Bit harsh as Leatherdale had taken 5 for 10 and helped Worcester beat the tourists on that occasion.

And the Worcester boys hadn't forgotten Waugh's dig four years on when the Aussies visited again. As Waugh prepared to face his first ball from Leatherdale, the slips were chirping: 'How about some sweet and sour', 'Would you like special fried rice with that?' and so on . . .

Waugh was so flustered he was nearly out lbw first ball, but survived and managed to score a few as the Chinese food orders continued to come in from behind the stumps.

FLIGHTS OF FANCY AND FEAR

Of course, the most infamous tour match incident of all was David Gower and John 'Animal' Morris's Tiger Moth fly-by which occurred during my first Ashes series. We were already down 2–0 after three Tests when we went to play Queensland at the Carrara Oval on the Gold Coast. On the third day, Animal made a century and was out just before lunch, as was David Gower.

At lunch, David told Allan Lamb and Robin Smith that he fancied a flight in the biplanes which we'd seen flying over the ground during the match. At first, David invited Mike

Atherton to come with him, but Athers wisely decided to go to the nets and practise his flipper. Animal overheard the conversation and said he'd come instead. So off they went.

Most of the players didn't know where they'd gone, but I'd heard what was going on. When they buzzed low over the stadium in these little planes, I was sitting with our skipper Goochy, coach Micky Stewart and tour manager Peter Lush watching from the pavilion balcony and keeping schtum. Down on the pitch, Lamby and Judge, who'd just completed his century, were less subtle, holding their bats up like rifles and miming shooting it down. Sadly, David didn't go through with his plan of lobbing onto the pitch the water bombs he'd prepared before take-off.

Aside from going for an aerial joyride during a match, which got David and John in very hot water (poor old Animal never played for England again), the thing I remember most was how they could easily have missed the start of Queensland's innings. Judge was out a few minutes after the fly-by and we collapsed from 411–5 to 430 all out.

The airfield wasn't that far away, but it was still a good 25 minutes' car ride to get there. It was lucky that when I went in to bat, I hung around for 20 minutes – above average for me. Just as I got back into the dressing room, Animal and David came in from the other side with goggle marks around their eyes before having a quick wash and brush up and going out to field. Their timing was spot on.

Talking of flying, any prospective Ashes tourist needs to know that they're going to be doing a lot of it. Australia is definitely not the ideal tour for the nervous flier, as Chris

Tavaré would tell you. Tav got married before the 1982/83 tour and decided to bring along his new wife for the entire trip. Lovely idea, but Mrs Tavaré had a terrible fear of flying, which meant she had to be sedated for every one of the 30-odd flights during the tour. As Derek Pringle remembers, 'If the drugs hadn't kicked in, every little bit of turbulence was met with a blood-curdling shriek from her, which made us a bit nervous.'

I was more than a bit nervous on a flight up from Adelaide to Port Pirie for a tour game once, a one-dayer against the South Australian Country XI. We were in a twin-engine plane just about big enough to accommodate a cricket squad and not many more and going over the mountains we hit an electrical storm and crazy turbulence. At first, we didn't have seatbelts on so all of our heads hit the ceiling and bodies were tumbling everywhere. The luggage dropped out of the overhead lockers – everything opened up.

People scrambled back into their seats, clicked seatbelts on and we just continued bouncing around for ten, fifteen minutes. I was sitting at the back of the plane with my head bolted back against the sheepskin-covered headrest and my hands gripping on to the armrests (or Ned Larkins) for dear life. Physio Laurie Brown produced a bottle of Famous Grouse, which was being passed round and gulped back between aerial bumps.

The stewardess was crying her eyes out which didn't exactly inspire confidence. We felt like we were going down. Even the boys who normally laughed at me for being terrified of flying were terrified themselves. I spoke to John Morris recently and he reckoned it was the scariest flight he'd ever been on. Me too, by a mile.

At one point, as we hit a huge bit of turbulence, everybody was screaming, and the door of the cockpit smashed open. I looked down the gangway, and I caught sight of a familiar figure sitting up there.

He turned round with a big smile on his face giving a thumbs-up.

The door smashed shut again.

'Bloody hell, was that Judge? Is he flying the plane?'

Robin Smith had somehow got himself into the cockpit to meet the pilot.

We all stumbled off the plane looking very pale – some kissing the tarmac – at the end of this nightmare flight. All except a very chipper Judge.

'Eh, you didn't need to worry, boys. I was up there, it was all under control!'

CLOSE ENCOUNTER

It was after journeys like that, I wished we'd taken the train instead, as they did more often in the old days. There's a brilliant tale the great *Test Match Special* commentator Brian Johnston used to tell in his 'An Evening with Johnners' show about one such journey during the 1950/51 tour.

The England squad were taking a train from Sydney to Newcastle to play a tour match, and there was a woman sitting in the carriage holding her baby.

The bloke sitting opposite couldn't take his eyes off this

baby and the woman eventually said, 'What are you looking at my baby for?'

'I'd rather not say,' he replied.

He kept staring though so she kept asking, and eventually he explained, 'All right, I'll tell you. It's the ugliest baby I've ever seen in my life!'

The woman burst into tears and was standing in the corridor crying her eyes out when the MCC players came past on their way to the restaurant carriage. Brian Close, on his first Ashes tour, asked the damsel in distress what the matter was and she tearfully told him that a man had insulted her.

'I'll tell you what,' Brian said. 'Before I have supper, I'll go along to the restaurant car and bring you back a cup of tea to cheer you up.'

A few minutes later, the chivalrous Yorkshireman returned to find her still in floods of tears.

'There you are, dear,' he said kindly. 'A cup of tea to cheer you up. And what's more, I've also brought a banana for the monkey.'

CHAPTER 6

DEBUT DAZE

THE DAY BEFORE THE MORNING AFTER

I went on my first Ashes tour not really expecting to play. I wasn't there just to make up the numbers, but every squad contains a couple of youngsters they want to blood for the future. I was a wide-eyed kid, but did quite well in the warm-up games and started to feel like an important member of the squad.

At the First Test in Brisbane, I helped out Martin Bicknell with twelfth-man duties, doing the drinks and drinking in the atmosphere. We got smashed by ten wickets and, if anything, watching that made me think to myself, 'Let me have a go – I could do better than that.' Certainly couldn't do much worse.

So when I was picked for the Second Test, while I was a bit surprised to be given a whirl so early in the series, I was bang up for it. My Test and Ashes debut was at Melbourne in the

1990 Boxing Day Test. We didn't train the day before. Instead, I got drunk. Why? Well, it was Christmas Day, wasn't it!

We all went to our Christmas lunch in fancy dress. I went as a sheikh. Lamby came as a bunny girl (just let that image sink in for a minute . . . I know, scary, isn't it?). There were pilots, cowboys and Indians, the odd Thunderbird, etc. It must have been quite bizarre for the other guests at the hotel to see us wandering around the place.

The new boys in the squad all had to do a skit for the other boys. In my wisdom, I decided that I would take the piss out of our captain, Goochy, in my little performance.

I came out and said, 'All right, lads', in my best high-pitched Essex estuary accent, then dropped and did a load of sit-ups and press-ups.

'You've got to ****ing get yourself fit.'

Goochy was always saying, 'Lads, you've all got to be ready whether you're in the team or not, because you could play at any time.' I repeated that as I got up and took a sip on my Christmas sherry.

The players were absolutely pissing themselves. Goochy had a slightly fixed grin on his face.

After lunch, around four or five o'clock, people started to drift away, but I cracked on. By about 8 p.m., I was the last sheikh wandering round the hotel bar, and with no one else to play with, I retired to my room, watched a bit of telly and crashed out.

THE LONGEST WALK

Woke up the next morning and it was debut day, the biggest match of my life so far. On the downside, I had a hangover. On the plus side, I'd been too busy enjoying Christmas the day before to get too nervous, and I was more intent on sorting myself out, getting ready, to worry too much about the enormity of it all.

But when I got inside Melbourne Cricket Ground and went out to warm up, it did start to register with me. I'd never seen anything like the place. The Gabba in Brisbane was quite a cute little ground in comparison. This was huge – we just don't have stadiums like the MCG in England. Due to reconstruction work, there was a hole where the Southern Stand used to be, so the capacity was down from its usual 100,000, but 60,000 Australians at the MCG was enough for me.

Goochy won the toss and decided to have a bat. Good result for me in terms of extra time to ease the hangover, and the boys did me a favour by batting well through the first day, with my drinking guru Ned Larkins (who was, by now, my ex-room-mate, as the management had realised the error of their ways and sensibly split us up) scoring 60-odd, and David Gower on his way to a century in a promising stand with Alec Stewart.

We began the next morning 239 runs to the good and just four down, but Gower and then Jack Russell were out in fairly quick succession triggering a bit of a collapse.

At the MCG, there is a viewing balcony for the players, but

the dressing room is downstairs and I was already pacing the floor down there.

I was not the most relaxed waiting to go out to bat at the best of times. And by the time I heard the wall-shaking roar that greeted Jack's dismissal, I was already in some distress.

Batting at number 11 (naturally), I was never quite sure when I should put my gear on. Is it at nine down? Eight down? I always had this fear of not being ready. Best be safe, start getting ready at six wickets down, Phil.

During the tour so far, I'd watched David Gower when he was waiting to go out to bat. He would just sit there serenely, looking absolutely immaculate, and, when his time came, collect his bat and off he went. Compare that to the sight of me wandering around wearing only my shirt, jockstrap, socks and helmet (yes, I even had my helmet on long before I had to go out and face Bruce Reid and Merv Hughes) – it was enough to make an Australian fly on the wall faint.

We could watch the game on TV in the dressing area, but as the wickets tumbled I'd repeatedly stagger up the stairs half-dressed to have a peek at the live action.

'What's going on? What's going on . . . ?'

'Chill out, Tuffers.'

Soon, the ninth wicket went down. I was in.

By that time I had remembered to put on my trousers, boots and every bit of protective equipment known to man.

Okay, here we go. C'mon, Phil, let's do this . . . Oh, don't forget the bat.

I walked up the stairs, opened the door, and in front of me

I could see these long, shallow steps stretching towards a circle of bright green in the distance.

I started wombling down the steps, beads of sweat running down my face underneath the helmet I'd been wearing for about an hour, listening to the hubbub of the crowd. When I looked up I saw I was surrounded by the packed three-tiered arena.

I kept thinking, 'I'm still on the steps . . . I'm still on the bloody steps.' It took me what seemed like 45 seconds just to get to the bottom.

Then I opened the little gate, looked up . . . and the players at the wicket were still miles away. It's the biggest ground I've ever seen in my life. I could feel all eyes on me and got really self-conscious as I trudged out towards the dots on the horizon.

The only thing I can compare it to was the time a few years later when I had a walk-on part in the old Channel 5 soap opera *Family Affairs*. All I had to do was to open a door, walk up to the bar and say, 'Hello, I'm Phil Tufnell, I'm here to judge the beauty contest. Can I have a pint of lager, please.' So I was standing there, a bit nervous, and the bloke went, 'Cue Phil.'

I opened the door and made my way to the bar. But under pressure, I'd suddenly lost the ability to walk naturally. Instead, I found myself strutting up to the bar like the Hofmeister Bear in those eighties' 'Follow the bear' adverts.

'CUT! Cut . . . Phil, what are you doing?'

I can comfort myself that I was not the first and won't be the last to feel the unique pressure of going out to bat on debut in an Ashes Test. For instance, there was a bloke called John Evans, who escaped a German Prisoner Of War camp during the First World War. That must have required a huge amount of courage, but come his Ashes baptism in the final Test of England's horrific 1920/21 series, he was a nervous wreck. According to his team-mate, Hon. Lionel Tennyson, Evans's 'knees were literally knocking together' when he went out to bat.

It was a similar story when I hit the turf at the MCG. I could barely put one foot in front of the other. But with my head tilted forward and chin tucked into my left shoulder, arms and bat waving around uncontrollably at my sides, I looked more like a toddler dragging his blankie along than a beer-guzzling bear with a funky walk.

When you watch the proper batsmen march out to bat, all their clothes and equipment seem to fit perfectly, but it felt like my gear was wearing me as I waddled towards the white rectangle.

After what seemed like an eternity I arrived at the wicket. And I must have looked a right state, a fact confirmed by the reaction of my batting partner Gus Fraser – he just burst out laughing – and of the Australian fielders. 'Who the **** are you?', 'What have you come as, mate?' were among the politer comments.

I was looking round cluelessly. What do I do now?

I'd played at The Oval, I'd played at Lord's, but this was different. The grass was bright green, the packed stands were a sea of colour, the sky was pure blue, the sun was beating down. Everything was shining and glinting. That was the first time I really realised, 'This is Ozzie, I'm playing in the Ashes.'

Somehow, I survived nine balls and thirteen whole minutes, before Gus was out to Terry Alderman, and I had to make the long trek back to the dressing room again.

I felt more comfortable when we went out to have a bowl. Gus took six-fer, I bowled well enough – 21 overs for 62 runs – without getting a wicket and we ended up with a lead of 40-odd runs. Then, after losing Athers early in our second innings on day four, Goochy and Ned dug in and were pushing us up towards a lead of 150 with just one wicket down.

By then, I was feeling quite relaxed. I had my shorts on, was having a bite to eat, chatting to my mates in the dressing room. This was normality, just like a match for Middlesex. And I had Gooch, Larkins, Gower, Smith, Stewart on my side – by the time it's my turn to bat again, we'd likely have a match-winning lead. All good.

But then their left-arm pace bowler Bruce Reid (backed up by their off-spinning all-rounder Greg Matthews) started to let rip through us and the wickets tumbled one after the other. As Australia took control, down in the dressing room I could hear the hum of anticipation filtering down and the roar that greeted the fall of a wicket shook the teacups. I'd never heard noise like it at a cricket game. I was used to hearing a cry of 'Howzat' followed by a polite round of applause, but the Aussie fans went mental. *Rooaaaaaaarrrrrrrrrhhhhhh . . .*

The intensity was something else. This wasn't just another game of cricket.

LITTLE DOC, SWINGING BOB AND THE BALL FROM HELL

My debut ended up runless (I got another 'not out' in the second innings, mind . . . okay, I didn't face a ball but still . . .) and wicketless (due to some scandalous umpiring denying me David Boon's wicket) and we lost by eight wickets, but I survived and earned my place in the next Test.

At least I was in good company. Graham Gooch got a pair and lost on his Ashes debut in 1975, but look what a great player he would prove himself to be. And as he said himself, 'It was quite convenient to have your first Test score in your surname . . .'

Goochy's old Essex mate Keith Fletcher also has bad memories of his debut against Australia, at Headingley in 1968. He came in for the injured Colin Cowdrey, and felt like an outcast in the England dressing room. He claimed later it was a case of each to his own with no encouragement for the new boy from senior players like Ken Barrington and Geoff Boycott.

To make matters worse, the Yorkshire crowd wanted local hero Phil Sharpe to play ahead of him. Then Fletch got bunged in to field at Sharpe's specialist first-slip position, a role he didn't like, and dropped two catches on the first morning.

His luck didn't get any better when it was his turn to bat, being given out caught behind for a duck, when the ball actually clipped his thigh pad, not his bat.

Poor old Fletch was immediately dropped to make way for

fit-again Cowdrey, but he managed to fight his way back and have a good Test career.

Others haven't been lucky enough to get a second crack at it. Take Frederick Martin who took 12 for 102 in his debut Ashes Test in 1890 but never played another Ashes match (and only one more Test, against South Africa). Or Arnold Warren, a fast bowler from Derbyshire, who took 124 wickets in the 1904 season, and, aged 30, earned himself an England call-up for the third Test of the 1905 Ashes series. After England made 301 at Headingley, Arnie opened the bowling. He took the prize wicket of Victor Trumper, clean bowling the legendary Aussie batsman for just 8, on his way to a fantastic five-fer as Australia slid to 195 all out. In the second innings, Arnie trapped Trumper again, this time for a duck. It was his only wicket as Australia hung on for a draw, but match figures of 6 for 113 were pretty impressive. Arnie's reward? He was dropped for the next Test at Old Trafford in favour of Lancashire's own Walter Brearley, who stepped up to the plate taking four wickets per innings as England clinched the Ashes. Poor old Arnie, with a Test bowling average of a shade under 19, was never picked again.

Best (and worst) of all was the case of Roy 'Little Doc' Park. As you can guess from the nickname, Park was also a doctor by trade and was called out on duty the night before his Test debut against England at Melbourne in 1920. Treating the sick wasn't the best preparation, and he was still wiping the sleep from his eyes when he was clean-bowled for a first-ball duck. Meanwhile, his wife, who was sitting in the stands, is said to have missed the one ball her husband faced in Test cricket because she was bending down to pick up her knitting at the time. Park did just as poorly with the ball, his single over of off-spin going for nine runs before he was withdrawn from the Australian attack. And with that, Roy's Test career was parked, having faced just one ball and bowled one over.

In contrast, Essex pace bowler Ken Farnes made a stunning debut in the opening Ashes Test of 1934, taking ten wickets at Trent Bridge. It was a great performance in a losing effort though as England slipped to defeat.

Farnes would appear in three Ashes series in total, but there was a tragic end to his story. Aged 30, just seven years after the start of his international career, he was killed when a plane he was piloting crashed, an accident that shocked the world of cricket.

Australia were soundly beaten in winter 1986/87, but they did grab a consolation victory in the final Test at Sydney and it was partly thanks to the unlikeliest of debutant heroes. When 30-year-old Peter Taylor was named in the twelve, people thought that the selectors had actually meant to pick the future Test opener and captain Mark Taylor, Peter's New South Wales team-mate, who was just starting to make a name for himself. The media and fans referred to him as 'Peter Who?' and their confusion was understandable. Australia had only selected one recognised opening batsman, so plucking from obscurity an off-spinner who had made only half a dozen first-class appearances and struggled to get a game behind NSW's three capped Test spinners, seemed a bizarre choice.

Instead, it proved inspired. He took a six-fer in the first innings and recorded match figures of 8 for 154. But that wasn't all – a left-handed bat, he went in at number nine and propped up an end for a total of four hours over two innings, allowing both Dean Jones (184 not out) and Steve Waugh (73) to make valuable extra runs. His second-innings stand with Waugh of 98 was particularly crucial as Australia won by just 55 runs, and he rightly took the Man of the Match award ahead of all the star names.

Probably the greatest Ashes (and Test) debut ever, though, was by Bob Massie at Lord's in 1972. Aged 25 and sporting a lovely pair of mutton-chop sideburns, Massie ripped through the England batting line-up bowling an array of inswingers and outswingers at a brisk pace. Nicknamed 'Fergie' by his team-mates after a tractor manufacturer called Massey Ferguson, he was more of a steamroller in that match, ending with incredible figures of 16 for 137 (a young hopeful called Dennis Lillee took the other four wickets in the match for Australia).

It was only a couple of years previously that Massie had been turned down by Northamptonshire, but he'd earned his place on the tour by taking a seven-fer against a Rest of the World team, including the wickets of Sunil Gavaskar and Garry Sobers. But almost as incredible as Bob's Ashes debut is how quickly he faded away. Just seven months later during a home series against Pakistan, he realised that he'd lost the ability to bowl his 'outie'. Bob could no longer swing it both ways and, after just six Tests, his international career was over.

Another hazard for the debutant is doing really well but being totally overshadowed by another player's performance. A classic example occurred when off-spinner Peter Such burst onto the Ashes scene with a magnificent six-fer in the first innings of the Old Trafford Test in 1993. I bowled all right in that innings too, actually. Then some blond Aussie kid went and dismissed Mike Gatting with the 'Ball of the Century' (or 'Ball from Hell' depending on which side you were on) and made everyone else look ordinary.

Ashes debutants also need to be careful what they say in advance of their big day. Before the December 2010 Test in Perth, Steven Smith, the promising Aussie leg-spinning all-rounder, was asked at a press conference why he thought he'd been selected. He talked about being funny and adding energy to the Australian team. No mention of his cricket ability then. Maybe he was trying to be humble, but it was a bit like *The Office*'s David Brent's declaration that he wanted his staff to think of him as: 'A friend first, and a boss second . . . probably an entertainer third.' He might as well have stood up and done a dance that 'fused *Flashdance* and MC Hammer shit'.

And, of course, the 'funny' remark gave the England boys rich sledging material when he came out to bat. Any poor shots were greeted with comments like: 'Is this what you meant when you said you were in for your jokes?'

Then again, you can be the most anonymous Ashes virgin and something can go wrong. In that same 2010/11 series, the refreshingly surnamed left-arm spinner Michael Beer was called up for the final Test at Sydney. He'd only played a handful of first-class games and even some Australian fans couldn't recognise him when he rocked up at the SCG.

Beer then suffered the nightmare of celebrating his first Ashes 'wicket', that of run-machine Alastair Cook, only for umpire Billy Bowden to call a no-ball after consulting DRS. Cookie, naturally, went on to score yet another big century, England scored 644 and won by an innings.

I don't know, a left-arm spinner overstepping the mark? Wouldn't have happened in my day . . .

CHAPTER 7

LIVING IN A SQUAD

SANTA GOUGHIE AND NAKED SHANE BURGERED

It has been said that I could be a disruptive influence on a cricket tour, but I did get selected for nine England tours so I can't have been that bad! In fact, I'd say that in a funny way I was a good tourist. Okay, there would be a little bit of argy-bargy along the way – 'Oh God, what's Phil done now' – but I was always bubbling along, looking to do something and get the players together. I was the joker and you need a player or two like that during these long trips away from home.

When Darren Gough played for England, he was another one who made people laugh. There was a good example of Goughie's attitude in the 1998/99 tour (I wasn't picked for that one). Australia had already retained the Ashes and

England were playing Australia A in Hobart on the flattest pitch in the world. This wasn't ideal for Gus Fraser who was trying to impress and get back in the Test team.

Athers declared early on day four, set them 376 to win and they knocked them off for the loss of one wicket. Back in the pavilion, the players were gutted, and Gus typically grumpy after a hard day running in and getting smacked around by the Aussie batters.

Goughie wandered into the dressing room dressed as Father Christmas, saying, 'Yo-ho-ho, I'm looking for Angus Fraser!'

Gus said, 'What the f*** are you doing?'

Unfazed, Goughie sat big Gus on his knee: 'Guess what I've got in my sack for you? I've brought you some wickets. How lucky you are. They are in very short supply at the moment. Yo-ho-ho.'

Gus almost smiled and the rest of the dressing room cracked up. It's great to have people who can lighten the mood like that when things go horribly wrong.

Dougie Walters, who played for Australia in seven Ashes series from 1965 to 1981, was also known as a big prankster in their team, but at the Perth Test in December 1974, his team-mates got their own back. At tea on the second day, Dougie came back to the pavilion 3 not out and declared he'd score a hundred runs in the next session, as he'd managed on a recent tour of the Caribbean.

With one ball remaining at the end of the day and 97 runs to his name, he needed one big hit to achieve his aim. He duly dispatched the next ball over the square-leg boundary for six and triumphantly ran to the pavilion through crowds of pitch invaders. But when he got back to the dressing room, it was empty.

Disappointed that he had no one to say 'I told you so' to, Doug sat down. As he started taking his pads off, Ian Chappell walked in.

'What the hell did you go and get yourself out for?' shouted Chappell.

'Out? Out? I didn't get out, I just hit a six,' replied Doug shocked.

Chappell remained poker-faced: 'Didn't you check the scoreboard? You were caught on the fence.'

Chappell carried on and on until Walters had tears in his eyes believing that he really had given his wicket away. It was only when his team-mates, who had been hiding in the toilets, burst in laughing their heads off that he realised he'd been pranked.

The funny thing was, Walters was out the next morning without adding to his score.

Shane Warne was introduced to Merv Hughes's sense of humour when he roomed with him in Adelaide before one of Warney's first Tests. The players had the team physio and dietician strictly monitoring their meals but, as Ian Healy put it, the young Warne's idea of a balanced diet was 'having a cheeseburger in both hands'. Luckily, Merv shared the same tastes and liked to top up his approved diet by wiping out the mini-bar and ordering burgers and chips from room service when he got back to his room in the evening.

One night, around midnight, they were both lying in bed

polishing off their secret Scooby snack. When they were done, Merv sent Shane to leave their empty plates outside a room a couple of doors down to put Errol Alcott, the team's physio, who used to patrol the corridors, off the scent.

So Shane, who was stark naked, looked out of the door to make sure no one was around and then scooted outside. He put the tray down and scampered back, but the door had swung shut and locked.

As Merv gleefully recalled: 'Just to hear his pleas for me to open the door – it would have been great to have on video or even audio – "Please, big fella, let me in. Someone's coming!" "Oh sorry, Warney, it looks like it's jammed . . ."'

'Left him out there for ten minutes. Never forgiven me for that.'

A roomie like Merv might be a nightmare, but when the Aussies stayed at Lumley Castle hotel in Durham in June 2005, all-rounder Shane 'Watto' Watson would have happily shared with anyone. The 700-year-old castle, where the staff dress in medieval costume and there are suits of armour all over the place, is supposed to be haunted and it certainly gave Watto the willies. He was so freaked out that he ended up going to sleep on the floor in Brett Lee's room rather than share a single room with a ghoul.

A journalist from the *Sun* called up the Australian squad's media manager, Belinda Dennett, to try and find out more about Shane's sleepover. Instead, she told them about her own experience, insisting she'd seen a ghost herself.

'I closed the blind in my room before I went to bed,' she recalled. 'But when I was woken at 4 a.m. by my phone the blind was up again. I looked out the window and saw a procession of white people walking past. It was amazing, very scary. Then I returned to bed and the blind went up again – and there was someone looking in through the window.

'Several of the players were uneasy although a lot of them in the morning said they were fine . . . but maybe they were just trying to be brave.'

As for Shane Watson, he got his hotel room changed and kept the lights and television on for the rest of his stay, because he reckoned ghosts didn't like light and noise. Then again, as Brett Lee pointed out, Watson is a man 'who once asked if *Planet of the Apes* was a documentary'.

The story of petrified Aussie cricketers was comedy gold for the British tabloids in the build-up to the Ashes series, and the *Sun*'s 'Scare Dinkum' headline is a classic. England fans kept the joke going, too, turning up for the next one-dayer at Chester-le-Street dressed in long white sheets, while Darren Gough sneaked up on Watto as he came out to bat and went 'Boo!'

FAVOURS FOR GRACE AND THE TEAM OF CAN'TS

There was so much going on in Oz, that, apart from my room-mate, I wouldn't necessarily see much of my team-mates when we were off the clock. We'd do a net in the morning and finish about two or three o'clock. Then some would go to bed, go off to play golf or lie around the pool.

On the 1990/91 tour, the likes of Ian Botham, Allan Lamb

and David Gower were very sociable, just not often with us younger boys. I wouldn't see them most nights because they'd be off with the mates they'd made on previous trips. Occasionally, we got invited along, but usually I'd just be hanging around with two or three of the younger lads in the evening. I'd always say 'See you in the bar at seven', but if a couple of members of my little mob had to go off and see their aunty who lived in Oz or a friend who'd flown over to see them, I'd be left sitting in the bar on my tod.

On a trip to, say, India, we seemed to do more things together. You don't want to be in each other's pockets all the time, but in Oz, it did get a bit cliquey. Mind you, that was nothing compared to the early Ashes history when 'gentlemen' amateurs and professional 'players' of the same team had separate dressing rooms. Even on the scorecards, the initials of a pro's name would be placed after the surname, while the gents' initials came first.

The amateurs were given all the privileges and allowed extravagant expenses. For instance, W. G. Grace earned far more from cricket than he did from his profession as a doctor. The cost of taking W.G. along with his wife and family on the 1891/92 tour was estimated to be about £3,000 (around £100k in today's money), more than the rest of the touring squad's fees put together.

Unsurprisingly, W.G.'s riches caused jealousy and in 1896, with the Ashes series poised at 1–1 after two Tests with one to play, five England players threatened to go on strike over their low pay compared to the England skipper. To be fair, W.G. was in spanking good form – the previous season he scored over 2,000 runs, including 9 centuries, at an average of 51. Not bad for a man turned 47 years old. The *Daily Telegraph* newspaper felt such feats deserved a reward and invited their readers to send in a shilling for the old legend.

The impromptu testimonial raised over nine grand. The total reflected how highly W.G. was regarded by the English public, but his poorly paid pro team-mates weren't so delighted at the riches being showered upon a bloke who was already well-off. They also suspected that he was getting far more than their £10 fee (plus lavish expenses) for playing for England. Before that Third Test at The Oval the following year, five top players – Tom Richardson, Billy Gunn, George Lohmann, Bobby Abel and Tom Hayward – demanded a 100 per cent pay rise to £20.

Four of them played for the host club, Surrey, who were responsible for paying the match fees, but they refused to fork out the extra cash. In the end, only their fast bowler Lohmann, who boasted an incredible record of 112 wickets at 10.75 in his Test career, and Nottinghamshire batsman Gunn, carried out their strike.

England won the Test without them, but a bitter taste lingered. W.G. was angry that his team-mates begrudged him money when it was mainly down to him that cricket was a mainstream sport at all, and the pros remained peeved at their poor wages.

Lohmann was never selected again, and sadly died a few years later from tuberculosis.

It is difficult enough to get a sense of togetherness in a squad without a class system, because you have so many different characters in the mix. I mean, with the best will in the world, in 1990/91 the young Tufnell and veteran Eddie Hemmings had a very different idea of a night out. We would have a drink together, but for Eddie it was a pint of mild and an early night.

That's where Mike Gatting did really well as captain of England's 1986/87 touring side, a great example of a series where the squad dynamics were just right.

Before the series, Micky Stewart came in as manager and he and Gatt were instantly on the same wavelength even though they'd never met before. Before selecting the squad, Gatt said to Micky – 'You pick your team and I'll pick mine' – and independently they chose virtually the same players.

They both went for strong characters and most of their choices proved inspired. There was Chris Broad, who they fancied against quick bowling on the bouncy Aussie wickets, and Bill Athey, who was a tough fighter, to go with the middle order of Gower, Lamb and Botham. They took a punt on my mate Phil 'Daffy' DeFreitas, who was 20 years old, talented and hungry. Bowling-wise, they had capable pace bowlers in Graham Dilley, Neil Foster and Gladstone Small. Then they had the Emburey–Edmonds spin combo – both great players.

When you look at the squad on paper now, you can see they were full of talent, but at the time, the press slated them as the worst ever because England hadn't won a Test since the previous Ashes series. Their poor performances in the warm-up matches didn't inspire much confidence either. Journalist Martin Johnson memorably wrote: 'There are only three things wrong with this England team – they can't bat, can't bowl and can't field.'

'We became a Team of Can'ts,' said Gladstone Small.

The senior players like Beefy, Lamby and Gower weren't taking those warm-up games too seriously, though. They were too busy, in Chris Broad's words, 'acclimatising to the wine and socialising'.

However, Beefy was buckling down to practice because Gatt had cut a clever deal with him. Sometimes in the past he'd caused friction within the team because he was no lover of practice and other players picked up on that and got lazy too – 'Both's not practising, so why should we?'

This time, Gatt put Beefy in charge of the bowlers and asked him to set a good example for the first six weeks of the tour by working really hard in practice. If he did so, Gatt told him that after that he'd be allowed to do what he liked. He also had Beefy rooming with Daffy early on to help him settle in, so the youngster didn't feel in awe of the great players around him.

The carrot and stick worked, because Beefy relished being given responsibility but also some respect as a senior player to enjoy himself. Indeed, Beefy later said this Ashes series was his greatest memory of touring.

Gatt got all the senior players mixing and socialising with the young lads – so they were all united and there were no cliques.

After the poor warm-up games, the big players knew they had to step up in the Tests and they did so. Micky Stewart worked out where they needed to bowl to each Aussie batter and drilled the team on their fielding. Gatt emphasised the need for disciplined bowling to plan and for the batters to dig in and make big runs when they got in.

On the eve of the series, he reminded the players about what the press were saying about them. Then Beefy made a short, inspiring speech:

'What we've just done is what any side does – practise. It's just practice. Tomorrow is about the real thing . . . If we play well, we've got a chance of winning. This is where it starts. You know what you've got to do. Now go out there and do it. Enjoy it and do it.'

It helped that Beefy backed up his words by going out and scoring a century in the first innings of the series. He was so up for it that he insisted on playing in the Fourth Test at Melbourne despite a side strain which meant he was only able to bowl at gentle medium pace. Typically, he took a five-fer despite bowling what Gatt generously described as 'the biggest load of pies I've ever seen'.

Beefy's mere presence in the side was enough to unsettle the Aussies, and everyone else in the England team was inspired by his example and Gatt's leadership to raise their game too. Chris Broad averaged 70-odd, equalling Jack Hobbs and Wally Hammond's record of scoring centuries in three consecutive Tests of an Ashes series along the way (note: Hobbs managed the feat twice).

England ended up winning the Ashes 2–1, only losing the final dead rubber. They won the one-day series to boot.

The Team of Can'ts had shown that with good leadership, team spirit and a can-do attitude, they, er, could. And I reckon that will probably be the last Ashes that England will ever win with such a lads-on-tour mentality, too. I wish I'd been part of it.

TUFFERS FOR SOCIAL CAPTAIN!

For the 1950/51 series Down Under, the England selectors, who made some very odd choices in their squad selection, also appointed a second manager, Brigadier Green. At the time, the counties were not happy at the decision to send another person which they'd have to pay for, and it didn't work out. The idea was for the brigadier to deal with social matters to ease the pressure on the captain, but of course, the Aussies weren't interested in the manager, they wanted the skipper to attend press conferences and functions.

Afterwards, the journalist E. M. Wellings suggested that in future it might be a better idea to choose a 'social captain' in the squad, who would be responsible for all social activities away from the ground.

As far as I know, England have never actually appointed an official social captain for an Ashes series, but there are usually a couple of players who take on the role unofficially. In the early nineties it was mainly Robin Smith, with help from Allan Lamb, who took on the responsibility. Judge's key duties were finding good places for us to go on days off, good restaurants and bars and to secure as much free drink for the team room as possible.

One time in New Zealand off the back of an Ashes tour, we were in the team room and Judge, Lamby and Beefy were nowhere to be seen. Suddenly, out the window we saw a helicopter coming into land. The three of them jumped out looking triumphant and for the next few minutes, the hotel bellboys were shuttling back and forth carrying in boxes of Cloudy Bay wine.

'We've filled up the fridge, boys!'

Even though I was never nominated as social captain for the team, I often selflessly took it upon myself to check out the local hostelries. My research was so thorough I sometimes didn't return until the following morning. Just doing my bit for team spirit.

SWANNY'S ASHES VIDEO DIARY

I count myself fortunate that digital camcorders weren't readily available when I went on my Ashes tours and smartphones and social media sites like YouTube and Twitter hadn't even been invented. Some of my off-pitch escapades captured on camera might have got a good number of hits, shares and retweets, but also could have cost me a few more hefty fines.

Modern-day England Test cricketers have embraced new technology, though. On their triumphant 2010/11 tour, the England and Wales Cricket Board (ECB) even let Graeme Swann loose with a camcorder to make a behind-the-scenes video of the trip. Swanny's Ashes Video Diary was released in seven episodes (plus a highlights episode at the end) via the ECB website and YouTube throughout the trip. They got hundreds of thousands of views and gave cricket fans a nice inside glimpse of life on tour and allowed Swanny to add 'Documentary Maker' to the many talents he thinks he has.

The series started slowly with Swanny sitting on his bed talking about the Xbox-playing habits of his team-mates (Jonathan Trott gloats when he wins and says the game's fixed if he loses, trivia fans) and his controversial views on the new roof at the Adelaide Oval (he doesn't like it), but soon hit its stride.

Swanny, who Andrew Strauss lovingly refers to as a 'buffoon', revels in his role as presenter, which allows him to rip the piss out of his team-mates and generally mess about. He hijacks a press conference with Steve Finn where he jovially describes Finn as 'the most boring man in international cricket'. Finn requests an apology which Swann gives in the next episode – 'I wholeheartedly apologise. Steven Finn, I am sorry that you are the most boring man in international cricket.'

He explains why he calls Alastair Cook 'Woody' after the *Toy Story* character – 'I promise it's not because he lives in a child's bedroom, it is because he runs like Woody out of *Toy Story*.'

Through it all, we also see the beautiful love story developing between Swanny and his room-mate Jimmy Anderson. We see sensual scenes of neck massage and the pair in mullet wigs doing a karaoke version of Waddle and Hoddle's 'Diamond Lights'. Then we witness Swanny's pain when Jimmy has to nip back to England to be with his wife for the birth of their child – he comforts himself by getting his team-mates to try and imitate Jimmy's grumpy face instead.

Probably the greatest achievement of the diary was making the 'Sprinkler Dance' go viral. Paul Collingwood has been credited with inventing the dance, and when Swanny asked fans back home to send in their videos of them doing it, he received over 5,000 in a week from everyone from schoolkids to swimmers, vicars to people wearing horse masks.

Swanny also used the diary as a way to set the record straight, like when Channel Ten aired a cleverly edited story which made it sound like he'd slated Australia's debutant bowler Michael Beer when he hadn't. And during his own version of the Queen's Speech on Christmas Day, he had a dig at my old mate Gus Fraser who'd suggested in print that the Sprinkler Dance had somehow contributed to England losing the Perth Test. 'That particular member of the press was in charge of Middlesex last year as they finished bottom of Division Two,' said Swann.

I'm sure the ECB press officer made sure that any footage of the boys' nights outs didn't see the light of day. Although, judging by the videos, the current players spend a lot more time than we did in the gym than at the bar. But we do see Swanny half-cut on Jägerbombs in the press room at the MCG a couple of hours after England retained the Ashes, and reviewing the match with rather impressive impressions of Richie Benaud and Tony Greig.

To cap it all there's a guest appearance by David Hasselhoff in Episode Seven where the Hoff wishes 'the England team to win the Ashes'. Okay, we'd already retained them by then, but it's the thought that counts.

DEPUTY DUCKIE'S BEEF SLICES

During an Ashes series, players will find themselves in direct competition for places in the team. This can lead to tension, but once the decision is made who's playing and who isn't, the captain and management hope that the lads who miss out don't sulk and remain supportive. And you couldn't ask anyone to be much more supportive than wicketkeeper George 'Duckie' Duckworth on England's controversial 1932/33 tour Down Under.

Les Ames was the first-choice keeper on that trip, but Duckie proved to be the best of deputies. In those days, wickie's gloves weren't as well padded as they are now, so while Ames was resting between sessions in the field, Duckie would stick slices of meat in his gloves to protect Ames's hands from the pounding they were taking keeping to Harold Larwood and co. (Steak tartare for lunch, anyone?)

'By the time lunch came round, when it was 100 degrees in the shade, the beef got a bit high,' remembered Ames. 'It had also been knocked to pulp by Harold Larwood's "expresses". Duckie waited upon me like a valet. He would be the first person to greet me when I got back to the pavilion. He would wash out my gloves, and, armed with a pair of scissors, he would cut up fresh slices of meat for my gloves before we went out again to field.'

This meat-exchange system worked brilliantly. The only problem arose at one Test later in the series. After another hot Saturday in the field, Ames chucked his gloves under a chair in the dressing room, took a shower, changed and forgot all about them. When the team returned to the dressing room on Monday, there was a terrible stench and a cloud of flies around the meaty gloves. Ames and Duckie had to get a new pair, while the other players opened the windows.

WILLEY SUPPORTS OLD ARSE

Mike Brearley told a nice story about team spirit during England's magical 1981 Ashes series win. It centres on Chris Old, the excellent bowler who joined Ian Botham at the wicket during Beefy's famous innings of 149 not out at Headingley. Old went in after a thrilling century-partnership between Beefy and Dilley, but England were still only 25 runs ahead with two wickets standing. They needed more runs to have a chance and, according to Brearley, the England boys sent Old on his way to the crease with 'a mixture of pleas, exhortations and threats'.

A right-armed seamer, Old batted left-handed and was a good striker of the ball, but he had a habit of backing away to the legside against quick bowling, an, ahem, technique that I later perfected.

That day he managed to keep in line more than usual though, scoring 29 and helping Beefy past his century and up to what proved a match-winning total. Whether that was because, back in the dressing room, Peter Willey was wedging a bat handle against the image of Old's arse on the television screen every time he faced a delivery is not clear. That's what you call giving your team-mate support.

GEORGE BRADMAN AND TIN ARSE

Being given a nickname is an important rite of passage for cricketers at any level of the game. Mind you, some of the nicknames Ashes players have got lumbered with have not exactly been flattering. Ian Johnson led Australia to two successive Ashes defeats in the mid-fifties when many felt that Keith Miller should have been made captain. While the golden boy Miller was known as 'Nugget', Johnson got tagged 'Myxomatosis' by his team-mates for his habit of bringing himself on to bowl when the tailender 'rabbits' came in to bat.

In England's 2010/11 touring side, Paul Collingwood was known to his England colleagues as 'Weed' for his wiry physique, while Matt Prior got pegged as 'Cheese' because of his cheesy taste in clothes. Crap dress sense is always a popular target. Shane Warne got saddled with the nickname 'Hulk Hogan' by his mates during the 2001 Ashes tour for his habit of wearing a bandana.

But has there ever been a sadder nickname than 'Poor' Fred Tate, as he was commonly known after his disastrous single Ashes appearance in the Fourth Test of the 1902 series. The Sussex medium-pacer made little impact with the ball, dropped a simple and crucial catch in Australia's second innings and coming in at number 11 with eight to win, was out fourth ball. Fred's son, Maurice 'Chubby' Tate, proved to be rather more successful, taking 155 Test wickets including 83 against Australia.

Trevor Bailey's nickname 'The Boil' might seem uncomplimentary, but he actually got it after his surname was pronounced wrongly at a football match in Switzerland when he was on tour with the Cambridge University football team. Bailey became 'Boiley' became 'The Boil'. It fitted well with his painfully slow batting style, as did his other moniker, 'Barnacle'.

What you don't want to do is leave your nickname to the spectators. The great Australian captain Warwick 'The Big Ship' Armstrong had become so lardy by the time of his final Ashes triumphs in 1920/21 and 1921, weighing in at around 22 stone, that some fans renamed him 'The Big Jellyfish'.

Alastair Cook has never been short of a nickname or five – 'Cooky', 'Chef', 'Golden Boy', 'Woody' (©Graeme Swann), 'The Run Machine' to mention a few. And he fared rather better than Warwick and co. when his team-mates added another to his list following his record-breaking batting performances in the 2010/11 Ashes: 'The Don', after the great Don Bradman.

Mind you, the actual Don Bradman, whose team-mates called him 'Braddles' when he was a youngster, was also called 'George' for no apparent reason. Everyone called Arthur Mailey, hero of Australia's whitewash triumph in 1920/21, 'George', too. Another random nickname I like was 'Lulu' for David Gower – Lulu's . . . I mean, *David*'s team-mate Bob Willis came up with it and no one ever knew why. As for Bob himself, he was called 'Goose' because when Bob couldn't remember someone's name, he'd just call them 'Goose' instead.

Bill Ponsford and Bill Woodfull, Australian batsmen in the Bodyline series, were known jointly as 'Mutt and Jeff' after the characters in a famous old American newspaper cartoon strip, but even the two Bills didn't know which of them was supposed to be Mutt and which Jeff. Another brave Aussie facing up to Larwood's missiles in that series was Stan McCabe, who gloried in the nickname 'Napper', because he looked like Napoleon.

I referred to Graham Gooch and Ian Botham mainly as 'Goochy' and 'Beefy'. However, on the 1978/79 England Ashes tour, Goochy was also called 'Zap' after the Mexican revolutionary Zapata, and 'Zorro' for his dark looks and Meh-ico moustache, while Beefy got renamed 'Tin Arse' because the previous year in Pakistan some of the locals had pronounced his name 'Iron Bottom'. During the 2001 series, the Aussies took to calling England's India-born captain Nasser Hussain 'Poppadom Fingers' because Nasser's fingers kept getting broken.

Steve Smith, Australia's fitness coach for the 1997 Ashes, was known as 'Tattoo' and on that tour he added a couple more to his collection of body art. On his left arse cheek, a Springbok being booted through the air in tribute to their recent series victory in South Africa. On his right, a freshly inked tattoo of a boxing kangaroo beating up a British bulldog.

Max Walker, who backed up Australia's famous 'Lillian Thomson' pace combo in the 1974/75 Ashes, had the fantastic nickname of 'Tanglefoot' or 'Tangles' in tribute to his unique bowling action. As Max himself described it: 'Right arm over left earhole, legs crossed at the point of delivery.' I'm also a big fan of Ashley Giles's 'King of Spain' moniker, the result of a mix-up when his club Warwickshire had commissioned a set of mugs in his honour that should have read, 'Ashley Giles King of Spin'.

But when it comes to nicknames, no one could ever really compete with 2006/07 Ashes winner, Mike Hussey, aka 'Mr Cricket'. Beat that.

WHATEVER WORKS

Daft superstitions are an essential part of the experience of being an Ashes player. It's a case of whatever works or, at least, whatever seems to work.

Probably my ideal superstition was that of England's dynamite new-ball duo, Sydney Barnes and Frank Foster in the 1911/12 series. They each got into the habit of drinking a glass of champagne at intervals. I would happily have joined them for a tipple in the interests of the team.

Big-hitting Adam Gilchrist liked to hang his yellow Wallaby scarf across the balcony for luck when he was batting. But in the Second Test at Lord's in 2001, he forgot to put it up before he went out. He called for the twelfth man just to get the message back to the dressing room to put it up. Before it could be done, though, Mark Butcher dropped him at slip. This might make you think his good luck wasn't dependent on scarf placement, but he did go on to crash 90 runs in quick time, being dropped four times along the way.

When things are going well, the superstitious members of the team don't want to break the spell and every one else has to fall in line. In Brisbane in 2010, Alastair Cook's diet was affected by his ability to bat for ever (or vice versa depending on your viewpoint). The night before England's second innings, he enjoyed roast lamb for dinner, then he went out and scored 132 not out by stumps the next day. Like it or not, his more superstitious team-mates demanded that he ate roast lamb again, and he went on to make a double-ton in an epic innings lasting ten-and-a-half hours.

In 1989 Allan Border put in his own marathon stint for the good of the team. In the Fifth Test at Trent Bridge, Geoff Marsh and Mark Taylor compiled a triple-century opening stand, becoming the first openers to bat through a complete day of a Test in England. AB spent most of the first morning of their partnership sat in his spot in the dressing room, watching the action on TV while writing some letters. With lunch approaching, he fancied a change of scenery and got up to go to the balcony to watch a bit of live cricket.

He had barely moved before his very superstitious bowler Terry Alderman called out: 'AB! You've been sitting there all morning and we haven't lost a wicket. What do you think you're doing?'

So he sat back down, stayed there the rest of the day as Marsh and Taylor racked up the runs. He was only allowed out to watch the next morning and the partnership came to an end soon after.

Personally, I didn't really have any major superstitions other than I liked the umpire to throw the ball to me when we went out to field. That did cause a problem when Jack Russell was playing because he liked to get his hands on the ball first too. So sometimes you did have a rather comical scene of both of us running towards the umpire, elbowing each other out of the way, saying, 'Over here, ump.' The irony being that I then spent most of my time in the field after that trying to get away from the ball!

WALKING STICKS AND CATHOLICS

Steve Waugh described his team of 2001 as a 'team without stars', which seems a strange thing to say about a side that included superstars such as Shane Warne and Glenn McGrath. But the Australian philosophy then was that the only way to succeed in the long term was through working hard together as a team rather than relying on the same individuals to produce match in, match out.

Under Waugh's captaincy, the Aussies began a tradition of inviting an honoured guest to their last team meeting before a Test and dinner afterwards. Before the Lord's Test in 2001, it was Francois Pienaar, South African rugby legend.

Pienaar told Waugh at dinner that he believed the key to success was 'the four Ds – desire, determination, dedication, discipline . . . Embrace them, and it will lead to delight.' I found that my four Ds – drink, debauchery, dancing and darts – also had the same effect.

The Australians obviously embraced Pienaar's version, though, because the series was done and dusted 3–0 in their favour by the end of the Third Test.

They were obviously a very tightly bonded group all playing hard for the baggy green. And for some the cap was not enough though – in Taunton between Tests, Michael Slater, Mark Waugh and Ricky Ponting all went along to the local tattooist to get numbers inked marking where they stood in the order of players capped for Australia. I can't match that, but I do have my wife Dawnie's name tattooed on my arse.

Don't think that they were always grimly focused on cricket though. For instance, the time when Steve Waugh came back into the dressing room, 101 not out at the end of the second day of the First Test. Normally, a centurion would expect to be clapped in and congratulated, but his arrival went almost unnoticed because the rest of his team-mates were huddled round the TV watching Aussie tennis player Pat Rafter in his Wimbledon semi-final versus Andre Agassi.

I liked the Aussie boys' present for Steve and his twin brother Mark on their 36th birthday during that tour too – walking sticks!

You don't necessarily need to be all happy families to succeed as an Ashes squad, however. Take the Aussie sides of 1934 and 1936/37. Don Bradman was the undoubted superstar, but it didn't mean he was the most popular member of the squad. The Don was a loner and once he'd piled up the runs, he preferred to head back to his room at the end of a day's play than mix with his team-mates.

As a Protestant who didn't smoke or drink, Bradman was hardly going to fit in with the Irish Catholics in the team such as Bill O'Reilly, Jack Fingleton and Stan McCabe who all liked a drink and attended Mass together during their voyages to England. (Fingleton, an opener in the Bodyline series who also became a fine cricket writer, really didn't like Bradman, and was seen laughing his head off when The Don was out for a duck in his final Test innings in 1948.)

And The Don was thought of as a tightwad. When a businessman gave him £1,000 following his record innings of 334 at Headingley in 1930, he didn't even buy a round of drinks for his team-mates, which didn't go down well with them. But Bradman averaged a shade over 139 in the series and the team won 2–1 so Aussie fans couldn't have cared less.

Tensions reached breaking point during the 1936/37 series when England jumped out to a 2–0 lead. After winning the Third Test to bring the score back to 2–1, the Australian top management singled out four players who they believed were giving captain Bradman grief. And without directly accusing them, it was insinuated that O'Reilly, McCabe, Chuck Fleetwood-Smith and Leo O'Brien were the ringleaders of late-night drinking sessions. The four thought that Bradman was behind the complaints – many years later, O'Reilly said he still hadn't forgiven Bradman for what happened. Actually, The Don hadn't been consulted and he was furious at being put in a compromising position with his team by the management.

Again, though, despite the divisions in the squad, the Aussies maintained their momentum on the pitch to clinch a memorable 3–2 series win, showing that ultimately the quality of the players in a team is most important.

Poor Graham Yallop was not so blessed with talent when he was made the captain of Australia at the age of just 26 and with only eight Tests under his belt for the 1978/79 Ashes. Captaining Australia in an Ashes series should be a great honour, but it was a nightmare from the start for Yallop because most of the top Aussie players had defected to Kerry Packer's cricket circus. The Australian public couldn't bear to watch and stayed away in their droves as England cruised to a 5–1 series win.

The only bright spot for Ozzie was the pace bowling of Rodney Hogg who snagged 41 wickets at just under 13 apiece. But even that didn't bring much joy for Yallop because he and Hoggy really didn't get on. Indeed, at the Adelaide Test, it got so bad they had a stand-up row during which Hoggy offered him outside.

TOURING AND STRIFE

In some ways an Ashes tour was an escape from normality, but real life was always there in the background to bite you on the arse. Rooming with team-mates you would find yourself involved in issues like marital strife, family illnesses, births, deaths. All sorts.

In 1994 I went to Australia after a traumatic year. In summary, my long-term relationship ended, I was denied access to my young daughter, my ex-partner's father smashed a brick over my head and tried to break my bowling arm, I got married again and I received telephone death threats. Things were not going too well.

Then, once I got to Australia, my new wife was telling me she was having second thoughts about our marriage (in hindsight, I wish I hadn't had first thoughts). From the start of the tour, we spent hours talking on the phone, but the more we talked the worse things seemed to get and we'd end up having huge arguments. When you'd just started rooming with a fella, getting to know each other, this wasn't an ideal scenario.

I'd be sharing a room with someone like Graham Thorpe or Phil DeFreitas; they had to bat/bowl the next day and I was on the phone having a screaming match with my other half. They'd go out for a walk to let me have some privacy, but when they got back the argument would still be raging. Then when I slammed the phone down, I was still stomping round the room, effing and blinding. We were all mates, but it's quite scary for the other guy. God knows what some of the boys thought of my carryings-on.

You got to know people's lives almost too well. The amount of times I saw people breaking down in tears on tours. Sometimes you were watching a life unravel before your eyes. Four months is a long time to be away from home when you are under pressure. Results on the pitch aren't good; you're fighting for your place in the side; your marriage is under stress; the kids are unwell; the boiler's broken . . . I'd see people get off the phone looking absolutely helpless.

'I'm in Australia. What the hell can I do?'

So many times you'd sit having late-night chats with your room-mate, trying to help or vice versa, when there was nothing to do except listen and try to be supportive.

The management never offered us a single room. I can understand that to some degree because maybe if you are locked away on your own, you can end up getting really depressed, but on the other hand it's not really fair on the room-mate. It's too much when he is already worried about his place, his next innings or bowling spell and on top of that he's taking on all your woes from home.

In 1994 everything just caved in on me during the opening match of the tour in Perth. I started the day with another long, hopeless phone conversation home. Everything seemed to have gone wrong in my life, I felt I'd caused it all and I was totally depressed. I rang physio Dave Roberts and told him that I couldn't do the twelfth-man job. I went back to bed, tried to sleep without success, but by lunchtime, I called Dave again at the ground and he was so worried by what I said that he came back to try to calm me down and gave me a sleeping pill to help me rest.

At the close of play, Daffy and Thorpey came and had a couple of beers with me as I poured my heart out. They were great, but it was all just too much for me. I ended up sobbing uncontrollably and totally trashing the room. I could hear them talking to me, trying to calm me down, but nothing was getting through. In desperation, they called for reinforcements, and Alec Stewart, Athers and Dave came to try and calm me down. By the time Athers arrived I was sitting on the end of my bed in tears wearing just a towel and holding a cigarette with a scene of total destruction around me. It must have been quite a picture.

I was taken in to the local psychiatric unit, sedated and a couple of days' complete rest was recommended. After leaving me in the hands of doctors, tour manager Mike Smith neatly summed up the general feeling among the management about my situation: 'He's ****ed then, isn't he?'

When they got back to the manager's suite at the hotel,

Mike, Athers, Dave and Keith Fletcher got round a table to work out what to do. Phone calls to Lord's were made to find a replacement, with Kent's Min Patel the favoured choice. Then there was a knock at the door. Athers opened it and I'll never forget his face when he saw me standing there! The shock of being put in hospital had hit me and almost immediately, I'd done a runner.

As Athers remembered it, 'He walked in aggressively and proceeded to do a kind of Michael Barrymore impression: "Awright? You awright? I'm awright!"'

I then apologised for causing such inconvenience and said that I was going back to my room to get on with my life and get on with cricket before shaking everyone's hand and leaving the room and them in stunned silence.

Athers reckoned I should be sent home to get professional help, but Mike Smith advised that was a legal grey area and instead they should give me an official final warning first. For good measure I also was given a £1,000 fine, as if I'd smashed my room up for some rock-star fun. Fined for having a breakdown – great.

The hierarchy were so bad in that respect back then. They didn't really care what was going on in your personal life. It was a case of, 'You're playing for England. Get on with it.' These days, I would have been assessed before the tour. 'Oh, you've been through a messy break-up, your ex's dad hit you with a brick . . . perhaps you'd better stay home, Phil, and join the tour if and when you feel ready.' But in those days you wouldn't dream of turning down the opportunity of playing for England because it might be held against you in future.

Say if your partner had a baby during the tour and you went home, that'd be a black mark against your name. Doesn't want it enough, bad attitude. Now that side of things is dealt with better.

WAGS, THE NURSERY END AND DAFFY ROSS

On the 1989 tour of England, Allan Border decided that the players' wives and girlfriends shouldn't join the players until the games were well underway, and no wives should be in the hotel during Test matches. He only relaxed the rule once the Ashes were won.

Previously, in 1981, their rule had been that the girls weren't allowed to stay with their partners in the team hotel, but that only meant that the players didn't bother staying in the team hotel at all. Not great for team spirit as the side was only getting together during the match. In 1985 the management went the other way and allowed the WAGs to stay in the hotel, which worked better except for those with young kids who ended up not getting enough sleep. So it is difficult to get the balance right.

Incidentally, while we're talking WAGs, Border tells a brilliant story about the wife of one of his players. She was really happy to be going to watch the game at Lord's because it had a crèche. When her husband told her that Lord's probably didn't have one, she replied: 'No, there must be one. I kept hearing the commentators talking about the Nursery End.'

In my time touring with England, wives and girlfriends

would only be allowed to come out for ten days over Christmas. They would join us for Christmas lunch, but until just a few years before it had been an all-male affair. That was something the England tour manager Peter Lush decided to change in 1986, inviting along any of the players' wives and girlfriends and kids who were in Oz and the family atmosphere was appreciated by everyone.

'It made the day,' said Gatt, whose family could not be with him in Melbourne, but he spent some time feeding Ian Botham's baby daughter instead.

David Gower organised the fancy-dress party that day, and looking at the photos, the players and their nearest and dearest were sporting some of the finest outfits ever seen in Ashes fancy-dress party history. Coach Micky Stewart was Julius Caesar, Lamby and his wife came as Sugar Plum Fairies, Bill Athey as a teacher complete with mortar board and cane alongside his wife dressed as 'teacher's pet' in short skirt, stockings and suspenders. The entire Botham family (and nanny) were bunny rabbits.

David Gower and his fiancée pushed the envelope, him dressed up as a Nazi SS officer and the future Mrs Gower in a nun costume, while Phil and Frances Edmonds must be the most well-spoken pair of Australian convicts of all time.

Daffy DeFreitas scooped the award for best outfit, though, glamming it up as Diana Ross in a revealing red dress, feather boa and curly black wig. If you half closed your eyes and ignored the moustache, it could have been Diana right there in the room.

Most worrying of all was Peter Austin, the team's scorer

and a man in his seventies, who turned up (un)dressed as a flasher, wearing nothing but red underpants under an old mac.

The Christmas presents organised by Gower caused a few laughs too. Left-handed bat Chris Broad, in the form of his life on that tour, was given a book on why left-handers are naturally superior (which is true of course). Gower gave himself a tube of champagne toothpaste, Micky Stewart received a can of disintegrating bullshit and Ian Botham, for some reason, was given a game called 'Grass'. Hmm. Other gifts included a pet cock, edible knickers and elephant-trunk undies for the well-endowed, um, members of the squad.

All good, clean, family fun, then.

Nowadays, the England players' wives and girlfriends are allowed to stay around the team for as long as they want and it's great that they have that option. Andrew Flintoff said that the presence of his wife, Rachael, in Australia during his nightmarish 2006/07 series was the only thing that kept him sane.

When I was touring, from the point of view of a partner back home, it must have seemed like while they were left dealing with screaming kids and day-to-day problems, us players were living the life of Riley. In some ways we were. The other side of it was that we were out there earning our corn, playing for England, achieving what we'd worked for. And what else could you do in the evenings, except stay in your hotel room and watch telly or read a book?

I think it was Shane Warne who once said that being a cricketer made you feel like you were only married for six months. Of course, that's not acceptable behaviour in normal life, but it was seen almost as the norm of touring life at the time. Going from town to town, doing what you wanted. It was a single man's game. It was fun, but at an expense. It was a very selfish sort of existence and made you a not particularly nice person. You were living the dream, but potentially building up huge problems, which was what happened in my case. The England hierarchy had to make changes because it was wrecking families.

Being part of an Ashes touring squad felt like being bounced around for four months. We bounced from town to town, doing well at cricket, doing badly, having painful phone calls home, arguments, tears, staying in great hotels, going out, laughing, eating amazing food, drinking and partying.

And for those plucked from county cricket to join an Ashes series, as I was in 1990, you suddenly went from being Joe Nobody to being really popular. Opportunities to sample the finer things in life were thrown in front of us every day. Mundane was out the window for the duration. Even when we were losing, it was like, 'Oh well, we tried our best. Do better next time. What's happening next?'

I just lived for the moment and tried to make the best of it.

TUFFERS' TEN ASHES QUICKS (I'M GLAD I NEVER FACED)

There's nothing like the feeling of going out to face a dynamite fast bowler in an Ashes Test. And there was nothing much I liked doing less. Here's a selection of ten great Ashes fast bowlers I'm most grateful I never had to strap on the pads to face. (I've chosen English bowlers as well as Aussies, because I didn't really like facing the quickies in the nets before an Ashes Test either.)

Harold Larwood

Sometimes it's the quiet ones you've got to worry about most. Wasim Akram was one of the most terrifying bowlers I ever faced and you hardly heard him as he approached the wicket because he shuffled in wearing spikeless sandshoes. Then in the West Indies' golden era, there was Michael 'Whispering Death' Holding, who glided in like a panther and generated horrifying speed. Harold 'Lol' Larwood, Douglas Jardine's number one Bodyline assassin, also had a chillingly soundless run-up.

Former Nottinghamshire and England batsman Joe Hardstaff described Larwood as a 'silent killer' and spoke of his 'carpet-slipper run'. Hardstaff claimed he could tell how fast Larwood was going to bowl by listening to his run-up. If he could hear Larwood's feet tap-tapping over the turf, he knew he was bowling within himself (although still bloody fast). But when Hardstaff couldn't hear anything he knew Lol was up to full pace: 'I used to look at the batsman and think, "You're a split-second from trouble, son," because I knew then that Lol was coming in on his toes. That meant only one thing – he was going to let slip the fastest he'd got.'

Larwood needed all that speed plus great control to consistently bowl on leg stump short of a length and keep a batsman of Don Bradman's genius tucked up during the Bodyline series. Those tactics upset the Aussies but impressed a Nottinghamshire brewery who sent Lol barrels of beer for the rest of his life, allowing the silent killer to have a quiet pint for breakfast every day.

Ray Lindwall

Ray Lindwall modelled his action on Larwood, and he was another bowling technician with a wonderful rhythmical run-up and bowling action that made him extremely rapid. Even Denis Compton admitted paying extra visits to the 'little room' before going out to face Lindwall and his mate Keith Miller.

During the Ashes series of 1948, when Lindwall was at his absolute peak, Compton and co. must have been delighted to be playing under a new law which allowed a new ball to be taken every 55 overs. Lindwall took 27 wickets as Australia streaked to a 4–0 win.

On the plus side for a player like me, Lindwall had a friendly attitude towards tailenders and saved his trademark skidding bouncer for the top batsmen. He believed that bowling a bouncer at numbers 8, 9, 10, Jack would be like admitting they could bat better than he could bowl – and they really couldn't. So while I wouldn't have lasted long against him, at least I might have avoided having my head knocked off. Most likely outcome, then:

P. C. R. Tufnell   b Lindwall   0

Bob Willis

With his curly mop of hair bouncing up and down, his bowling arm revving beside him like a jockey whipping his horse as he ran in from near the boundary and the cold, dead eyes of a shark staring you down, I would not have fancied facing Bob Willis when he worked up a head of steam.

Brave bloke, too, was Bob. He had operations on both knees in 1975 and still came back for more, bowling through pain for the rest of his career. And England fans will be pleased to note that we have an Australian doctor to thank for helping Bob stay around long enough to destroy their team with his famous eight-fer at Headingley in 1981. A Dr Arthur Jackson advised him to do slow long-distance running to build up stamina, and all of that slow running helped Bob to bowl faster for longer. Bonza advice, mate.

Fred Spofforth

Known as 'The Demon Bowler', Fred Spofforth was Australia's first superstar fast bowler and can take some credit for the very existence of the Ashes series. It was his career-best figures of 14 for 90 at The Oval in 1882 which gave Australia their first Test win against England on English turf and led to the joke obituary published in *The Sporting Times* newspaper marking the death of English cricket.

Fred stood 6ft 3in – way above average height in those days – and was as skinny as a whippet. He also had a very large hooter. One observer described Fred's action as 'all arms, legs and nose' and he could bowl hostile spells while keeping excellent control of line and length.

Fred first came to the attention of the English public in 1878, when he was part of the Aussie touring side that bowled out the MCC twice in a day at Lord's for 33 and 19. Fred took ten wickets, including the prize scalp of W. G. Grace. Back in the dressing room at the end of play he shouted 'Ain't I a demon?' over and over again. No one disagreed and The Demon Bowler tag stuck.

Ernie Jones

Australia's second great fast bowler after Spofforth. Working in a coal mine had strengthened Jonesy's shoulders and he could ping the ball down at a rapid rate. Famously, on a lively wicket in Sussex, he parted W. G. Grace's bushy beard with a bouncer.

'Sorry, Doctor, she slipped,' Jones told a shocked W.G.

Jones was not above bending his arm to generate extra pace. Indeed, at Sydney and Adelaide in the 1897/98 Ashes series, he became the first bowler to get called for throwing in a Test match. He still managed to take 22 wickets in the series at around 25 runs a pop.

He added another first in 1899 at Lord's when he arrowed the first recorded beamer in Test history. Again, W. G. Grace was the man facing, this time just getting his whiskers out of the way.

Jack Gregory and Ted McDonald

Six foot three and powerfully built, Jack Gregory ran up fast and put everything into the delivery, whereas his mate Ted McDonald glided to the wicket and had an ultra-smooth bowling action. Together in 1921 they formed Australia's first all-pace new-ball partnership, causing almost as much cricket carnage as England's more notorious Bodyline bowlers would a few years later. Before then, Australia tended to pair a quick and a slow bowler to open the bowling, as did most teams of that era.

Gregory was the all-round star performer in Australia's 5–0 whitewash triumph at home in 1920/21, poaching 23 wickets and scoring 442 runs at an average of 70-plus. McDonald took just six wickets in that series, but come summer in England, he claimed 27 Ashes wickets at under 25 runs apiece. The duo's combined tally of 46 wickets helped Australia to a 3–0 series victory, and they would have shared a half-century of dismissals if it hadn't been for some typically English summer weather.

John Snow

The son of a vicar and a poet in his spare time, John Snow transformed into 'The Abominable Snowman' when he had a ball in his hand. A rebellious sort with a very nasty streak as a bowler, Snow left a trail of carnage on the 1970/71 Australian tour.

He didn't give a toss about the unofficial fast bowlers' union rules about not bouncing tailenders, which would get him in my bad books straight away as a potential opponent. Mind you, Snow argued blind that he wasn't actually bowling bouncers because he aimed the ball at armpit level rather than head-height. Whatever, whether it hit you in the armpit or on the bonce, it hurt.

Like Frank Tyson before him, The Snowman built up his fast bowling muscles by chopping down trees. He was a nightmare for opposition batsmen to deal with, and very painful for those who couldn't. 'I never let them forget the game is played with a very hard ball,' Snow wrote after taking 31 wickets on that 1970/71 tour.

Australia would have to wait four years to get revenge for Snow's brutality with the arrival on the scene of a Sheila who was hell-bent on out-Snowing The Abominable Snowman . . .

'Lillian Thomson'

The combination of Dennis Lillee and Jeff Thomson was so destructive in the 1974/75 series that two (long-haired blokes) became one (girl) called 'Lillian Thomson'. So I'm counting her as one bowler in my ten.

Before the 1974/75 series, Lillee wrote: 'I try to hit batsmen in the rib cage when I bowl a purposeful bouncer, and I want it to hurt so much that the batsman doesn't want to face me any more.' Works for me.

England batters knew what Lillee was capable of too since he took five wickets in the first innings of his Test debut against them in Adelaide in 1971.

Thomson, on the other hand, was a mystery to them. The 24-year-old did play against them in a tour match before the start of the series, but Greg Chappell had told him to 'just **** around' so he bowled well below his full pace. He did such a good job of not impressing the England players that when they saw the surname 'Thomson' on the Australia team sheet, they assumed it was Victoria's Alan 'Froggy' Thomson who had been picked. They soon discovered the painful truth though.

Within the first hour of England's first innings in the First Test at Brisbane, he broke Dennis Amiss's thumb. With his fifth ball of the Second Test in Perth, he hit Brian Luckhurst's hand off a good-length ball and Luckhurst wasn't able to field the next day. Worst of all, in the second innings, he caused David 'Bumble' Lloyd to retire hurt after hitting him right in the 'Bumbleballs'.

In a team meeting before the game, Bumble had joked, 'I could play Thomson with my dick,' but I don't think he planned to test the theory in an Ashes Test.

Thomson's team-mate Max Walker recalled Bumble's agony like this: 'I don't think all the equipment was inside the little triangle . . . He went down like a bag of cement. He went from a pasty English tan, to an ashen grey and then a squirmy green. I can see now if I shut my eyes, two guys dragging him off the ground.'

As Bumble collapsed in agony on the pitch, Thomson walked down, stood over him and said: 'Now you can't.'

The 'dick' comment had obviously got back to the Australian dressing room.

Back in the hutch, Bumble assessed the damage to his equipment: 'Everything that should have been in the box was forced through the holes and was now on the outside. I needed a welder to separate the remains of the box from its contents.'

Later on Thomson did go to check on Bumble. 'Sorry mate, I didn't think it would hurt that much,' he told him. And that was about as near to sympathy as you ever got from Thommo.

Thomson actually didn't sledge that much on the pitch, he just bowled really fast and with bad intentions. 'I enjoy hitting a batsman more than getting him out,' he said in '74. 'It doesn't worry me in the least to see the batsman hurt, rolling around screaming and blood on the pitch.'

Thomson wasn't the biggest bloke but he was as flexible as a yoga teacher – he could pin his legs behind his head – which allowed him to slingshot the ball at crazy speeds, some say up to 100 mph. He wasn't too concerned about technique – 'I sort of shuffle up and go whang,' he claimed – but he whanged it very fast indeed.

His long, hurling arm action where he virtually had his back to the batsman and the ball shielded from view until a split-second before he released it, made him more erratic than Lillee, but that wild unpredictability only made him more scary. He generated such pace and bounce that the ball could lift up to waist or even chest height from a full length. Before the batter knew it, if he was lucky enough to avoid getting hit, the ball was past him and slamming into the gloves of Rod Marsh standing back 35 yards behind the stumps. I can feel my right leg twitching back towards square leg just thinking about it.

The umpires did nothing to limit the short stuff aimed at the England batsmen, so Thomson often bowled a couple of bouncers per over while Lillee sometimes pinged down three or four. Lillian Thomson dominated the series, taking 58 wickets, as Australia triumphed 4–1. The Thomson half took 33 of them in just four-and-a-half of the six Tests and looked set to beat Arthur Mailey's record of 36 set back in 1920/21.

Thankfully though, for the England batsmen, the man responsible for causing them so much hurt, hurt himself playing tennis on a rest day and missed the rest of the series. The only question left was whether the Bumbleballs would ever recover?

Frank Tyson

Like Jeff Thomson, Frank 'Typhoon' Tyson once bowled a ball that bounced on the wicket, airmailed the outfield and hit the sightscreen. I don't know if that counts as six byes, but I do know that requires ludicrously fast bowling. Typhoon Tyson didn't bother with trying to swing the ball to outwit batsmen, focusing instead on express deliveries which meant that slip fielders needed to stand 40 yards back to have a chance of taking the edges. Don Bradman and Richie Benaud both rated him as the quickest they'd ever seen.

Luckily for the Aussies, the Typhoon only had a 17-match Test career due to the stress bowling so quickly put on his body, but the impact he made as an unknown 24-year-old on his debut Ashes tour in 1954/55 will never be forgotten.

Tyson had got his Test call-up after breaking Bill Edrich's cheekbone at Lord's. Edrich made the mistake of trying to hook Tyson, but even though he was a great hooker of the ball, Tyson was too fast for him.

However, in Oz young Frank looked all at sea in the First Test. It was only when he chopped his run-up down a few strides in the Second Test in Sydney that he found his, well, his stride, taking ten wickets. He followed that with another match-winning performance, a six-fer bowling downwind in Australia's second innings at the MCG, taking all six wickets for 16 runs off 6.3 eight-ball overs to clinch victory for England. Witnesses to that wind-assisted Typhoon reckon it might just have been the fastest spell of bowling in history.

In the rain-affected Fifth Test, with England enforcing the follow-on and chasing victory against the clock, Tyson bowled off just half a dozen yards but was still rapid enough to have five slips and two short legs against Australia's top-order batsmen. I wonder what field he would have set to me? Maybe a couple more slips . . .

CHAPTER 8

TEAM SELECTION

HAWKE EYE

In Chapter 1 I talked about squad selection. Once the Ashes series gets underway the selection fun and games really begin as injuries, players' poor form and blind panic can kick in. With the introduction of central contracts, and England actually winning the Ashes again, team selection has become far more consistent, some would say dull. Instead, let's look back to the golden eras (and there have been a few) when selections were made on a whim and a prayer.

Our old friend Lord Hawke was instrumental in one of the most bonkers team selections of all time for the Old Trafford Test in 1902. Three of England's best players – ace bowler Sydney Barnes, Yorkshire's swing-bowling all-rounder George Hirst and Gilbert Jessop, a quick bowler and monster hitter –

were dropped for no obvious reason. When captain Archie MacLaren was handed the team sheet, he wasn't impressed. 'Look what they've given me!' he said. 'Do they think we are playing a blind asylum?'

England lost by three runs.

England's skipper at the start of the 1921 series (and a man with a lot of initials), J. W. H. T. Douglas, was equally miffed by the side given to him for the Lord's Test. 'What's this damnable side of picnickers they've sent me?'

The 'picnickers' were particularly bad at fielding. *Wisden* reported that 'an England side so slow and generally inefficient had never previously been seen against Australia'. Unsurprisingly, they lost.

In 1909 England's Ashes selectors made some outstandingly schizophrenic choices. Lord Hawke was leading the way of course, but MacLaren and new selector Leveson Gower assisted in the mayhem.

England got off to a great start in the series, winning the First Test by ten wickets, despite our best bowler, Sydney Barnes, being mysteriously omitted. Australia were struggling, but Hawke and co. ignored the principle of sticking with a winning team, dropping four players for the next Test at Lord's. It was a ridiculous blunder and Australia won comfortably against the reshuffled side. The one bright spot for England was the bowling of medium pacer Albert Relf who took a five-fer in the first innings. Naturally, Relf was dropped.

Barnes was finally drafted in for the Third Test, and took 6 for 63, but by then Australia had got their confidence back and won it to take a 2–1 lead.

Jack Hobbs got the chop for the Fourth Test which ended in a draw.

Needing to win the final Test to draw the series, the selectors surpassed themselves, bringing in a bloke called Douglas Ward Carr, a 37-year-old who'd only started playing first-class cricket for Kent earlier that summer. Even more oddly, he was a leg-spinner who couldn't bowl leg-spinners – a few years earlier, in mastering the art of bowling googlies, he'd somehow forgotten how to bowl his stock ball!

Carr, who opened the bowling with Sydney Barnes, actually started amazingly in the Test, taking three wickets in seven overs. And although he eventually took a bit of hammer, his match figures of seven wickets for 282 from 69 overs were pretty creditable against one of the most dangerous Australian batting line-ups ever.

Of course, Carr never played another Test.

Another draw meant the series ended in defeat. Twenty-five different England players had been selected during the series and only England captain Archie MacLaren and wicketkeeper Dick Lilley had played in every Test.

Sixteen of those 25 never played against Australia in a Test again.

Despite the spectacular shambles, Leveson Gower would appear on a few more selection committees, but the legendary Lord Hawke would not be recalled for selection duty until 1935.

LORD TED/TED LORD

In the modernish era of Ashes selectors, another sort-of-lord, 'Lord' Ted Dexter, was hard to beat for entertainment value. A dashing, brilliant player in his day, Ted was less successful in his time as chairman of the selectors from 1989 to 1993.

Even though he didn't always pick me, I got on well with Lord Ted, actually. Very interesting fella. I remember sitting next to him at a pre-match dinner once and having a long chat about riding motorbikes which he was mad about. Unfortunately, he ended up with a reputation for being, if not mad, a bit of a space cadet. I prefer to think of him as an original thinker.

When he got the job, succeeding Peter May, the general buzz was that it was an exciting appointment. He had charisma and was never short of a bright idea. In the eighties, Ted and Bob Willis led a brewery-sponsored *X Factor*-style contest to try and find England's next great fast bowler. Okay, what they mostly discovered were a load of pub regulars who filled in the application for a laugh while half-cut at their local, but it's the thought that counts. Tom Stancombe and David Dismore won the contest from 3,000 hopefuls/hopelesses and went on to become, um, England fast-bowling legends.

What worked better was Ted's idea for a players' world ranking system which the International Cricket Council later adopted and we take for granted today. In his time as chairman of the selectors, he would also sort out the structure of the county game, bringing in four-day matches.

One of his first tasks was to choose a captain to face Allan

Border's team in the 1989 Ashes series. Ted wanted to put Mike Gatting back in charge. Gatt, of course, had lost the job following alleged shenanigans with a barmaid (allegations which he denied), but just before he got the chairman's job, Ted had made it clear that what players did in their hotel room was not relevant to their ability to play for England. 'If it is embarrassing then it is wrong, but if it is private, and hopefully delightful, then what could be better – even in the middle of a Test Match?' he said. In many ways, Ted was my ideal selector . . .

However, Ossie Wheatley of the old TCCB (Test and County Cricket Board) told Ted that appointing Gatt was out of the question, so instead he went for the horizontally laidback David Gower. The feisty Gatt might have been a better match for Border, who was hell-bent on revenge after finishing on the losing side two Ashes series running.

Diplomatically, Ted told the press that Gower was 'the choice of the England committee' for the captaincy. Well, it's true, Gower was chosen, even if he was the second choice!

Despite being undermined in his first crucial decision, and having an operation on his heel which left him on crutches, Ted was still zipping around the county grounds on his motorbike looking for the right players to take on the Aussies. Little did he know that by halfway through the series some very good players – including John Emburey, Graham Dilley and Phil DeFreitas – would be announced as part of a rebel squad led by the outcast Gatt to tour South Africa.

Sadly, once the series got underway, even the things Ted did have some control over went horribly wrong. He selected four seamers and no spinners for the First Test at Headingley and suggested Gower chose to bowl first. Australia scored 600 and won at a canter.

Then, with England one down, Ted did what any responsible selector would do in the circumstances – he wrote a hymn and suggested the players sang it in the bath before matches. A born-again Christian, Ted has a healthy regard for the power of the Almighty and, in fairness, the Aussies were so much better than England at the time that acting on a hymn and a prayer was probably as good a tactic as any.

'Onward Gower's Cricketers' (to the tune of 'Onward Christian Soldiers') was a cracking little ditty. The first verse went like this:

> *Onward Gower's cricketers*
> *Striving for a score*
> *With our bats uplifted*
> *We want more and more*
> *Alderman the master*
> *Represents the foe*
> *Forward into battle*
> *Down the pitch we go*

Very inspiring. Okay, it didn't actually inspire England to win a match in the 1989 Ashes – we lost 4–0 – but inspiring all the same.

The strange thing throughout that series was that for all his enthusiasm going out to look at potential Test players at county games, Ted rarely went into the dressing room to speak to the players he actually selected. The impression that he was distant from the players wasn't helped when he said in a press conference: 'And who can forget Malcolm Devon.' After that fans of Derbyshire, Malcolm . . . I mean, Devon's home county, started calling Dexter 'Ted Lord'.

To be a selector you do need self-belief no matter what, and Ted had that in abundance. After a crushing series defeat, he declared: 'I'm not aware of any mistakes I've made.'

Ted presided over two more Ashes series, and while the results on the pitch never got much better, his comical ability to say the wrong thing never deserted him.

After David Gower got the push, his next captain was Graham Gooch (Ted had described Goochy's previous appointment as England skipper as 'being hit in the face by a dead fish').

Ted selected me for my first tour in 1990/91, and he flew out to join us in January 1991, by which time we were already losing 2–0. Could the good lord be our saviour? Er, no. As Ted told the press: 'I pondered two hours in the middle of the night, but don't think there's anything I can do to help.'

Sheer genius.

Back home in 1993, and with England 2–0 down again after two matches, having just been smashed by an innings at Lord's, Ted said boldly: 'We can still win this series 3–2 and if that proves to be the case there is no question Graham [Gooch] will be the man pouring the champagne at The Oval.'

By the Third Test at Trent Bridge, when Ted dropped five players (including me), he had gone astrological in his hopes for the newly capped players. 'I just hope the stars and planets will be propitiously aligned for the young cricketers starting out on their Test careers.'

The new boys did help England to a draw, but after losing the next match and with it the series, Goochy resigned. Ted followed suit during the Fifth Test to cheers from the crowd, a sad end for the Lordster's colourful selection career.

Ian Botham concluded that Ted 'crossed the line between eccentricity and idiocy far too often for someone who was supposed to be running English cricket'. And, yes, okay, we won only one Test in three Ashes series under him, and no one was much clearer what our best team was by the end of his reign (mind you, 'only' 24 England players were used in the 1993 Ashes compared to 29 in 1989 so I guess you can call that progress), but as Ted was fond of saying, 'winning isn't everything'.

And maybe it's time England revived one of his most imaginative wheezes. Altogether now, 'Onward Cooky's cricketers, striving for a score . . .'

WHEN SELECTORS GET IT RIGHT . . .

As Australia were piling up a massive first innings total at Lord's in 1993, an MCC member asked ex-Australian captain Ian Chappell how come his country always produces good young batsmen.

'We play them,' was the deadpan reply.

Chappell felt England selectors were overcomplicating things (Lord Ted overcomplicating? Never!) and not giving promising youngsters like Somerset's Mark Lathwell a go.

Maybe Ted overheard Chappell, because Lathwell was picked for the next two Tests. But by then the Aussies were in total control of the series, Lathwell made little impact and, in the typical England selection style of the time, rather than stick with him, he was dropped and never picked again.

Sometimes England selectors have got it spectacularly right though. For instance, during the 1956 Ashes series, they got on a roll making some inspired picks. With England one down, controversially, they recalled Cyril Washbrook for the Third Test. Washbrook hadn't played a Test for five years, and as an MCC member, his selection seemed like jobs for the boys. But Cyril proved the doubters wrong, putting on 187 with Peter May after England won the toss and batted first, the best partnership by an English pair since the war. May scored a century and although Cyril just fell short, his 98 runs helped to set up an innings victory by England to bring the series level at 1–1.

For the next Test at Old Trafford, the selectors plucked another golden apple, bringing in Reverend David Sheppard. The game is remembered for Jim Laker's 19 wickets, but a century by Sheppard, coming in at number three, was key in setting up another chance to enforce the follow-on and take a 2–1 series lead.

Even though England were assured of retaining the Ashes, the Aussies were keen to even up the series in the last Test at The Oval. But again the England selectors made another shrewd recall, bringing back 38-year-old Denis Compton, who'd been sidelined by recurring knee problems. After a sticky start against hostile bowling by his old mate Keith

Miller, Compton showed his class with a stylish innings of 94, the highest score by a batsman on either side, and Australia could only just hang on for a draw. All in all, the selectors had had a great series.

Who to select can be a really fine judgement call. One great example of that from Ashes history was the Third Test at Headingley in 1981. After the first day, Mike Brearley thought he'd made a terrible ricket on his return to the team and captaincy, by picking Bob Willis over John Emburey. Bob had been struggling with a chest infection and was only brought into the squad at the last minute, but Brearley preferred him to Emburey, even though Graham Gooch and Ian Botham reckoned the ball was going to spin from day one. England selectors Alec Bedser, Charles Elliott, Brian Close and John Edrich were also inclined towards picking Embers, but let Brearley have the team he wanted.

The Aussies, who shared Goochy and Beefy's view, were miffed that England's premier spinner was being left out too. When they saw the England team sheet, captain Kim Hughes took Dennis Lillee and Rod Marsh out for another look at the pitch to make sure their plan to bat first was the right one. When Marsh visited the England dressing room later, he even asked Brearley if leaving out Embers had been a bluff to get them to put England in to bat!

Hughes won the toss and they did bat first, scoring a comfortable 203–3 on the first day, Bob Willis not looking like taking a wicket. Meanwhile, off-spinner Peter Willey, who with all due respect was not in Embers's class, was making balls turn and bounce sharply – and that was despite Willey having a bruised index finger which stopped him giving the ball his usual tweak.

Brearley was having kittens. Near the close of play he told umpire David Evans that bowling a team out for 90 should have been doable on this pitch. After a fairly sleepless night, he even apologised to Embers, saying that it was his personal decision to leave him out.

However, after seeing the Aussie pace attack bowl out England for 174 in our first innings, Brearley started to think that maybe it wasn't such a bad call after all. On Sunday he even called Embers, who was back playing for Middlesex by then, to say that maybe he hadn't been wrong. And by the Tuesday, when Bob Willis uprooted Ray Bright's middle stump to complete one of the greatest displays of fast-bowling in Ashes history and a miraculous victory, Brearley's decision looked utterly inspired. From selection 'cock-up' to cockahoop.

ONE HILL OF A PUNCH-UP

Brearley had the confidence of the selectors to get his unpopular selection of Willis through. Clem Hill, the skipper of the Australia team which slid to a 4–1 home defeat in the 1911/12 Ashes, did not have quite such a cosy relationship with his chairman of selectors, Peter McAlister.

McAlister didn't rate Hill's captaincy skills. In return, Hill and the Australian players were not great fans of McAlister, who had a reputation for selfishness after picking himself for the previous Ashes tour of England when he was regarded as a spy in the camp for the Australian Board of Control.

The mutual hostility spilled over in February 1912 during a meeting in Sydney to choose the side for the next Test in Melbourne. Australia were already losing the series 2–1 and tensions were running high. When McAlister called Clem the 'worst captain in living memory', Hill, who was a fairly calm chap normally, lost it, leaping across the table and punching McAlister. A proper bare-knuckle fist fight lasting a quarter of an hour followed, reaching a dramatic climax when Hill tried to chuck McAlister out of a third-floor window. Luckily, an official managed to drag the raging Hill away and prevent the first-ever case of murder during an Ashes selection meeting.

CHAPTER 9

HOW TO BE AN ASHES CAPTAIN

To captain an Ashes team is both a huge honour and a massive responsibility. A skipper is carrying the weight of history of this great sporting event and the hopes and expectations of a nation. You need a lot of personal qualities and skills to handle all the requirements and pressures.

For some reason I was never called upon to lead my country into battle against the old enemy (stop giggling at the back . . .), but many different characters have been given a go. So what can future Ashes captains learn from the great, the good and the not-so-good ones of the past?

Poshness can help . . .

Well, actually, this isn't true any more – even though our recent ex-captain Andrew Strauss is frightfully well-spoken – and it never has been for Australians. But it is worth remembering that, crazy as it seems, before the gentlemen/players divide was removed in 1963 it was almost impossible to become England captain unless you came from a privileged background and played cricket part-time. A downtrodden old full-time professional simply wouldn't do.

James Lillywhite was the first pro to captain England versus Australia – in the first-ever Test match, at Melbourne in 1877. But after Arthur Shrewsbury led the team on the 1886/87 tour it wasn't until Jack Hobbs was made stand-in captain for the ill Arthur Carr during the Fourth Test of 1926 that another pro was allowed to take charge.

'A rotten captain . . . but then, I am afraid, most pros are not much good at the job,' was Carr's sniffy assessment of Hobbs.

Wally Hammond took a job as director of a tyre company in 1937 to give himself a chance of the captaincy, and even then the egg-and-bacon ties at the MCC were none too keen, and it was only the fact that Wally's mate Plum Warner was chairman of the selectors that his appointment went through.

Although it caused MCC traditionalists to faint, a professional was appointed to lead England into the 1953 series – Len Hutton. But old habits die hard, and when his former captain Freddie Brown was recalled to the side for the Lord's

Test, Len naturally found himself doffing his cap and calling Freddie 'Skipper'.

If only I'd been around then. With my private-school education (okay, it was only a brief education because I was expelled) I'm sure the MCC members would have preferred me for the job.

... But self-hypnosis doesn't

Bob Willis was regarded as a better vice-captain than skipper, but he was England captain in 1982/83 when other candidates such as Graham Gooch went off on a rebel South Africa tour.

Bob had used hypnosis tapes in the mid-seventies to focus his mind and help his bowling, but a trance-like state is not ideal for the captain's role.

Mike Gatting recalled: 'Bob would be in a dream world half the time. At Headingley, he was running in and we had to stop him to point out that he had neither a third man nor a fine leg!'

Be a top tosser (and carry a threepenny bit)

If I had to choose one captain from history to toss a coin for my life, it would probably be England's captain in the 1905 Ashes series, Stanley Jackson. Stanley's fag at Harrow School had been none other than Winston Churchill. The son of a lord, he went on to become an MP, chairman of the Conservative Party, president of the MCC and Yorkshire and chairman of the England selectors in 1934 and 1946. Oh, and he was knighted. Very similar to my life story, then . . .

Stanley could play a bit too. In that 1905 series he averaged 70 with the bat and took 13 wickets at 15 apiece. Not only that, he was a lucky tosser, winning the toss in all five Tests as England triumphed 2–0.

On the other hand, you wouldn't want my mate Alec Stewart tossing for your life. Stewie incorrectly called heads in every Test of the 1998/99 series. This meant that Mark Taylor became the first Australian or English skipper to 'coinwash' his opposite number since Lindsay Hassett in 1953. That year, England captain Len Hutton got so hacked off with Hassett's luck that when he lost his fourth toss in a row at Headingley, he chucked away the coin in disgust. Hassett put England in, and Ray Lindwall bowled Hutton second ball in front of his adoring Yorkshire fans just to rub it in. Despite his tossing misfortunes, Hutton led England to a first series victory for 19 years anyway, nicking the final Test after four draws.

Although nothing much went right for England captain David Gower against Australia in summer 1989, he did manage to freak Allan Border out with his habit of producing various random coins for the toss. Gower pulled out everything from a French franc to an old threepenny bit during the series and Border later admitted that he found this 'unnerving'.

AB always called 'heads' and thought that maybe Gower was using coins of different weights because they'd give him an advantage. Not sure how that works; I suspect it was just David being his normal cultured self – not many captains I knew wandered round with a threepenny bit in their pocket.

If you do win the toss, make the right decision

It only takes a second to say 'We'll have a bat/bowl', but get it wrong and your team could pay the consequences for days. It could even cost you the Ashes series.

The coach and senior players will have a say in whether you bat or bowl, but ultimately it's the captain who makes the call out in the middle and cops most of the blame if it goes horribly wrong.

England fans look back fondly on Ricky Ponting's decision to put England in in the Second Test at Edgbaston in 2005, even though his legendary strike bowler Glenn McGrath had just tripped over a cricket ball in the warm-up. McGrath had torn ankle ligaments and was out of the game. My *Test Match Special* colleague Geoff Boycott summed up Ponting's choice with typical understatement as 'the most stupid decision he'll ever make in his life'.

That day, England carted a McGrath-less Australian attack all around the park, racking up 407 all out at about five an over and changing the course of the series which Australia had begun with a win.

It's easily done though. Two-and-a-half years previously, by the time of the opening Test in Brisbane, things were already going badly wrong for England. Our main strike bowler Darren Gough had got seriously injured and was on his way home and Freddie Flintoff also had a niggle, so captain Nasser Hussain had a lot on his mind. When he examined the wicket the day before the game it looked a bit green, so he thought it would help his under-strength seam-bowling attack if they bowled first.

The next morning, Nass had a quick check of the wicket and reckoned it looked a lot browner. But after a quick consultation with coach Duncan Fletcher in the dressing room, he decided to stick with his original plan to bowl.

He won the toss, the ball hardly moved off the straight and Matty Hayden scored 197 as Australia built up a match-winning total. 'The Aussie crowd were actually laughing at us,' recalled Nasser, but the funny thing was that his opposing captain Steve Waugh said he would have bowled first too.

In the First Test of the 1954/55 series, with England defending the Ashes, Len Hutton put the Aussies in at Brisbane, which looked a huge gamble on a good wicket. Having lost every toss in the previous series, perhaps Len had forgotten what it was like to have the choice? Anyway his decision proved to be a shocker as Australia scored an unprecedented 601–8 declared against England's all-pace attack.

To be fair to Len though, England's fielding was woeful, grassing no fewer than a dozen catching chances.

Possibly one of the bravest toss-winning decisions in Ashes history was made by Aussie skipper Mark Taylor at Old Trafford in 1997. He surprised everyone – his team-mates included – by winning the toss and opting to bat first on a green, greasy wicket under grey skies. It seemed even bolder or madder (depending on your point of view) given that Taylor was opening the batting himself and Australia were 1–0 down in the series.

Before he'd gone out to do the toss, he'd told his players they'd bowl if he won, but changed his mind when he reached the middle. The sun had come out, he felt the pitch wasn't too bad after all and he had happy personal memories of scoring a hundred at Old Trafford back in 1993 when Goochie had stuck them in. He also fancied Shane Warne to wreak havoc in the last innings, which was always a good bet.

When he got back to the dressing room, knowing he'd won the toss the Aussie boys were getting their whites on ready to field. They thought Taylor had lost his marbles when he told them they were batting and started pulling on his own pads.

At 160 for 7, the straitjackets were being prepared, but Steve Waugh pulled out a match-turning century. Then Warney got to work quicker than Taylor predicted, taking a six-fer in England's first innings. Australia won comfortably to level the series and went on to win the next two matches to secure the Ashes for the fifth time in a row.

A naturally gifted player doesn't necessarily make a great captain . . .

Greg Chappell was a natural player, but he himself admitted that captaincy didn't come as easily to him, unlike his older brother and former Aussie skipper, Ian Chappell. 'Ian was a better captain than I was,' said Greg. 'I did a workmanlike job, but he did a very skilful job.'

According to leg-spinner Kerry O'Keeffe, who played under him, Ian Chappell's skills included keeping his team talks simple. Apparently, his instructions for how to deal with English batsmen would mostly consist of 'Bounce the ****'. As for the bowlers? 'Slog the ****'. Even I could have got my head round that.

Greg took a bit longer to get the hang of it. His team-mates said that it was when he was given the captaincy again in 1981/82 and endured a rare bad run with the bat that he became a better skipper because he finally found out how hard the game could be for other players. Dennis Lillee recalled: 'Almost overnight he became a more understanding captain.'

David Gower, Ashes skipper in 1985 and 1989, was another wonderfully gifted player who admitted some weaknesses as a captain. For instance, he wasn't one to hang around and talk to his players after a day's play, and sometimes a player does need a few words of encouragement from his captain.

'I wasn't good at the added extras, because as a player I didn't want too much of that,' said Gower with the benefit of hindsight. 'But I am now a firm believer that you do have to spend time to get your message across and look after people.'

Andrew 'Freddie' Flintoff is another brilliant player who found skippering an England Ashes team very difficult. It was between Freddie and Andrew Strauss to lead England into the 2006/07 series, and after his inspirational performances in 2005, Freddie got the nod. But he was struggling for fitness (as were other 2005 heroes including Steve Harmison, Marcus Trescothick and Ashley Giles) and up against an Australian side desperate for revenge. With England's bowling attack struggling to bowl out Australia, the workload for Freddie on the pitch was so great that he didn't have the energy to do all the man-to-man captaincy that Michael Vaughan had been so successful at in 2005.

Captaincy didn't suit Freddie, who was at his best being one of the lads, playing instinctively and inspiring his team-mates with his performances, rather than having to constantly think about tactics.

Ian Botham was similar. Beefy always claimed the captaincy didn't affect him, but the spectacular things he achieved when he was freed of the extra responsibility told otherwise. When he was captain in the first couple of Tests of the 1981 Ashes series he even seemed reluctant to put himself on to bowl, which was a handicap to the team as he was always capable of match-turning bowling spells.

Kim Hughes, Beefy's (and then Mike Brearley's) opposite number in 1981, was another richly talented player who didn't thrive as skipper. However, years later he claimed: 'Good players in your team make good captains. Great players make great captains . . . Too much is made of the captain's role. At the end of the day the captain can't bowl or most captains aren't bowlers . . . if the bowler can't get the bloke to bowl it in the right spot it doesn't matter.'

Ted Dexter would probably have sympathy with that argument as he had that problem in a very big way as England captain trying to get his fast bowler Freddie Trueman to do what he was told. Bluff Yorkshireman Freddie never took kindly to anyone telling him what to do, least of all an ex-public schoolboy like Lord Ted. In the 1964 Headingley Test, their feud reached breaking point. In the first innings, Trueman wanted to bowl bouncers at Australian batsman Peter Burge and the tailenders, but Dexter was against it. Trueman did it anyway, but Dexter refused to put a square leg or deep square leg in and the ageing Freddie's less-than-fiery bouncers were continually hooked to the boundary by Burge who scored 160, an innings which changed the whole course of the match.

Kim Hughes did have bowlers of the calibre of Dennis Lillee, Geoff Lawson and Terry Alderman at his peak, though – would another captain have been able to get more out of them?

Hughes openly showed weakness to England too – after failing to reach a small second innings target at Headingley against a rampant Bob Willis, Mike Brearley overheard Hughes at a drinks gathering during the Edgbaston Test saying, 'I hope we don't have 130 to get again.' Can you imagine Steve Waugh saying something like that?

To be fair to Hughes, he didn't have a say in selecting the squad (for instance, he had little faith in their spinner Ray Bright and was reluctant to bowl him at crucial times in the 1981 series) while, oddly, Greg Chappell, who would have been captain if he'd chosen to join the tour, did have a say, because he was skipper when the squad was picked.

Overall, Hughes found it impossible to gain the respect of the senior players, because most thought Rodney Marsh should have been made captain. Marsh denies there was any animosity between the likes of Lillee, himself and Hughes, but on the pitch there were some arguments. Hughes himself said he always felt he was up against the old guard.

... And you don't have to be a great player to be a genius captain

Mike Brearley never scored a Test hundred, averaged only just over 20, but will be remembered as one of England's greatest-ever captains. Not many people realise that he did score over 25,000 first-class runs during his career, so he was no mug with the bat, but it was his man-management skills that made him an outstanding character in Ashes history.

He captained Cambridge University, had 11 years as Middlesex captain and only lost 4 of his 18 Ashes Tests as England captain (11 wins). It was hardly surprising that he became a psychoanalyst because he had an amazing ability to get very different characters to perform to their best whether they were jazz hats like him or more working-class fellas like Graham Gooch or Ian Botham. As Beefy once said: 'I took stuff from him that I'd clip others round the ear for.'

He actually gave up the England captaincy for a while to focus on his psychoanalysis training and Botham took over. Of course, he came back when it went all wrong for Botham as skipper in the 1981 series, which allowed Beefy to focus on what he did best – flaying Australian bowlers to all corners of the ground and swing-bowling their batsmen into submission. Before the famous Headingley Test, he actually asked Botham, who'd just resigned the captaincy, whether he felt okay to play. There was no way he wanted Botham to rule himself out, but he just wanted to show him that he understood he'd had a tough time. Of course, Beefy said he was good to go, and with Brearley encouraging him to play his natural attacking game, he produced one of the greatest Test batting performances ever.

Brearley's own batting average was just 17 in that '81 series, but his captaincy was key to England's comeback victory.

Put others before yourself

Mike Brearley admitted, 'I was better at helping others than I was at helping myself, at least at Test level.' That unselfish attitude is important.

Mark 'Tubby' Taylor, who followed Allan Border as Australian captain, was a much more successful batsman than Brearley at Test level (making 19 centuries and taking a world record 157 catches) and was a great player in his own right. But he was also such a good captain that when he went through a major slump in his batting form that lasted well over a year, he still kept his place in a great Australian side.

All his team-mates were amazed how he remained so upbeat when he was getting criticised left, right and centre. The Australian selectors' wisdom in sticking by him was shown at the start of the 1997 Ashes series when he scored a battling century at Edgbaston under mega pressure.

'Allan Border was a better player than I was and a great leader by example, but he wasn't a great communicator,' said Taylor. 'People would follow him because of the example he set and I didn't think I could lead the side that way.'

And, like Brearley, Taylor was a fantastic man-manager. He could get across to the players what he wanted to do, but also talked to them, listened to their ideas and adjusted his tactics. A good bloke, who played hard and wanted to win, Taylor summed up his attitude saying, 'Not too many people die over a game of cricket.'

Get the team to do as you say, not as you do!

During their 1921 Ashes tour, the legendary Australian captain Warwick Armstrong ordered his players to go to bed before 11 p.m. before and during Test matches, but allowed himself to stay up until 1 a.m.! By this time the 'Big Ship', as he was nicknamed, weighed in at around 22 stone, so maybe he wanted to get a midnight snack before getting his head down?

His later nights and the extra rest for his players obviously did no harm, because having led his team to an Ashes whitewash victory Down Under a few months earlier, they followed up with three more wins at the start of the Ashes series in England to earn a 3–0 series victory.

A 'queer' hatred for an entire country's people can go a long way

No cricketer had more 'queer' hatred for Australians than Douglas Jardine. He seemed to judge every Australian by the people who abused him at matches, and considered them 'an uneducated and unruly mob'. The team manager Plum Warner said about Jardine: 'He is a queer fellow. When he sees a cricket ground with an Australian on it, he goes mad.'

His old schoolmaster at Winchester College had predicted

that while Jardine might win England the Ashes, 'he might lose us a Dominion', and it is true that his brutal Bodyline tactics caused an international diplomatic incident. From the moment the boat carrying his team docked in Australia, Jardine set out his stall, refusing a gift of a bottle of Scotch for every man in the team and dismissing a request for team information from an Aussie journalist.

On the other hand, his loyalty to his players encouraged many of them to follow him unquestioningly all the way to victory. Batsman Herbert Sutcliffe had described Jardine as a 'queer devil' on the previous tour of Oz in 1928/29, but he was converted to the ways of Douglas on this notorious tour: 'His fighting power was a wonderful source of inspiration to us all. He planned for us, cared for us, he fought for us on that tour and was so faithful in everything that he did that we were prepared on our part to do anything we could for him,' he said.

Gubby Allen was not so sure, though. In a letter home to his wife in November 1932, he wrote: 'Jardine is loathed more than any German who ever fought in any war . . . sometimes I feel I should like to kill [him] and today is one of those days.'

Jardine knew how to keep everyone on their toes. He would not even tell his players, let alone journalists, the eleven until he'd been out to toss up. All members of the squad would be dressed in their whites, ready to play, and he'd just pin the sheet on the wall.

Get touchy-feely Richie-style

Richie Benaud was a surprise choice as Australia's captain in 1958/59, but did brilliantly leading his team to a 4–0 victory after three successive series defeats.

One of the great man's innovations was to encourage his players to celebrate wickets with more than just an old-fashioned handshake. He had his boys high-fiving and hugging in the style of football players, and the love and affection clearly paid off.

Pick the right ball

David Gower famously made a calamitous call in his first Test back as skipper at the start of the 1989 series, ignoring the advice of the groundsman and sticking Australia in on a road of a pitch at Headingley. The pitch had been relaid and although the odd ball kept low, there was little encouragement for the quicker bowlers and spinner John Emburey had been left out so the England team had very little variety to fall back on. Apparently, the theory of Gower and the new chairman of selectors Ted Dexter was that cloud cover would offer some movement in the air, and swing bowler Phil Newport, who'd been drafted in for his Ashes debut, could cash in.

There were two main reasons why, in reality, the ball hardly wobbled off the straight. One, it was too cold in Yorkshire for swinging.

For the second reason, you have to look back at Australia's tour match against Worcestershire. In a low-scoring game,

Newport took ten wickets on the first day and this match-winning performance earned him a place in the England side. He had bamboozled the Aussie batters in that game using a high-seamed ball manufactured by Readers. So it was hardly surprising that Allan Border suggested using the smaller-seamed, less swing-friendly Dukes ball for the First Test. What was surprising was that Gower agreed to the request!

So poor old Newport was neutralised before he started, and Australia scored 600, courtesy of centuries by Mark Taylor and Steve Waugh – even Merv Hughes scored 71.

Newport's reward for being given the wrong ball was being dropped and not appearing in the rest of the series. As for Gower, it was just the beginning of a captaincy nightmare . . .

Anything doesn't go

When Ted Dexter appointed Gower, he said he was looking for him to set the 'tone and style' for the team. Obviously, there was no more stylish player than Gower, but as I mentioned earlier he did things his own way and when things went wrong the media slammed him for it.

It didn't take long for this to happen in 1989. On the Saturday of the Second Test at Lord's, Australia completed their innings, topping 500 runs, and then England lost three quick second-innings wickets. After a bad day in the field, Gower was not in the best of moods when he came in to meet the press. Critical questions about his tactics didn't lighten the atmosphere either, so he cut his own interrogation short and left the room saying he had a taxi waiting to take him to the theatre. He was going to see a preview of the Cole Porter musical *Anything Goes*. Which didn't go down well.

He got a telling-off from the management and a mauling in the press.

But after a stimulating night at the theatre, and a rest day on Sunday to read all the negative headlines about his captaincy, Gower came out to bat on Monday determined to prove people wrong and scored a fighting four-hour century to start an England fightback. 'It occurred to me that I had never needed a century more than I needed one that day,' he said later.

It wasn't enough in the end though, as Australia ran out winners again.

Gower's enjoyment of press conferences didn't increase either. At Edgbaston he got so frustrated he ended up bending forward and headbutting the table over and over again Basil Fawlty-style.

It's not a popularity contest

Gower's other massive problem in the 1989 series was that he was up against Allan Border. Border had been the losing captain in two previous Ashes series and he'd had enough of being the nice guy who came second.

It's hard to believe now about a man who ended up becoming one of the most determined cricketers and captains who ever lived, but as a youngster Border preferred surfing and messing around on the beach to cricket. He didn't rate himself as a natural leader either, but former captains Greg and Ian Chappell persuaded him to give it a go when Kim Hughes resigned and Australian cricket was in the doldrums.

Ian Chappell had said Border was too matey with the England boys in 1985, but it wasn't until a humiliating defeat inside three days at the MCG in 1987, which meant another series defeat, that he finally flipped.

They'd been expected to walk the series, but they'd been beaten by Gatt's infamous 'Team of Can'ts'. It was the lowest point of his captaincy. Just to rub it in, the television in the dressing room was showing tennis star Pat Cash leading Australia to success in the Davis Cup. Afterwards, Bob Hawke appeared on the screen saying, 'It's a pity there weren't more Pat Cashes at the MCG today.' Even the Australian prime minister was having a pop at them.

Later that evening, after sinking many beers, AB made an announcement, as Merv Hughes recalled: 'He said, "Right, boys, this is it. I'm sick of being seen as a nice guy and losing. If I'm seen as a prick from now on, that's alright, but we're going to start winning some games" . . . After that we became more verbal, tried to become more intimidating and tried to come together more as a team and that was virtually all off the back of Allan Border, who was a fantastic captain.'

Mike Brearley said 'playing a cricket match against a side captained by Ian Chappell turns a cricket match into gang warfare' and Border wanted to recapture the aura of that great Aussie side of the mid-seventies. When Chappell took over the captaincy from Bill Lawry in 1971, Australia hadn't won any of their previous nine Tests. He lost his first match in charge, but never lost a series against anyone after that.

Chappell got in trouble with administrators because he always spoke his mind, but he always backed his players and built great team spirit.

Border knew that he had to put the needs of Australian cricket before his friendships with the likes of Beefy and David Gower, and when he switched off the charm, he didn't do it by halves.

'Border was everybody's mate in 1985, but nobody's mate in 1989,' said Gower. 'In 1985, we talked all the time, but in 1989 I only heard him say "heads" or "tails" until about August . . . He sledged pretty fiercely too, which is something that doesn't normally bother me too much, although on this tour he was hyper-unfriendly.'

He banned his team from having a post-match drink with the England boys as had been the tradition. And when Robin Smith called for a drink when batting during an innings, Border spat: 'Can you have a drink? No, you ****ing can't. What do you think this is? A ****ing tea party?'

It was only when the Ashes were won that he relaxed his attitude and accepted an invitation from David Gower to his place for a barbecue (what Australian could say no to a barbie?).

With typical grace, Gower got the champagne out to toast the Aussies' victory. He did his party trick of sabreing the bottle open with an axe and as well as sending the cork flying, a little bit of glass hit Border on the face. 'Congratulations, serves you right,' joked Gower.

To be fair to AB, later that evening he apologised for being a miserable git and explained his behaviour: 'I thought we had a bloody good chance to win and I was prepared to be as ruthless as it took to stuff you.'

Being a miserable git had worked and AB kept up the grumpiness when the Ashes were at stake – Australia didn't lose another Ashes Test till 1993.

You need a bit of Aussie mongrel (or pedigree British bulldog) in you

It would have been interesting to have seen how Mike Gatting, the chairman of selectors' Ted Dexter's first choice as captain for the 1989 series, would have fared against Allan Border. Gatt was the best captain I ever played under and he had proved his Ashes-winning credentials when he led England to an unlikely victory in the previous series.

Steve Waugh once wrote, 'As a captain you have to have a bit of a mongrel streak.' Well, Gatt was more of a pedigree British bulldog in appearance, but he had all the qualities Waugh was talking about. As Micky Stewart, England's coach on the 1986/87 tour put it: 'Gatt was red, white and blue through and through – so was I. He loved playing the Aussies; loved stuffin' them.'

Batsman Chris Broad, who thrived on that tour, described Gatt as 'My kind of captain. He had get-up-and-go, loved a challenge.'

Positive and aggressive, Gatt led from the front, setting an example by the way he played and battled. He had learnt a lot playing under Mike Brearley but he knew he was a different type of captain and went about things his own way. 'I learnt a lot under Brears, but he had unique gifts as a captain and there wasn't any point in me trying to emulate him,' he admitted. 'From a tactical perspective I obviously wasn't as astute as Brears but if I made tactical mistakes at least they'd be bold ones.'

So it was a shame that the Test and County Cricket Board hadn't forgiven him for the on-pitch row with Pakistani umpire Shakoor Rana and the tabloid story which cost him the captaincy in the first place and blocked his appointment in 1989. He might have been a tougher foe for Allan Border, who had chosen that series to really channel his inner mongrel. Gatt ended up leading a rebel tour of South Africa instead when England could have done with him on Ashes duty.

Play it as straight as Herbie

The Australian squad of 1924/25 was captained by a bookmaker called Herbie Collins. At Adelaide, a large man chomping on a cigar sidled up to Collins and offered him a hundred quid to lose the game. Herbie might have been a bookie, but he was not a bent bookie. He turned to his team-mate Arthur Mailey nearby, told him what the guy was offering and suggested they throw him down the stairs!

Don't act like an old Wally

At the tail end of his career, forty-something Wally Hammond was a disastrous leader of the 1946/47 tour. He travelled separately to matches in a Jag and didn't mix with his team-mates at all except for at the actual games. Denis Compton said it was the 'worst example of mismanagement from the top I encountered on tour'.

Embrace individuality! Embrace the shovel!

One of the big difficulties a captain has is getting the balance right between giving talented individuals their head and the team ethic. I saw this first-hand on my first Ashes tour when Graham Gooch clashed with David Gower (him again!). Both great cricketers, and actually good friends, but their personalities and approach to cricket clashed. Graham was all about hard work and long hours of training, whereas David's preparation was more relaxed, an approach that worked for him.

I remember them once having a big row in a team meeting. We were losing the series and Goochy was giving us a pep talk. He was talking about how the long sessions fielding in the sun in Oz can sap the energy from the team, and when we feel that is happening it's up to someone to do something about it.

David, who had been perched elegantly on his chair, legs crossed, looking fairly uninterested in proceedings, suddenly put his hand up. Everyone turned round. As a young, impressionable bloke, I was keen to hear what this icon of the game had got to say.

'I'll tell you what we do at Leicester,' he said in his beautiful Queen's English. 'We have a trigger word: shovel. So whenever anyone feels like the energy is dropping, they shout "Shovel! Shovel!"'

What? We're all cracking up and Goochy is looking at him daggers.

'David, look, if you've got nothing constructive to say, just shut up.'

'Oh . . . oh . . . well, I actually thought that was quite a valid point.'

But Goochy wasn't having it.

'Well, if you don't want me to contribute to the team meeting, I may as well not be here . . .' sniffed David.

Goochy got fed up as the tour went on because he'd spoken to David a few times about setting a good example to the younger players, basically by doing things his way. But David just wasn't that sort of person, and after the Tiger Moth incident, he was called in for a meeting with Graham, Micky Stewart and Peter Lush.

'It took them an hour and a half to talk total bollocks about motivation, team spirit, conforming to what they wanted, etc.,' said David.

When they questioned his motivation levels, David pointed out he'd top-scored twice in Brisbane and made centuries in Melbourne and Sydney.

They just couldn't find a middle ground and from there it was all downhill in their cricket relationship.

When you compare how Gatt managed Ian Botham on the 1986/87 tour (see page 97) and got the best out of him, you have to think a bit more flexibility would have helped. Graham wasn't on that tour and said: 'It's not for me to cast aspersions because I wasn't there, but you hear stories about some players' behaviour and there's no doubt that questions could have been raised. But ultimately they won and that's all that matters, so everyone turns a blind eye.'

In fairness to Goochy, he has since said he regrets not giving David more freedom in between matches – 'What David gave you was when he took guard.' He was just trying to introduce a diet and fitness regime that is normal nowadays, but other senior players weren't buying into it.

As Alec Stewart said, 'He wanted to mould us into a Graham Gooch side and he didn't want David Gower telling young players that the way to do it was to have a glass of wine and a bottle of champagne.'

Stewie adopted a similar approach when he later captained an Ashes team himself. Which is probably why he didn't pick me!

Let players play their natural game

Steve 'Tugga' Waugh was a disciplinarian too like Graham Gooch. He expected players to be dressed correctly, turn up on time and respect each other, but he also encouraged them to play their natural game.

'If you think you can hit the first ball for four or six, then go out and do it,' he said. 'My advice was for them to play their way rather than the way others thought they should play. We had such a talented line-up we could be aggressive.'

Michael Vaughan had a similar attitude to Waugh – he liked to give players the freedom to play: 'I am not a big one on technique. Once you're at the highest level it's been embedded for years.'

Players like Freddie Flintoff, Matthew Hoggard and Steve Harmison thrived under Vaughanie in the 2005 Ashes series doing it their way.

Gain a psychological edge when the other team are celebrating

After Australia hung on to draw the epic Third Test at Old Trafford in 2005 courtesy of tailenders Glenn McGrath and Brett Lee, the Aussies were celebrating wildly on the balcony and out in the middle. Michael Vaughan used that to motivate his disappointed players. He got them round in a huddle and pointed out that the all-conquering Aussies were celebrating a draw like they'd won the Ashes. Even though the team were gutted not to get the last wicket, Vaughanie had turned it into a positive. They took that attitude into the next game at Trent Bridge, which proved to be another thriller, but this time England edged it.

Get reluctant players playing for you

In 1950/51 there was a suspicion that England all-rounder Trevor Bailey didn't want to be on the tour, and it took a telling-off from captain Freddie Brown to put him right.

In a warm-up game against South Australia, Bailey ran in to bowl wearing a thick MCC sweater as if each step was killing him. Watching on, legendary fast bowler Harold Larwood commented: 'If A'ad booled in sweater in Australia Dooglas [Jardine] would have walked oop an' ripped it oopen at seams.' An English journalist put it more simply: 'I don't think Trevor wanted to come on this tour.'

Bailey and the team read the comments in Adelaide, and before the second innings Freddie Brown was seen sending Bailey to the nets behind the George Giffen Stand with half a dozen balls. Freddie then watched from the rear window of the MCC dressing room as Bailey bowled each ball at full pace, before running down to collect the balls and repeating the process again and again.

Bailey bowled brilliantly the following week in Melbourne.

Later that summer, Bailey's right thumb was fractured/broken by a fast ball from Ray Lindwall in the first innings of the Third Test at Sydney. The injured thumb was put in plaster and Brown refused Bailey permission to bat in the second innings. But later he went out and joined his skipper at the crease anyway.

Aussie captain Lindsay Hassett went across to tell Bailey he shouldn't have come out to bat, saying that in a Test match his bowlers were entitled to bowl flat out, but couldn't against an injured player unable to hold a bat properly. Luckily for everyone, the innings ended soon afterwards with Bailey nought not out and no further harm done.

Some Aussie cynics questioned whether Bailey came out to bat just to be seen as a hero rather than to help his team, but let's give him the benefit of the doubt. And Brown deserves some credit for inspiring someone who didn't look like he even wanted to be there earlier on the tour to want to bat despite a broken thumb a few weeks later.

Don't be a 'weak dick' (and have better players than the other team)

Steve Waugh inherited a great team from Mark Taylor and wanted to make them even better. He hated complacency and looked for any small detail he could improve on. One problem he identified was Australia's habit of easing up once a series was won – what he called 'dead rubber syndrome'. And it's true they had lost the final Test in 1993 and 1997. Now, I like to think that when we won the final Test at The Oval in 1997 rather than them losing, it was because I helped bowl them out, but Waugh felt that it was down to their level of concentration dropping from earlier in the series.

Generally, Waugh thought Aussies were mentally tougher at key moments in matches. On the pitch, a favourite sledge of theirs was to call a Pom a 'weak dick'.

I'm more with Nasser Hussain, who captained against Waugh's teams in 2001 and 2002/03 and lost. Nasser reckons we had mentally tough players, too, but theirs were just better and they had greater strength in depth to replace injured players. Nasser was a shrewd tactician who came up with his own imaginative field placings to try and put the opposition batting line-up under pressure, but the Aussies were too good.

He deserves a lot of credit for laying the foundations for Michael Vaughan when he took over as captain. Nasser didn't succeed in an Ashes series, but he instilled more fight and character in the team and when the sides were more evenly matched in 2005, Vaughanie reaped the benefit of that.

Mike Atherton rated the 2001 Australian team as the best

he played against. And Waugh's players were so superior and set such a fast pace, he often didn't pay much attention to the pitch in choosing what to do when he won the toss. His attitude was to win and win as quickly as possible. Even on a good wicket where most teams would bat first, he knew Warne, McGrath and co. could skittle us for a below-par score and then their batsmen could quickly build a lead, giving them loads of time to bowl out the opposition in the second innings.

In the words of Graeme Swann, 'A trained chimp could have thrown the ball to Warne and demanded a six-fer to win a Test match.'

If you feel like giving up, recall your old favourite temperamental left-arm spinner to cheer you up

Mike Atherton was on the brink of resigning as England captain before the final Test of the 1997 Ashes series. England were 3–1 down, the Ashes were lost and everything seemed gloomy. Then he recalled a mercurial left-arm spinner who had actually been in the squad for each of the previous five Tests, but mysteriously left out of all of them.

England won a thrilling match at The Oval, with the leftie nicking 11 wickets and everyone lived happily ever after. Well, Athers decided to carry on a bit longer as captain anyway.

TUFFERS' TEN ASHES BLOCKERS

Ashes matches have never been won on flair alone. You need batters who can dig in, and these boys knew how to dig deep . . .

J. W. H. T. Douglas

Johnny Douglas was England's captain in twelve Ashes tests between 1911 and 1921 and earned the nickname 'Johnny Won't Hit Today' from Australian fans for his inability to score runs at a decent rate against their star bowler Arthur Mailey. I doubt many people were brave enough to call him that to his face though, because Johnny actually packed a punch when he put his bat down, having previously won a boxing gold medal at middleweight in the 1908 Olympics.

Ken Mackay

'Slasher' Mackay succeeded the flamboyant Keith Miller as Australia's premier all-rounder, but whereas Miller was devil-may-care in all respects, Mackay was a grinder of the highest order. They did share a great eye for a cricket ball, but whereas Miller used that to smash the ball around the park, Slasher used it to let balls that were marginally off line skim pass his stumps without offering a stroke. A nurdle through midwicket or a nudge past cover point was about as attacking as he got. He set his stall out on his Ashes debut at Lord's in 1956, batting for over six hours in two innings for a total of 69 runs.

A left-handed batsman, he bowled right-handed and his miserly, accurate medium pace frustrated opponents in a similar way. If he wasn't going to play any shots, why should they?

Tedious to watch he might have been, but he was a very important member of Australia's Ashes teams in the late fifties and early sixties. And when it came to blocking, Slasher saved the best for his last Ashes (and Test) series in 1962/63, making 86 not out at Brisbane, an innings of such stunning dullness that he was dropped by public demand.

Trevor Bailey

Back in 1953, there had been jokey calls for a single-wicket match between Trevor 'Barnacle' Bailey and Slasher Mackay, the two deadest bats in England and Australia.

The cricket-loving poet Alan Ross once wrote: 'Bailey's batting in Test cricket is limited to three strokes, the forward defensive, the late cut and the swing to leg with a ratio in favour of the first about a hundred to one.'

Bailey did occasionally cut loose though – in the First Test at Brisbane in 1954, he earned himself a £100 prize put up by a local businessman for the first English player to hit a six. (Mind you, he did take nearly five hours for the other 82 runs in that innings.)

The value of the Barnacle's dig-in ability was most clearly seen in the Lord's Test against Australia in 1953, when his marathon block-fest in partnership with Willie Watson on the final day saved England from defeat.

Keith Miller, who bowled against him that day, once said, 'Trevor was so often such a pain if you were playing for Australia against him – a damned nuisance in fact.'

Barnacle scored 71 runs in four-and-a-quarter hours at Lord's in '53, but that was nothing in comparison to his effort Down Under in 1958/59, his final Ashes series. In a legendary innings in Brisbane, Barnacle took a mind-blowing seven-and-a-half hours to score 68. That's under ten an hour, folks – who said Test match cricket is boring?

During the innings, an Aussie journalist asked the England scorer, George Duckworth, when Bailey had scored his last run.

'Twenty minutes past two.'

'Today or yesterday, George?'

Bill Lawry

Bill took the concept of a 'captain's innings' to another – and not necessarily good – level during the 1970/71 Ashes series. The Aussie skipper spent 25 hours at the crease to score 324 runs – that's an average of over seven-and-a-half hours per 100 runs.

In the Second Test, Australia were set 245 to score in 2 hours and 25 minutes. A tough assignment but worth a crack. Bill was probably not the best man for this job, though. Once he'd reached his 5,000 runs in Test cricket and his 2,000 runs against England with his second and third runs of his innings, he really pressed the pedal to the metal, scoring 6 in 68 minutes. When time ran out, Australia were just the 145 runs short of victory with seven wickets still remaining.

Australia lost the series and poor old Bill was sacked as a captain and dropped from the team for the final Test in the cruellest possible way, finding out the selectors' decision from reporters who'd been told before him.

Godfrey Evans

An incredible wicketkeeper, Godfrey Evans also played some dashing innings for England, but he makes this list for an epic display of blocking during his first Ashes tour in 1946/47. At Adelaide, England were eight wickets down in their second innings and needing to get more runs on the board to set

Australia a decent target when young Godfrey joined Denis Compton at the crease. Doing the ultimate job of 'propping up one end', Godfrey batted an amazing 95 minutes before scoring his first run, while Compton moved towards his second century of the match.

At one point, Keith Miller bowled two successive bouncers at him before apologising: 'Sorry Godfrey, but I have to do it – the crowd are a bit bored at the moment.'

Bob Woolmer

Bob made his England debut against Australia in the Second Test at Lord's in 1975 and was immediately dropped despite making a couple of thirties. He was recalled for the Fourth and final Test of the series at The Oval though. With Oz one up, England lost all hope of squaring the series when they were skittled out for under 200 and forced to follow on. Victory was out of the question and defeat looked likely in this six-day match, but for Bob's legendary display of dig-in ability. Coming in at number five, he batted for eight-and-a-quarter hours, chiselling out 149 runs, to save England's bacon.

It took Bob a few minutes over six-and-a-half hours to reach his ton, which at the time was the slowest-ever Ashes century by an England player – my old team-mate Athers set a new record at Sydney in 1990/91 in a two-coats-of-paint-drying 451 minutes. Top blocking.

Monty Noble

A dentist by trade and a wonderful Australian all-rounder, Monty's batting efforts in the three-day Old Trafford Test of 1899 were as painful as root canal for English bowlers. Monty had all the shots, but was happy to wait for the bad balls before playing them.

In that game, with wickets falling all around him, Monty made a relatively spritely 60 not out in three-and-a-bit hours in Australia's first innings. But that wasn't enough to save the follow-on, so he really dug himself a trench at the wicket in the second innings, chiselling out 89 over five hours and twenty minutes to break English hearts and save the game. His batting was described in *Wisden* as 'a miracle of patience and self-restraint'. A most noble effort.

Geoff Boycott

No list of the top digger-inners would be complete without my *TMS* colleague, Boycs. You only have to take a look at your 'Boycott Bingo' card to understand his attitude to batting.

'Show the maker's name' . . . 'It's not how good you look, it's how many you score' . . . 'Batting's all about grafting' . . . 'Now 'e's got an 'undred 'e's got te knuckle down fer a really big score' . . . 'You can't get runs in the pavilion', etc. . . .

And if you don't understand all that, you've got 'no more brains than a pork pie'.

Difficult to highlight one Ashes innings from Boycs's brilliant career because he was always so hard to get out, but his century at Trent Bridge in 1977 was a bit special on the grafting front. It took Boycs three hours to score his first 20 runs in his first innings back after three years' self-imposed exile from Test cricket. He was dropped on 20, but ended up sharing a double-century stand with Alan Knott, reaching three figures in roughly six hours.

In that game, Boycs became the first player ever to bat on every day of a five-day Ashes Test. And by the end he could have hit everything the Aussies bowled at him with a stick of rhubarb.

Bill Woodfull

Bill was the captain and opener for Australia in the Bodyline series, not something I'd wish on anyone. A straight-batter in every sense, English players jokingly called Bill 'Wormkiller' because his backlift was so short that it was only good for beheading worms if they strayed onto the wicket.

Bill makes the cut in my blockers list for once scoring an Ashes century in the Fifth Test at Melbourne, 1929, which included just three boundaries. Even better, in 1926, he scored a century in the Australians' tour match against Surrey without hitting a four before reaching three figures. Many worms were harmed in scoring that century.

Chris Tavaré

Tav turned blocking into an art form and used his crazy dead-batting skills to drive the Australians round the bend. Tav actually had some flair – smashed a few quickfire hundreds for his county in his time – but in Ashes games he was totally focused on boring the hell out of the Aussie bowlers. He gets added dig-in ability points for his opponent-maddening habit of doing a little circular walk towards square leg and back again after every ball he faced.

When England toured Oz in 1982/83, they were lacking Gooch and Boycott who were serving bans for going on a rebel tour of South Africa, so Tav, who preferred batting three, was pitched in as opener under orders to protect middle-order stars Gower, Lamb and Botham. Tav took his duty extremely seriously.

The first day of the First Test in Perth he gave Dennis Lillee and Terry Alderman a taste of what was in store, taking a whole day to score 66 not out – brilliantly, he managed not to score any runs at all in the last 73 minutes of play. He was stuck on 66 for a total of 90 minutes and was eventually out just before lunch the following day for 89, after 7 hours and 46 minutes and facing 337 balls.

If you look at some of his scores on that tour, you'd say he failed a few times, but the genius of Tav was that even when he wasn't scoring he was occupying the crease. In the second innings at Perth, he took over two hours to score nine runs – at that rate, it would have taken him just over

21 hours to score a century. Even his ducks took a while.

In total, he spent 18-and-a-half hours at the crease to score 218 runs over the five Tests. Now that is dig-in ability. Just the man you need in your team, if you're a bowler and like a decent 'Cat nap' between stints in the field . . .

CHAPTER 10

BETWEEN MATCHES

FLEA BITES AT THE CRAZY HORSE

You will have probably noticed by now that most of my own personal Ashes tales are from tours Down Under. There are a couple of reasons that most of my great memories are of touring rather than home series. First of all, I was always a bits-and-pieces player, picked for the odd Test at home. Although I appeared in three Ashes series in England, I was selected for a grand total of four games – two in 1993, and the final Test in both 1997 and 2001. I never had a run at it and consequently never really felt like an integral part of the whole thing.

Playing at home was like doing your job – you played a match and then went home. Or in my case in 1997, I was in the squad initially selected for the first five Tests but not selected for the team and sent back to play for my county each time.

All the boys were split up – you'd just meet up a couple of days before. There would be a great buzz at the grounds, but we just sort of rocked up, put our coffins down and played the game.

At the end of a day's play, we all got in our own cars and drove back separately to the hotel where we were staying. Of course, there would be excitement about the series among the people at the hotel, but most of the players would likely go off to meet their family and friends. If I went down to the bar, there would be few if any of my team-mates there, so I'd just sit and have a chat with the punters, then if someone I knew did turn up, we'd maybe go to a restaurant for a bite to eat. We would never go out and hit the town in the same way as we would on tour – it was a bit too close to home so I'd tend to keep my nut down.

Even though I was very proud to be representing my country, there wasn't the same feeling as an Ashes tour. We were getting spanked on the pitch and there was no sense of belonging at all in those days, before central contracts brought a bit more stability. It was a case of if you didn't do well, then you'd be dropped. And if you were a spinner like me, even if you did well and it was a seamer's pitch next you wouldn't play either.

So I enjoyed playing Australia in Australia more than I did playing them in England.

Everyone in the squad stayed in the vicinity and it all just felt more contained.

I can't recall ever having room service or sitting at the hotel with a couple of the boys having a quiet dinner in Australia. We went out every night. Why wouldn't you? There was a lot of mental pressure to deal with, so win or lose, you needed to wind down. Even if it was just going to a local bar for something to eat and getting back at half eleven. But in the gaps between matches there was always the chance that it cracked on into the night. 'Ooh, is that a party going on? Shall we pop in?'

In 1991 we stayed in a hotel on Hindley Street in Adelaide, which I soon discovered was *the* street in the city for nightlife. Coming from England, where pubs closed at 11, to an area where things just started getting lively at that time was rather appealing to the 24-year-old me. I found myself in a place called the Crazy Horse on my first night there. It must have been one of the first lap-dancing establishments in Australia and, I don't know what it's like now, but it wasn't exactly the Playboy Club back then.

The tables looked better suited to pasting wallpaper, the sofas were the type you might find fly-tipped by the road and you could buy Castlemaine XXXX lager by the six-pack. On the plus side, it was open all night and a lady would occasionally wander out and perform a strip show.

However, my abiding memory is of coming out early in the morning with the birds tweeting, feeling itchy and flea-bitten (those sofas . . .) doing the walk of shame back to the hotel while trying to avoid the attention of England fans out for an early-morning constitutional. 'Morning Tuffers . . .'

Being in the England cricket team was a useful calling card

on our nights out. Naming no names, but some of the boys used to go out wearing their England blazers to help them get noticed. I didn't do the blazer trick myself, but I have to admit there were times when we were out and about and perhaps people didn't recognise us and we'd start talking about the day's game in raised voices.

'PLAYED WELL TODAY. BEEFY GOT FIVE-FER . . . Oh, hello, Phil Tufnell, England.'

So we did start egging on the buzz occasionally.

If a group of players were standing at the bar, people would often just congregate around us, four or five deep. That was the norm. Obviously, some players found that less enjoyable than I did, so they might say, 'Right, then, let's go to the table.' And after dinner they might get a cab home, but I'd usually go back to the bar and start up again.

There was booze available to us everywhere we went. You'd always have a drink in your hand whether it was a High Commissioner's do or a local place. You wouldn't dream of having an orange juice. It was almost polite to have a drink.

But it wasn't like we were shit-faced all the time. A couple of pints and a couple of glasses of wine. We were just enjoying the adulation and recognition. It was what boozing should be – a merry, happy buzz. Oz is a great place for that. It's a very free country. There's sun, space and a feeling that people want to enjoy themselves. The women seemed to be much more forward than back home as well. It was, like, 'Hiii, you wannnna have a paaaahhrttty?' and my answer was pretty much always yes.

Australia was also the place where I first really discovered seafood. In Sydney we'd often go for a walk around town. Nothing specific to do, so we'd just have a wander. And more often than not we'd end up finding a restaurant near Sydney Harbour Bridge and have fantastic oysters, lobster or crayfish, washed down with a crisp white wine. Everything was so fresh and it was all a step up from the fish and chips I was used to at home.

One of our favourite places to go was the famous Doyles seafood restaurant on the beach at Watsons Bay. It's been there since the late nineteenth century and we'd get on a boat at Sydney Harbour and go across there for fish and chips and a few drinks. Actually, my most memorable visit there was not on an Ashes tour but back in 1992 on the eve of our World Cup semi-final against South Africa.

Even though he was trying to hide it, Robin Smith was a bit upset because he'd hurt his back and it looked like he'd be injured and miss the match. And while the rest of the lads sat down on the veranda at Doyles, Judge parked himself on the beach with a wine cooler and a bottle of wine. He sat there all evening at the water's edge letting the waves gently massage his bad back – we had a very different approach to injury rehab in those days. Sadly for Judge, the wine-and-water massage treatment didn't work and he missed the big game.

At the end of a Test match in Sydney, the lads might go their separate ways for dinner, but come the early hours, the livelier members of each team and fans would gravitate towards a watering hole called the Bourbon and Beefsteak in the Kings Cross district. You could always find a friendly face down at the Bourbon. Although Ricky Ponting may not agree, after he infamously got in a fight there back in 1999.

LIFESTYLES OF THE RICH AND FAMOUS

One of the most surreal parts of my first Ashes tour was suddenly to find myself mixing with celebrities. I'd see Mick Jagger, Ian Botham would just waltz up and chat to him and I'd get dragged along in the slipstream.

Mick has always loved his cricket and he'd hung out with the Aussies during their 1972 tour of England. That summer the very hairy, very heavily medallioned Australian team of Ian Chappell, Dennis Lillee and co. stayed at London's Waldorf Hotel and lived like the rock 'n' roll band they looked as if they were in, boozing it up and socialising in the bar with celebrities.

Beefy first met Jagger at his debut Test match against Australia at Trent Bridge in 1977. 'One of the strangest conversations I saw in my first Test match was Derek Underwood and Mick Jagger in the corner of the dressing room discussing field placings for left-arm spinners,' he recalled.

Personally, I never discussed my arm ball in depth with Mick, but just being around someone like him and big cheeses who ran corporations was a totally different world for me. From knocking around with my mates, I was suddenly chatting with important people and they'd be talking to me like a mate, saying things like:

'Do you lot want to come on my boat for a steam under Sydney Harbour Bridge and then back to my place [a multi-million-pound mansion] for drinks?

'What, you want me to come? Me? Too right I want to come!'

Aussie ex-player-turned-writer Jack Fingleton, reporting on the 1950/51 tour, wrote of the England team spending an evening at the home of a well-known citizen. The players were told they were welcome to bring along friends and one unnamed young member of the squad took along 'a very smart blonde'. However, there was an awkward moment when the blonde lady was introduced to the hostess who explained that she had recently sacked her as a maid from this home for being 'too perky'. Not sure if that would hold up in a court of law these days, but anyway the blonde lady was allowed to stay and apparently enjoyed her night immensely.

No one had ever asked me to go to posh dos like that before. All these things had opened up to me because of the Three Lions. I didn't have any money, but suddenly I had access to a great lifestyle.

Nowadays, the players on Ashes tours still do some glamorous stuff, but we seemed to be doing it all the time. It'd be, like, 'What are you doing tonight?'

'Oh, I'm going down to Kerry Packer's. He's picking me up in a helicopter, going to go down the winery and have a bit of dinner.'

We used to see Packer, the media tycoon and World Series Cricket creator, at the casino quite often. He was a massive gambler. I once saw him playing blackjack and he was betting on seven different boxes at once, tens of thousands of dollars each hand.

I was not quite such a high roller myself, but I did win a couple of grand playing blackjack once. I split two queens. Everyone said don't, but I did anyway. I wanted to put £200 on each split, but didn't have enough money on me so asked all the boys to lend me some. They didn't want to, but I kept bugging them till I got the stake. Drew Ace-Ace. Lovely.

FROM WARR TO PSYCHOCHEESEOLOGY

Of course, the gaps between matches also give a squad a chance to regroup and get in training for the next match. And members of the press would be keeping a close eye on proceedings, just as E. M. Wellings was during the 1950/51 tour. He was not impressed. After England's 4–1 series defeat, he was scathing in his criticism, particularly of the young players.

'The modern young player will not work at his game,' he wrote. 'Practice to most of them is obviously a tedious routine to be got through as quickly and with as little expenditure of effort as possible.'

Perish the thought.

Fielding practice was lackadaisical too, said Wellings. John Warr, a controversial selection for the tour (see page 10) apparently had never been shown how to hold his hands to make catches. And it showed during matches. After missing one sitter in the middle of the tour, one team-mate said Warr looked like 'Frank Swift [the great England goalkeeper] turning the ball round the post for a corner'.

'He dropped catches around Australia as prodigally as the

cockney drops his aitches,' wrote Wellings. I'm just thankful he wasn't around to report on 'The Phil Tufnell Fielding Academy' in 1990/91 . . .

Wellings also reckoned that the MCC players preferred playing golf to working on their game, noting that the squad's baggage manager had to lug about as many golf bags as cricket bags. 'I have even heard a player arranging for someone to take on his twelfth man duties to free him for the golf course.'

There was no excuse for a lack of practice, said Wellings, because sometimes the England boys might not play a match of any sort for over two weeks.

The mighty Australian touring team of 2001 under their coach (and Ned Flanders lookalike) John 'Buck' Buchanan were rather more professional in their approach. Although some of Buck's methods were rather unusual, as I'd discovered when he was Middlesex's coach for a year – revolutionary techniques like making us train, which we didn't like much. On the 2001 tour, Buck had the Australians in one team meeting discussing what cheeses they liked and disliked and which they would like to taste. I'm not sure how expressing a preference from English Cheddar over Camembert improves your cricket, but this training concept was based on a book called *Who Moved My Cheese?* Buck had left copies in each player's hotel room and they were supposed to read it before the meeting. However, Brett Lee, who'd joined the tour late, had never received a copy of the psychocheeseology tome and thought the coach and team had literally gone mental.

KANGAROO TAILS AND CUDDLY TOYS

When we had a break between matches or an up-country game for which some players were being rested, people would just disappear for a few days. I'd turn up to training sometimes and wonder where everyone had gone. When you asked, it was 'Oh, he's gone fishing in Manly' or 'He's gone up into the hills for a little R and R'.

It was usually the senior players who were given the extra time off. I didn't mind that, only no one ever asked me if I wanted a break. Perhaps they felt my long nights out were enough leisure time!

In the early days of the Ashes, the players seemed to have more space between matches, partly due to the extra time it took to travel overland between venues. But when they did have some leisure time, many of them liked nothing better than going out killing Australian wildlife.

After the First Test of the 1897/98 series, the touring party from England had a week off for Christmas and to travel down from Sydney to Melbourne, and some players did gun and rifle shooting from the boat on the way down.

The shoot-fest continued on arrival at their hotel as the players headed out for a day's hare shooting, but, as their elegant batsman Ranji reported in his diary of the tour, they got even more than they bargained for: 'We had some lively shooting at geese, duck, coot, and other wild fowl that had assembled in great numbers at the mouth of the Nicholson river, and for a quarter of an hour, there was great excitement on board the steamer, and everybody was delighted at the unexpected good fortune.'

Later that day, as they looked for hares, they got a bit of a fright when they came across two large black snakes in the scrub. But no problem when you've got team-mates carrying guns. 'Richardson shot one, and Storer the other of these poisonous reptiles,' wrote Ranji.

Blimey. When we went to visit a nature reserve on my first Ashes tour, we weren't so well armed. Although I could have done with some sort of weapon when an emu went for me. 'Don't worry, they won't bite . . .'

The koala I held seemed to like me better – well, he only crapped all over me.

Fast bowler Ken Farnes told how a local furrier in Perth took the team out kangaroo shooting on the 1936/37 tour. Ken had no desire to shoot animals himself, but he was assured that they were a pest and numbers had to be kept under control by occasional drives.

So he had a go, but missed with every shot. The professional hunters did make a kill though, and Ken ended up coming back to the hotel carrying a poor little orphan joey which had jumped out of his dying mother's pouch. The baby kangaroo was placed in expert care. Meanwhile, the players were happy the next evening when they were served up part of its mother in the form of kangaroo-tail soup. 'The finest soup I have ever tasted,' said Ken.

Er, yum.

When the Australian team of 2001 came to England, their leisure activities weren't quite as bloody, but they still caused carnage for the vendors on Brighton Pier one day. Brett Lee,

Glenn McGrath and Jason Gillespie went along and put their cricketing skills to good use, winning armfuls of cuddly toys. All their fielding practice came in very handy as they knocked down cans, skittles and whatever else stood in their way. Indeed, their throwing arms were so deadly that the poor chap at the basketball stand was forced to close down until they left.

In the old days, when the tour fees were not so great, some players would take the opportunity to make a bit of money on the side between games, too. Godfrey Evans, who was a partner in a jewellery business in Birmingham, took a display case of brooches and rings with him on the 1954/55 tour Down Under and tried to flog his wares whenever he had a chance. Meanwhile, the Bedser brothers, Alec and Eric, did a bit of networking looking for potential importers of their company's office equipment.

If only I'd thought of that – could have got the Tufnell family's silversmith business exporting Down Under!

CHAPTER 11

CONTROVERSIES

GRACE-FUL GAMESMANSHIP AND BIG SHIP MISBEHAVING

An Ashes series just wouldn't be the same without a good dollop of controversy. Strangely, I was never really involved in any big Ashes disputes – just the odd minor incident like calling an umpire a '****ing bastard' on my debut when he scandalously denied me my first-ever Ashes wicket . . . have I mentioned that? [*Yes, you have, Tuffers. Let it go . . . Ed.*] And there was that time at the MCG in 1994 when Athers was trying to slow the pace of the game down to give us a chance of salvaging a draw. I bowled 48 of the slowest overs ever by a spinner in their second innings (I tied and retied my shoelaces a lot and made many fine adjustments to field placings that day. We still lost.)

But with two teams who desperately want to win and national pride at stake, the temptation for players (and coaches and officials) to stretch rules to breaking point to gain an edge has been there since day one. In fact, before day one – it was the dubious behaviour of the legendary W. G. Grace that indirectly inspired the idea of the Ashes in the first place.

This is what happened 1882 at The Oval. Australia 110 for 6 and just 72 ahead.

The Australia number 8 Sammy Jones left his crease to prod the pitch. Grace whipped off the bails and appealed. Even though the ball was to all intents and purposes 'dead', and Grace's behaviour lacked any of the grace you'd expect of a Victorian gentleman, the umpire felt he had no choice but to give Jones out.

Between innings, Aussie fast bowler Fred 'The Demon' Spofforth, a man with a clinical middle-parting and an impressive moustache, bundled into the England dressing room to confront Grace, calling him a cheat and telling him he'd regret his treachery.

A man enraged, Spofforth went out and bowled his devilish heart out, taking 7 for 44 as England crashed to 77 all out and lost by 7 runs. This defeat would inspire the famous mock obituary written in *The Sporting Times* by Reginald Shirley Brooks, a boozy journalist with an arch sense of humour:

In Affectionate Remembrance
OF
ENGLISH CRICKET
WHICH DIED AT THE OVAL

CONTROVERSIES

ON
29th AUGUST, 1882
Deeply lamented by a large circle of sorrowing friends
and acquaintances
R.I.P.
N.B. – The body will be cremated and the ashes
taken back to Australia

The legendary Australian all-rounder Warwick 'Big Ship' Armstrong, whose Ashes career spanned three decades from 1902 to 1921, was cut from the same cloth as Grace. A massive, imposing figure at 6ft 3in with an ever-expanding waistline, Armstrong had an appetite for battle. And he didn't care about winning prettily, or necessarily fairly, he just wanted to win.

He excelled himself at the Headingley Test in the 1909 series, after an Australian appeal against Jack Hobbs for 'hit wicket' was turned down. Armstrong refused to accept the decision. Hobbs described his behaviour as 'nasty and un-sportsmanlike' and it affected him, because when play eventually restarted, Hobbs was out a couple of balls later not offering a shot.

Two games later, Armstrong stretched gamesmanship to quite unbelievable lengths, keeping debutant Frank Woolley waiting for a reported 19 minutes to face his first ball in Test cricket while he bowled practice balls. Yes, I'll spell that out – nineteen minutes! Okay, bowl some practice balls but how do you waste that much time? That is some achievement.

A future great all-rounder, Woolley only managed eight

runs that day. Australia won the series 2–1.

The Big Ship didn't make himself too popular with the English public on his final Ashes tour in 1921 either, when he complained about everything from playing hours to the lack of a rest day before Tests. In the Fourth Test, when the England skipper Hon. Lionel Tennyson declared England's first innings closed half an hour before stumps, Armstrong kept his players on the pitch after his wicketkeeper Sammy Carter (rightly) said it was against the rules. The crowd booed, but actually in this case he was right: because the first day's play had been abandoned and the match had reverted to a two-dayer, England shouldn't have declared. When play resumed, Armstrong bowled the next over having bowled the last one before the stoppage, thus breaking the rules himself.

Armstrong was no fan of time-limited matches either. He didn't believe in draws and thought every match should be played to a finish. When a result was not possible in the last Test of 1921, he took off his proper bowlers and went out to field in the deep rather than his customary position at second slip. Just to emphasise his boredom, as he was fielding near the boundary, he grabbed a newspaper that had blown across the pitch and started to read it. Asked later why he did it, he joked, 'To see who we are playing.'

BORDERLINE CATCHES

In the days before the Decision Review System was introduced, disputes over catches were more common and harder to resolve. Even the great Don Bradman found himself embroiled in controversy in the first session of the first Ashes Test after the Second World War. At Brisbane, Bradman appeared to be caught in the slips for 28 by Jack Ikin off Bill Voce, but he didn't walk, and when Ikin finally appealed to the umpire the finger stayed in the pocket.

England skipper Wally Hammond didn't hide his anger, saying loudly at the end of the over as he passed by Bradman and the umpire, 'A fine bloody way to start the series.'

Bradman later argued his innocence saying he wasn't sure whether the ball had carried and so he had waited for the umpire's decision. And unlike the Big Ship and W.G., The Don was known for his sense of fair play so he probably deserves the benefit of the doubt.

Bradman went on to score 187 and Australia topped 600, and even worse luck was to come for England. With perfectly terrible timing, violent thunderstorms juiced up the wicket for the Aussie bowlers before each England innings, and Australia won the match by an innings and plenty.

Another memorable one occurred during the Fifth Test at Edgbaston in 1985, an incident which Australian skipper Allan Border claimed cost them a draw in a rain-affected match.

In the second innings, wicketkeeper-batsman Wayne Phillips was on 59 and going along nicely, when he smashed a ball from spinner Phil Edmonds straight onto the foot of Allan Lamb who was trying to get out of the way at silly point. The ball looped up to David Gower who claimed the catch.

Umpire David Shepherd wasn't sure, so he consulted his colleague David Constant at square leg who told him that in his opinion the ball hadn't hit the ground. Watching from the pavilion, Border was furious. He thought the umpires should have given his batsman the benefit of the doubt. With Phillips gone England rattled through Australia's last four wickets and wrapped up victory within the hour.

Okay, AB might have felt hard done by, but what about Lamby and his poor foot?

In more recent years, Ricky Ponting has been particularly vocal in his opinion that batsmen should 'walk' when a fielder claims a catch without waiting for the umpire's decision. For instance, there was an incident on the first day of the Adelaide Test in 2002 which infuriated Ponting and co. Michael Vaughan drove a ball from Andy Bichel uppishly to cover where Justin Langer claimed a low catch. The Aussie lads ran over to celebrate, but Vaughanie stayed where he was and waited for the verdict of umpires Steve Bucknor and Rudi Koertzen. They consulted but couldn't reach a decision so they referred it to the third umpire, and after viewing the replays, he gave Vaughanie the benefit of the doubt. It happened again at Melbourne later in the series when Jason Gillespie was sure he pouched Nasser Hussain, but the decision went England's way.

The day after Langer's disallowed catch, *The Australian* newspaper ran the headline, 'RIP: THE DAY THE GAME LOST ITS VERY SOUL'. Which was a bit extreme.

My opinion on 'walking'? Well, ask yourself if you were batting nine down, final Test match, one run to win the Ashes, you hit the ball and you're not sure the fielder's taken the catch, would you walk off?

PITCHING FOR GLORY

Pitch conditions can influence the outcome of a cricket match like few other games.

Take the 1938 Ashes series, when Australia were leading 1–0 going in to the final Test. But the match at The Oval was played on arguably the friendliest batting wicket in Ashes history. So when Wally Hammond won the toss for the fourth successive time, the England batters absolutely filled their boots. They racked up an incredible 903 for 7, with Len Hutton compiling the highest-ever Ashes innings of 364. As an added bonus, Don Bradman, who was averaging over 100 in the series up until then, broke his ankle bowling so he couldn't bat, and England ended up winning by a monstrous innings and 579 runs.

Afterwards, spinner Bill O'Reilly, who'd worn the skin off a finger from bowling 85 overs (yes, count them – eighty-five overs) in England's innings was looking for the groundsman: 'If I had a rifle, I'd shoot him now.' In that case though, if Australia had won the toss and Bradman had had first dig on that pitch, the England players might have been the ones on the warpath.

There have been other occasions when the pitches have been more obviously prepared to suit the home team. In the summer series of 1997, five of the six pitches were unofficially tailored to England players' strengths – just one match was played on a flat wicket. We still lost.

And if you are going to blatantly rig a pitch, you should at least have the decency to come up with an imaginative excuse.

Headingley 1972 will always be remembered for the 'fusarium' explanation used by the authorities for a ridiculously spin-friendly pitch which helped 'Deadly' Derek Underwood to ten wickets and England to an easy victory.

It was claimed that a freak thunderstorm a few days before the game had left the pitch riddled with a microscopic fungus called fusarium. Luckily, the symptom of the fungus was a crumbling wicket perfectly suited to Deadly, by far the best spinner on either team. Strangely, the rest of the grass around the ground seemed perfectly fine. And when Aussie captain Ian Chappell looked up 'fusarium' in the botanical dictionary, he discovered that it needed temperatures of 75 degrees-plus to flourish and it hadn't been that warm in Yorkshire.

Luckily, for England, the Aussies didn't want to be seen as whingers so they didn't make too much of a fuss about it even though they felt they'd been stitched up.

CHUCKERS AND DRAGGERS

I was accused of 'throwing' when I was in New Zealand before the 1992 World Cup, which was staged in Australia and New Zealand. Their wicketkeeper Ian Smith accused me of chucking my slower delivery, which was a bit odd – not sure why anyone would want to do that. The authorities looked at video evidence and rubbished the claims and I never had any more trouble in Ashes games.

Another left-arm spinner, Tony Lock, was not so fortunate. Lock took a series-winning five-fer in the final Test of the 1953 series at The Oval, but the Aussie captain Lindsay Hassett was not gushing in his praise for Lock. Instead, at the presentation ceremony after the game, Hassett claimed that Lock 'chucked half our team out'.

Lock's killer delivery was a fast yorker, and there were widespread doubts about his action when he bowled it. Indeed a few months later in the Windies, he was no-balled for throwing. Lock did have an excuse though. Apparently, he used to train in winter indoors in a building with a very low roof and had to bend his arm to avoid leaving the skin of his knuckles behind on the ceiling. That's a good 'un.

The controversy went up another notch in the 1958/59 Ashes. This was a series which featured some of the dullest, slowest, most negative cricket in Test match history. One day in Adelaide, England bowled only 51 eight-ball overs. That's the same as 68 six-ball overs. And the first four days in Brisbane, the average total runs scored per day was 130. Thankfully, there were some disputes to liven things up a bit.

In the First Test Colin Cowdrey was given caught out by Lindsay Kline when the ball seemed to clearly bounce in front of the fielder, but that was nothing to allegations of not just 'chucking' but 'dragging' too.

On England's side, they had Lock and fast bowler Peter Loader: whereas Lock tended to give his faster ball a bit of extra elbow, Loader's arm tended to bend when he bowled his slower ball. But in this series most attention was focused on the Aussie bowlers, particularly left-arm quick bowler Ian Meckiff and burly pace man Gordon Rorke. Meckiff himself later admitted he was a chucker and although his action made him wildly inconsistent in his line, it also, quite literally, threw England's batsmen's timing off.

The Aussies' part-time bowler Jimmy Burke also admitted delivering his off-spinners with a bent arm and Keith Slater, who switched between spin and pace bowling, could sling it down at suspiciously high speed when he decided to.

Rorke was brought into the side for his debut in the Fourth Test to replace the injured Meckiff, only to be accused of the double whammy of throwing and 'dragging'. His arm action was not as jerky as others, but Rorke apparently played fast and loose with the old no-ball law where the back foot was supposed to be behind the bowling crease at the point of delivery. It was said that although his back foot started behind the line, he dragged his toe along the ground well beyond the bowling crease before actually delivering the ball. A 6ft 5in, 15 stone, blond stormtrooper of a man, Rorke was an intimidating figure, and he looked even bigger to batsmen because by the time he released the ball, he was a couple of yards closer to them than any modern bowler would ever get today. Like Meckiff, Rorke was an erratic bowler, but when he got his line right, the ball arrived so quickly as to be almost unplayable.

Freddie Trueman, never a man for understatement, said the Australian umpires were biased, no-balling the England boys while allowing Rorke, in his words, 'to bowl with both feet over the front line'. Ironically, Richie Benaud, who was captaining the Australian side, reckoned Freddie himself was a dragger and was also one of the players, like Rorke, whose bowling habits led to the authorities introducing a front-foot law in 1963.

Perhaps bearing in mind that the Australians hadn't lodged

an official complaint about the rigged pitches in England during the 1956 series, captain Peter May didn't complain in 1958/59 either. However, when the series was over the English players did make their feelings clear to both Sir Don Bradman and the MCC.

In fairness, I should point out that the Aussies' demolition job on us in 1958/59 wasn't all down to chucking and dragging. Peter May's team was supposed to be the best in the world, but they got beaten up 4–0. The post-series inquest pointed to the poor wickets in England which meant that our batsmen's confidence had been destroyed before they got Down Under, while our bowlers struggled when they went abroad and played on flat pitches where you had to work for wickets.

Then there was our lack of quality all-rounders and the reliance on specialist batsmen and bowlers meant England had a long tail, while Australia boasted the all-round talents of Benaud and Alan Davidson who took 55 wickets between them in the series at an average of under 20 runs. And both of them bowled with lovely straight arms.

As for Mr Meckiff, he didn't even make the next Ashes tour of England as umpires clamped down on the bent-arm brigade.

You might think that the introduction of a front-foot law would have eliminated any no-ball issues for umpires, but this was only if they chose to enforce it. David 'Bumble' Lloyd always used to say that Jeff Thomson was pacier in Australia than England, partly because the home umpires seemed to allow him to bowl from past the popping crease.

One time, back in the dressing room after batting his

way through a typically hostile spell by Thomson, Bumble mentioned to his team-mates that Thommo was over the front line for most of his deliveries. They said he should tell the umpires after the break, so he made the point early in the next session.

'He gets quite close, doesn't he, sir?' he told the umpire. Quite tactful and polite, considering he couldn't see any foot markings actually behind the front line.

'He's close enough,' replied the umpire bluntly. 'And anyway, we don't agree with that law over here.'

'You do when we're bowling,' grumbled Bumble.

SUCKER AND LEAKS

Millions of words are written on every Ashes series, and a nice dispute always gets plenty of column inches.

Hard to believe now it has become such a normal part of top-level cricket, but when the idea of a 'Man of the Series' prize was first floated, even that caused a media hoo-ha. Before the First Test of 1950/51, a company offered £1,000 to the 'player whose team-play was most highly rated by two former Test players – Arthur Mailey (Aus) and Arthur Gilligan (Eng)'.

At the time, the idea of offering an individual reward in a team game, even if it was for 'team-play', was seen as rather undignified. Our old friend E. M. Wellings called it 'absolutely farcical' and 'contrary to the spirit in which cricket should be played'.

Mailey and Gilligan used a bizarre points system to judge

the award which seemed to favour all-rounders as points were awarded for both batting and bowling. Credit due then to batsman Len Hutton who ended up top of the points table having averaged close to 90 over the series. Not that Len got to keep all the money, because the players of both sides had agreed to split the prize between them long before.

Sometimes journalists can be too eager to jump on a story and not check their facts properly. Like when Marcus Trescothick published his autobiography and revealed that he had been the chief Murray Mint sucker in the England side, assigned to spit sugary gobbets on the ball when the team needed a little extra to get the ball to swing. Aussie journalists got quite irate when they found out, implying that the 2005 Ashes had been won by cheating. Which would really have sucked. But they obviously hadn't read the book too carefully – Trescothick was talking about the 2001 series which England lost 4–1.

Of course, there's nothing better for a journalist than when a story literally lands on their desk. Like before the Third Test in 2001 when the team notes of Australian coach and leading psychocheeseologist John Buchanan were misplaced and found their way to the press.

Buck compared where the Australian Ashes campaign had reached in relation to Sun Tzu's philosophy on the nine types of ground to be covered for a battle to be won, as written in *The Art of War*.

The leaked document gave an insight into the Aussie coach's thoughts on England. 'Overall this English team is hanging onto excuses (e.g. injuries, toss, bad luck, dropped catches etc),' he wrote. 'By gradually taking each of these away, ultimately, there is no place to hide.'

All pretty fair comment really, as they were killing us at the time.

The *Daily Mirror* newspaper adapted the original *Art of War* book cover image to read 'The Art of Waugh' in tribute to Aussie captain Steve Waugh.

Waugh himself felt Buck was a 'performance manager rather than merely a coach', 'ahead of his time, a bloke I have always found helpful and stimulating'. Twin Mark Waugh, on the other hand, read a few words of Buck's Sun Tzu notes and concluded they were 'rubbish'. Diff'rent folks, diff'rent strokes.

A similar storm in a teacup occurred during the 2006/07 series when someone nicked England's bowling plans for each of the Australian batsmen and leaked them to the Australian press. Now, I never saw the plans, but I'm guessing they probably repeatedly mentioned bowling 'top of off stump'.

The ECB took the leak terribly seriously and dispatched their press officer to read out a statement on this grave breach of tactical security. Unfortunately, no one had told bowler Matthew Hoggard, also on the stand at the press conference, of the gravity of the matter. When quizzed further about the ECB investigation that was supposedly underway, Hoggy replied: 'We are continuing our enquiries, and when we find the culprit we're going to string him up by his ding-dang-doos and chop them off. We've got our finest detectives on the case – Inspector Morse, Sherlock Holmes and Miss Marple.'

WHEN BRADMAN BATTED LIKE ME

Of all the controversial tactics used in Ashes history, none has been more infamous than Bodyline (see pages 25–27). As I described in Chapter 2, Jardine's tactics in that 1932/33 series were not actually very original – it was basically 'leg theory' as used by Plum Warner two decades previously, only with faster bowling – and he wasn't even that sure of using it against Bradman and co. until after he arrived in Oz. One reason he might have been worried about it was that Larwood hadn't had much success on his previous Ashes tour in 1930. It was only when they got out there in 1932 that he discovered that Larwood, aged 28, had found a couple of yards' extra pace from somewhere. Which was handy.

Another odd thing that many people don't know is that Jardine wasn't actually playing when leg theory was first used on Bradman in a tour match against an Australian XI at Melbourne. He'd left his deputy Bob Wyatt in charge while he went fishing. And while Jardine was out hooking trout, Larwood had Bradman trapped lbw for 36 in the first innings after Wyatt had moved all the slips to the legside. He then bowled him for just 13 in the second, Bradman playing a very un-Bradman-like cut shot backing away.

Wyatt claimed he only moved the slips across to stop batsmen getting easy onside runs that day, but once Jardine and the selectors realised the potential, it evolved into what became known as Bodyline.

When Jardine returned from his fishing trip, Wyatt reported that the tactic had definitely unsettled Bradman.

'Oh, that's interesting,' said Jardine. 'We'll have to give him more of it.'

He had the chance in the MCC's last tour match before the Ashes proper, when they played New South Wales at the SCG. And it was clear that they were on to something when Bradman was bowled by Bill Voce in the second innings, by a ball that Bradman tried to evade but hit middle stump.

'This was batting from the Phil Tufnell handbook,' wrote author Simon Briggs, in his book *Stiff Upper Lips and Baggy Green Caps*, probably the only time my batting skills have been mentioned in the same breath as The Don. I am honoured.

Once the Ashes series got underway, Bodyline bruised many Australian batsmen and caused an international incident. On the second day of the Third Test in Adelaide, one of the darkest days in Ashes history, Aussie opening batsman Bill Woodfull was moved to tell England's manager Plum Warner, 'There are two teams out there on The Oval; one is trying to play cricket, the other is not.'

Woodfull was lying on the physio's table in the dressing room at the time having been hit over the heart by a missile delivered by Harold Larwood, so he knew what he was talking about.

Plum deadbatted the complaints, so the Australian Board of Control sent a cable to the MCC saying that this 'unsportsmanlike' ploy was 'likely to upset the friendly relations existing between England and Australia'.

The MCC and Jardine didn't like the accusation of bad sportsmanship one bit and Jardine said he would not play another match unless it was withdrawn. The Aussie Board of Control backed down and the series was allowed to continue, which it did without further serious injury. But the bitterness remained and spread beyond cricket. Politicians were talking about the threat to economic relations between England and Australia – US president Franklin Roosevelt was even told about it. All this over a game of cricket.

England ended up winning the series 4–1, and even though Bradman still topped the Aussie batting averages, keeping him down to a mere 56.57 was seen as a triumph. Former captain Warwick Armstrong, by that time working in the media and always good for a provocative comment, reckoned that The Don was 'frightened of fast bowling'. Bradman had moved around his crease when Larwood was about to bowl, which his critics claimed showed he had a yellow streak, but that seems unlikely. In fact you could also say he was ahead of his time. Moving your feet to leg or off as the ball is delivered was seen as unorthodox and reckless then, but in modern times great batsmen like Kevin Pietersen have used such techniques to mess with the bowler's line and length and gain the upper hand.

Despite the uproar, new versions of leg theory bowling have since been used in Ashes series. The Bodyline bowling employed to shackle Bradman was short-pitched and aimed at the batsman's head and shoulders, with good-length balls used only as a surprise delivery, whereas the 'modern leg theory' bowling operated by Len Hutton in the fifties was a slightly fuller length. It was not about bowling bouncers and physical intimidation, but keeping the ball just short of a length and taking the drive, square cut and late cut away from the batsman.

England skipper Hutton had Trevor Bailey bowling leg theory almost from the start of the First Test at Brisbane in 1954, and Lindsay Hassett, who'd been opposing captain to Hutton a year before, complained in print during the match. 'Leg theory at any time is an ugly spectacle,' he wrote, 'but leg theory forty minutes after the start of a day's play in a Test match before a near-record crowd is a tragedy.'

It didn't work very well, either, as Australia romped to victory by an innings. Hutton changed his approach as the series progressed and the novel tactic of generally aiming at the stumps was more successful as England won three of the last four Tests.

Mind you, things still got a bit spicy in that series between the fastest bowlers on either side, Frank 'Typhoon' Tyson and Ray Lindwall. Tailender Lindwall had scored a useful 64 not out in Brisbane, and when he walked out to bat in the Second Test, Tyson was determined not to let that happen again. He'd bowled a bouncer at Lindwall in Brisbane, which caused a stir as it wasn't the done thing to bowl bouncers to tailenders, and he did so again to try and soften Lindwall up. This time it worked and soon after he had him caught behind.

When it was Tyson's turn to bat in England's second innings, Lindy wanted revenge for his breach of the fast bowler's unwritten code of behaviour – thou shalt not bounce thy fellow rabbits.

Lindwall's low delivery arm meant that from Tyson's viewpoint, the ball was delivered outside the white sightscreen and he completely lost sight of a very fast, short-pitched delivery. He turned his back on the ball, was struck a sickening blow on the back of his bonce and fell in a heap.

'As I slipped in and out of consciousness, I was dimly aware of the players gathering around my prostrate body,' recalled Tyson. 'Indistinctly, I heard my fellow batsman Bill Edrich saying, "My God, Lindy, you've killed him."'

Luckily, Frank had a tough nut and after an X-ray was able to go back to the batting crease later that afternoon.

Getting knocked out by a cricket ball would put a lot of people off, but with Tyson, it sparked him to bowl even faster in the next innings when he took a six-fer, leading England to a narrow victory.

His 28 wickets were key to England's series triumph, and he had Lindwall in his pocket whenever he batted from then on, as Frank gleefully noted: 'From this juncture in the series, Ray was always on the look-out for the bouncer when he batted. Knowing this, I kept the ball well up to him – and he never made another score!'

As for leg theory, Mike Brearley did his own version at Sydney in 1978/79, placing seven men on the legside much to the disgust of the Australian fans who still associated such fields with Jardine. But, in fairness, the Aussies had already got their own back in the 1974/75 series when, under Ian Chappell's captaincy, Messrs Lillee and Thomson had bloodied our boys' stiff upper lips with arguably the most intimidating bowling in Ashes history.

Chappell's grandpa Vic Richardson had played for Australia in the Bodyline series. Vic had argued at the time that they should fight fire with fire and bowl at the body too, but no other senior player agreed with him. So when his grandson was let loose to lead the Aussies against the Poms in the 1970s, he did, in his words, 'like my granddad would have done, to stick it up them'.

Anyway, whatever the rights and wrongs of Bodyline, leg theory and all that, I can now die a happy man in the knowledge that my batting technique has been compared to the great Don Bradman's. Just call me 'The Don' . . .

BRANSON REWRITES ASHES HISTORY

During my Ashes career, debate started bubbling about the actual ashes and the 10.5cm-tall urn containing them. Australia were dominant through the nineties and people started to suggest that they receive the urn and be allowed to retain it until the next series. But, since it was given to them by Lady Darnley in 1927, the MCC have kept the urn at Lord's almost continuously and have been reluctant to ever let it be moved. As a compromise, they instead commissioned a Waterford Crystal trophy, in the shape of the original urn only larger, which was first presented to Mark Taylor, captain of Australia's winning team, at the end of the 1998/99 series.

By the end of the 2010/11 series, Australia had won the Ashes series 31 times against England's 30 series wins (five draws), and yet over the course of the competition's history, the actual little urn had only visited Australia twice since it was given to Hon. Ivo Bligh: first in 1998 as part of the Australian Bicentenary celebrations and, second, to coincide with the 2006/07 Ashes tour when it was put on display at the Museum of Sydney and then shown in other states around the country. Otherwise, the Aussies have had to improvise, like at the end of the 1982/83 series when an Australian supporter gave Greg Chappell a silver cup. The fan claimed it contained the ashes of one of the bails used at the Sydney Test during that series. 'Who said the Ashes never come back to Australia?' quipped Chappell, and the cup was kept at the Australian Cricket Board's offices.

Sir Richard Branson's airline Virgin Atlantic sponsored the transportation of the real urn in 2006/07, but, bizarrely, at one point it looked like Virgin might not bring it back. It all started with a conversation between Branson and Ian Botham over dinner aboard Branson's yacht moored in Sydney harbour. The Aussies were already 4–0 up and set to close out a whitewash win, and Beefy argued that they deserved to keep the real urn when the series ended rather than just a replica. His argument was that if you win the Ryder Cup or European Cup, you get the trophy.

Branson then took it upon himself to launch a campaign for the urn to stay Down Under. Encouraged by a phone call from the Australian prime minister, John Howard, he called a press conference at Sydney Football Stadium down the road from the SCG. There he sat, flanked by Beefy and Allan Border, to state his case.

'Australia should be proud to have won the Ashes and they should keep the Ashes until England win them back,' he said, adding that as the airline responsible for bringing the Ashes to Australia he felt 'uncomfortable' flying them back to England.

'It seems very strange that England players should be flying back to England with the urn,' he continued. 'It just doesn't stack up . . . Cricket is meant to be a fair game and it seems fair for Australia to keep the Ashes until we take them back fairly and squarely.'

When he was challenged, though, it became clear that Sir Richard's grasp of cricket history was, to be polite, shaky. Three times he tried to explain the origins of the Ashes series and each time he got it very wrong. His second effort went like this: 'In 1882 the idea was that the Ashes would come to Australia, and they would then come back to England, but then an English captain grabbed hold of them and they have kept them at Lord's ever since. It's wrong.'

Told that the urn was actually a private gift, he hurriedly checked his briefing notes and replied: 'I think the MCC are mistaken. I think it was originally a trophy, not a gift. The Ashes were burned when Britain, erm, when England, lost the 1882 game and it was turned into a trophy which the Australians took back to Australia and I think, and I may be wrong, but I think the MCC may be rewriting history.'

At this point, the highly acclaimed cricket writer Gideon Haigh told him what had really happened and that actually it was Sir Richard who was rewriting history.

Shaken by the public lesson, Sir Richard then ended up referring to the 'MCC' as the 'MMC' which didn't help his case much either. However, he still concluded 'Australia should have the Ashes' as Ian Botham believed too.

So is it fair that the urn is kept at Lord's no matter who wins? Before the urn was given to the MCC in 1927, there was no physical object representing 'The Ashes', it was just symbolic, but that didn't stop both teams competing as hard as if there was a trophy at stake. And the urn was never meant to be a trophy anyway, it was just a jokey present to a friend.

It is unusual for a major sporting event not to have a trophy, as the Ashes didn't for many years before the Waterford Crystal version was awarded, but that's part of the unique charm of the event. And do the players really look at the Waterford Crystal trophy as the Ashes trophy? When you see the teams celebrating the Ashes, you tend to see the players holding the cheap little Ashes replica aloft instead.

It was argued by writer Matthew Engel that if the Aussies had a permanent cabinet set up at one of their great grounds where the real Ashes urn could be displayed as it is at the Lord's museum, an empty plinth could be a great incentive for the losing country to want to get the urn back next time.

My opinion? Well, having carefully weighed up the pros and cons, the delicate arguments as to whether a 'gift' has evolved to be a 'trophy' and whether it's fair that Australia have only had the urn twice in over a century, I have come to the considered conclusion that . . . sod it, we should keep the Ashes in England!

TUFFERS' TEN ASHES BASHERS

A small selection of Ashes big-hitters who've dented a few fine bowlers' figures (and some pavilions) down the years . . .

Matthew Hayden

Matty Hayden was one of the guys who revolutionised the way Test openers play, taking the attack to the bowlers from ball one and setting the tone for other batsmen to follow. Built like a brick outhouse, he hit the ball with enormous power and when he was on form he was a nightmare to bowl to.

My lasting memory of Matty will be from my final Test match at The Oval in 2001. Coach Duncan Fletcher had reluctantly brought me back into the side. And when I say reluctantly, he actually told the media I was only in because there was no other option. So that made me feel good, and then the Aussies won the toss and batted on a belter of a wicket.

Matty and Justin Langer, who I had played with at

Middlesex, came out to open the batting and Justin was chirping away cheerily as we walked out: ''Allo Tuffers. Laaahhv-ly day for cricket, mate.'

I wasn't having it, but he carried on regardless.

'I think I know what you're going to be doing today, mate. You're going to be tossing it up, aren't ya. Looking forward to you coming on, mate.'

He knew how to wind me up, in a nice way, but the message was clear – they were planning to smash me out of the attack.

I'd been out of Test cricket for eighteen months, and when I came on to bowl, there was a nice cheer from the crowd. Matty was facing. I got my field set and started my run-up with my usual hop, skippety-skip. No sooner had I got to the skippety than Matty was picking his bat up like a caveman's club and walking down the pitch, growling.

'Rrrraaaaaaauuuuuggghhh!'

I was so taken aback that I nearly stopped my run-up, but I thought I'd better carry on.

He just smashed the ball for four.

I thought to myself, 'At least have a little block first ball, Matty – I might have developed a chinaman since you last batted against me. At least have a look at me!'

I did actually get Matty in the end that day, but that was my one wicket for loads, and Aussie went on to score 600, made us follow-on, job done.

Frank Woolley

Of all the bashers in this list, no one bashed as elegantly as Kent and England's Frank Woolley. This left-handed all-rounder had picture-perfect technique and could also hit the ball miles without any seeming effort. During the 1924/25 Ashes, he hit leg-spinner Arthur Mailey out of the SCG – and that is a very big cricket ground – causing a ten-minute delay as a search party went out to look for the ball. Mailey saw the funny side, quipping, 'At last I've found a way of slowing his scoring-rate down.'

Doug Walters

Aussie legend Dougie and I had quite a lot in common as cricketers:

Didn't like training. Tick.

Liked drinking, smoking and staying out late. Tick.

Scored 100 runs or more in one session of a Test match three times. Er . . .

Known as the 'Dungog Dasher', Dougie was a little fella, but had strong forearms and amazing hand–eye coordination. Indeed, some people said he had such a quick eye that it could cost him his wicket because if the ball moved off the pitch, he was able to adjust his shot and get an edge on balls that others missed.

He announced himself on the Ashes scene in 1965/66 with

a century in his debut Test innings at the Gabba and followed up with another one in the Second Test at Melbourne. But his most extraordinary Ashes knock was 103 on a super-fast wicket at Perth in 1974, starting at 3 not out after tea and completed before close of play with a hooked six off Bob Willis (although, Ian Chappell wouldn't let him believe that – see pages 90–91).

His biographer and former team-mate Ashley Mallett wrote, 'Doug loved a beer, a smoke, a bet and a bat, not necessarily in that order.' He used to terrorise bowlers and then invite them for a drink at the end of the day's play. And with Dougie, his drinking sessions would often last a lot longer than his destructive innings.

On a short trip to Ireland during their 1968 Ashes tour, he couldn't locate his hotel room after a long night on the lash. He bashed on the hotel manager's door.

'Hey mate, what have you done with Room 22? I can't find it, it's disappeared.'

The manager shook his head in confusion: 'There is no Room 22. Our rooms only go up to 18.'

Dougie was in the wrong hotel.

Kevin Pietersen

An exceptional talent with the capability to destroy any attack, no one will ever forget his innings at The Oval in 2005 when England needed to bat out the final day to claim the Ashes. KP came in during the morning session with Glenn McGrath on a hat-trick, was dropped twice and generally looked all at sea as he prodded and poked around.

At lunch, captain Michael Vaughan advised him to 'stop messing about and go and express yourself'. KP listened, taking 35 off 13 balls from a stunned Brett Lee straight after the interval.

'Pietersen was unbelievable,' recalled Lee, who was bowling at speeds up to 95 mph. 'In my first over I bounced him and he hooked me about 15 rows back. An over later I put a man back for the trap and he launched again. This time I was hit about 20 rows back.'

He also played a couple of incredible flat-bat smashes straight back past Lee and bulleting into the fence. And so it went on as he dismantled the Aussie attack with more and more outrageous shots. His innings of 158 included seven sixes, breaking Ian Botham's record for the most sixes in an Ashes innings, and more importantly it clinched the Ashes.

That innings was truly great. Unlike the skunk haircut.

Keith Miller

Born in a place called Sunshine in the suburbs of Melbourne, having fun on and off the pitch was the priority for Miller, who thought nothing of going out all night during a match. A former Royal Australian Air Force fighter pilot, he famously said 'Pressure is a Messerschmitt up your arse, playing cricket is not', so taking a few risks when he was bowling or batting was neither here nor there to him.

Miller is widely regarded as Australia's greatest ever all-rounder, he hit three tons in Ashes matches and played many other great attacking innings. English fans were first wowed by his big hitting when he hit a century for the Australian Services team in the first 'Victory Test' at Lord's in 1945. He soon topped that with an innings of 185, again at Lord's, for the 'Dominions' all-star XI against an England side, when he belted seven sixes, an innings earning his place in the hearts of all cricket fans, English and Australian.

Bob Barber

A tall, naturally gifted left-hander, his coaches at Lancashire didn't think there was anything they could teach Bob about batting when he was growing up. And by the time he went to Oz in 1965/66, he had developed into an aggressive opener with the ability to smash the shine off the cherry. He scored a thousand first-class runs on that tour, highlighted by a thrilling innings of 185 at the SCG, including an opening partnership of 234 in even time with Geoff Boycott (not sure how many of those Boycs scored).

Even the Aussie fans loved his style, but that proved to be his only Test century, as Bob's cricket career went down the toilet . . . in a good way for him, though, as he got more involved in his father's business and made a fortune out of toilet disinfectant tablets. Top of the plops.

Adam Gilchrist

Gilchrist's motto was 'just hit the ball' and at the WACA, Perth, in 2007, the most destructive wicketkeeper-batsman in history whacked the ball a lot. He bludgeoned a century off 57 balls, an all-time Ashes record, missing Viv Richards's world record by just one ball.

Gilchrist wouldn't have got anywhere near Viv's record but for a misunderstanding, though. He was batting with Michael Clarke, who had also just reached his century, and they signalled to the dressing room to find out if captain Ricky Ponting wanted them to go for fast runs and a declaration or bat through till stumps. They thought they saw Punter give them a thumbs-up, which Gilly took as a green light to give it some welly.

When he reached his hundred, Ponting called them in. Back in the pavilion amid the backslaps from team-mates thrilled by his innings, Punter came up to him and said: 'What was that about? I wanted you to bat through to stumps!'

Ian Botham

England's greatest-ever all-rounder was a beast with a bat in his hands. His approach was best summed up when tailender Graham Dilley joined him at the crease during his famous innings of 149 not out at Headingley, which sparked England's remarkable comeback in the 1981 series. 'C'mon, let's give it some humpty,' he told Dilley.

What I didn't realise was that he borrowed Graham Gooch's Duncan Fearnley bat for that innings. Goochy had scored 2 and 0 with it. 'Graham hadn't used it much during the match, and I thought there were a few runs left in it,' he reckoned.

He was even more murderous in scoring 118 at Old Trafford in 1981, hitting 88 of the runs in boundaries (including six sixes). He played some absolutely incredible shots, including two sixes off fast bouncers from his mate Dennis Lillee. Both were dead straight, arrowing at his head (he wasn't wearing a helmet), but he ducked at the last minute and went through with the shot anyway, depositing the ball way back into the stands over long leg. Genius.

Charles Macartney

The stocky Macartney had a technique all his own, but his brilliant eye and timing made him one of Australia's greatest-ever destroyers. In his last Ashes series, his innings of 151 in under three hours on a tricky wicket at Headingley in July 1926 was a game-changer. When he came in at number three with Australia 0 for 1 after one ball, he reportedly told bowler Maurice Tate, 'Let's have it!' and then proceeded to give it to the English bowlers.

However, Charlie's most remarkable innings was in a 1921 tour match, when he pulverised the Nottinghamshire bowling, scoring 345 in less than four hours – the most runs scored by a batsman in a single day in first-class cricket until Brian Lara pummelled 390 in one day during his 501 not out in 1994. To put that in some sort of context, Chris Tavaré scored at 12 runs per hour in the 1982/83 series, so it would have taken him just about 29 hours to score that many runs.

A couple of matches later, in the Test at Headingley, Macartney only managed to score one century before lunch – he must have been taking it easy that day. Just amazing.

Gilbert Jessop

Just 5ft 7in tall and weighing around 11 stone, the Gloucestershire and England all-rounder Gilbert 'The Croucher' Jessop could unleash shots of monstrous power from a hunched-up batting stance. His finest Ashes moment came in the final Test at The Oval in 1902. Australia already held a 2–0 lead, so England were just playing for pride. And with England five down for under fifty in their second innings, still needing over 200 to win, The Croucher came to the rescue. He smashed 104 runs in 77 minutes, 68 of them in boundaries, including three mighty swipes into the pavilion and an all-run five, paving the way for a nail-biting win for England.

Good man to have in your T20 team . . .

CHAPTER 12

SLEDGING

THIS IS WAUGH!

I didn't really bother sledging Aussie players. Maybe the odd 'You lucky bastard' if they got away with a mistake, but I never got in a war with one. Generally it wasn't worth it because, if anything, it just seemed to make them more determined.

My first Ashes series in 1990/91 was against the Australian team skippered by Allan Border, and they were tough. When Border walked on the pitch, he gave you nothing and the rest of the players followed suit. Their attitude was, 'I'm playing for the baggy green, mate. I might have a laugh and a beer with you afterwards, but when I cross the white line, I'll fight and I'll scrap until I drop.'

As a bowler, it was impossible to get inside an Australian batsman's head. Any of them. Impossible. Even the tailenders would come back at you: 'Why don't you **** off, mate? You say what you want, Tufnell, you ****ing little arsewipe. Who do you think you ****ing are?'

Even the great Ian Botham, who loved sledging, said he was selective in his targets: 'I'd only sledge someone I thought it would affect. I'd never sledge Border or Waugh because I didn't want to wake them up.'

Maybe Jack Hobbs had the right idea during the 1948 series against Don Bradman's Invincibles. Hobbs went up to The Don and delivered the most complimentary sledge in the history of the Ashes. 'You're too good, you're spoiling the game,' he told him.

The Aussies sledged us much more than we did them through the nineties because they had the upper hand and they knew it. They kept turning us over. McGrath, Warne, Gillespie, Gilchrist, Waugh . . . if you said anything, they'd just dismiss you: '**** off, mate. Have a look at the scoreboard, you prick!'

I never felt that any Australian I played against was mentally fragile. They were mentally strong and they let you know that without saying a word from the moment you turned up at the ground.

I remember doing some close-catching practice before play one morning with Robin Smith and a couple of others. I mean, Robin Smith is an excellent player, but Mark and Steve Waugh walked past and sort of sniggered to themselves. They had a great way of looking down their noses at us. They kept beating us, so the superiority complex was understandable.

Australian cricketers from local to Test players are naturally competitive. Aussie cricket is full of what they call 'mongrel' – people who fight hard and will do and say whatever it takes to gain an advantage. The national team captained by Ian Chappell in the seventies was probably the first Ashes team to take sledging to extremes – they were labelled 'Ugly Australians', not for their long hair and 'taches, but for the verbal abuse they dished out. In the eighties, peace broke out between the two teams – Allan Border was playing county cricket for Essex at the time and personal friendships developed between opposing Ashes players. That changed when Border got tired of losing and from 1989 it was all on again.

Although there have been some strong contenders for the title before and since, the Australian Ashes team led by Steve Waugh, which blitzed England in the 2001 series, was nominated by a former Aussie great, Neil Harvey, as 'the greatest bunch of sledgers there's ever been'. Harvey didn't mean it as a compliment, adding: 'All I can say is that I'm disgusted and the sad thing is I'm not the only one.'

Steve Waugh didn't see it as sledging at all, though. He called it 'mental disintegration' and there was a lot of mental disintegrating going on in the summer of 2001.

The tone was set when Dizzy Gillespie broke England captain Nasser Hussain's finger in the First Test at Edgbaston. After Nasser had been patched up and prepared to face the next ball, Ricky Ponting called from slip: 'Follow it up with another good one', much to Nasser's annoyance.

Waugh was unrepentant, saying, 'For me, the entire incident was an excellent example of what Test cricket is all about: testing your opponent, physically and mentally, when he's vulnerable.'

The Aussies knew that with Nass, who was a very fiery in-your-face competitor himself, it wouldn't be difficult to get a reaction so they loved winding him up.

Steve Waugh always had a line or two ready for him such as: 'When you're gone, Nass, who's going to shore up the middle order with a stodgy 29 off 117 balls?'

And wicketkeeper Ian Healy came up with a very funny one captaining Queensland in a tour match against England, telling a fielder he wanted him to 'stand right under Nasser's nose' and then placed him half a dozen yards away.

At Edgbaston in the 1997 series, Nass scored a double-century but had to put up with plenty of sledging all the way through. However, he drew the line when substitute fielder Justin Langer joined in too. 'Look, I don't mind this lot chirping at me, but you've just come on,' Nass told him. 'You're just the ****ing bus driver of the team, so you get back on your bus and get ready to drive it back to the hotel this evening.'

In 2001 Mark Ramprakash returned to the side for the Third Test and the Aussie fielders tried to get him freaking out about the number 14. He was dismissed for 14 in the first innings and, bizarrely, that was the fifth time in six innings against Australia he'd made that score. When he made it to 14 not out in the second innings, Waugh piped up: 'Let's make it six 14s for Ramps!'

It seemed to affect his concentration as he played and missed a few times and the Aussie fielders amped up the pressure. 'Let's chip up on number 14!' said keen gambler Shane Warne.

Ramps did eventually get past 14, but that didn't stop the Aussies, who then kept telling him that he was in unknown territory. Soon he got out to a very un-Ramps-like slog, bowled Warne, stumped by Gilchrist. 'To me this is gamesmanship, or mental disintegration, but it's not sledging,' said Waugh.

Whatever it was, it worked. We got annihilated in that series and by the time I got my Test recall for the final match (which proved to be my last-ever Test), the Ashes were long since lost.

At least Jimmy Ormond, making his Test debut in that game, salvaged a little sledging pride for us when Steve Waugh's brother Mark tried a bit of disintegrating on him.

'**** me, look who it is,' said Mark. 'Mate, there's no way you're good enough to play for England.'

Without missing a beat, Jimmy replied: 'Maybe not, but at least I'm the best player in my family.'

RANJI GETS EVILS

The term 'sledging' first started being used in the mid-sixties. There are a few tales about how the word came to describe making insults to opponents that are about as subtle as hitting them with a sledgehammer, and not surprisingly most point to it originating in Australia. Grahame Corling, a workmanlike fast-medium bowler from New South Wales who played in the 1964 Ashes, generally gets the credit. One story has him making a rude remark at a barbecue, while another claims that he led his team-mates in a chorus of 'When a Man Loves a Woman' by Percy Sledge when a batsman came in (the batter's wife was allegedly having an affair with one of his team-mates). Ian Chappell reckoned it started when a cricketer swore in front of a woman at a Sheffield Shield match and the woman reacted 'like a sledgehammer' (whatever that means . . .).

Anyway, no matter when the practice of sledging got its name, on-pitch verbals designed to put opponents off have been part of the Ashes experience since the earliest days. For instance, W. G. Grace was one of the finest sledgers of the 19th century – his favourite trick when fielding close to the wicket was to talk while the ball was being bowled. And spectators have also been having their say in Ashes matches from behind the rope for over a century. During England's 1897/98 tour Down Under, Prince Ranjitsinhji got himself in hot water with Australian supporters for suggesting that England had had to bat in poor conditions in the Second Test. This is what he had written in a column for an Australian magazine: 'A good many opinions were from day to day expressed by old cricketers and by spectators of the game as a whole, and on the wicket in particular, and in most cases the bias in favour of the home team was so great and pronounced, that the opinions expressed by most of these "accepted authorities" were in anything but harmony with the truth, principally as regards the pitch.'

In summary, what I think he was trying to say was that the pitch was crap and anyone who said different was talking out of their arses.

He did qualify his comments by adding: 'The English

players only wish to justify their apparent poor display in their two innings by the state of the wicket, and they have no intention of minimising in the slightest possible degree the superiority of the Australian players in this, the Second Test Match, a superiority which has shown in all departments of the game.'

This didn't cut any ice with the Aussies and after his comments were published he got sledged mercilessly during his first innings in the next Test at Adelaide.

'I was at the wickets for about quarter of an hour, and during the whole of that time uncomplimentary and insulting remarks were hurled at me from all parts of the field,' he said later. 'That such behaviour is unfair to a player of any side is too apparent.'

However, Ranji claimed that the abuse didn't affect him personally, saying that a hand injury caused the poor stroke which cost him his wicket.

Ranji wasn't best pleased when the crowd at the Fourth Test at Melbourne were equally rowdy, though. They groaned and hissed at every English appeal for a wicket and he noted afterwards that the umpires were getting it in the earhole too.

'It was very noticeable, also, that when the Australian bowlers or stumpers suffered the same fate at the hands of the umpires, the crowd was disposed to jeer – not at the players making the appeal, but at the umpire who dared give the decision against their men. Such inconsistency, to put it mildly, is hardly fair to the visiting team. Players on either side are at perfect liberty to appeal if they think fit, and therefore they ought not to be treated in this uncivil and unjust manner.'

As you can tell, Ranji was never a man for a short sentence when a really long one would do.

At the end of the tour, Ranji admitted that the 'barracking' (as he called it) had affected the England players' performance at times and called for the Aussie authorities to take action. He wrote: 'I sincerely hope that the good sense of the people, and the representatives of the press, who have done so much to make the game what it is today, will prevail, and they will gradually but effectually abolish the mischiefs under which cricket at the present day suffers in Australia.

'Unfortunately, several journals, misunderstanding our protests, have taken them as condemning Australian crowds and press, rather than as a rebuke of an evil which visitors and local players alike suffer from; so they have to a certain extent encouraged this evil.'

JAZZ-HAT JARDINE

The 'evil' was here to stay though, and the Aussie fans found their perfect target when one Douglas Jardine rocked up in Australia for the first time in 1928/29. Educated at Winchester College and Oxford University, Jardine was as posh as they come. He was such a jazz hat, he insisted on wearing one – a multi-coloured Harlequin cap – when he was playing. Didn't he realise it was like having a target on his head? The only time he didn't wear it, in the last Test, he made a duck.

'When are you going to get a move on, Rainbow?' a fan shouted at Jardine as he slowly compiled the second of three centuries in a row at the start of the tour (yes, Jardine could play a bit, too).

'Eh, Mr Jardine, where's the butler to carry your bat for you?' sneered another when he walked out to bat.

A bloke on the Hill at Sydney renamed him 'Sardine' (well, it rhymes I suppose . . .) and when Jardine was dismissed, he sent him on his way, shouting: 'Now you can get back into your tin.'

Not that Jardine was that bothered what they thought of him. Booed as he walked off after scoring a century against New South Wales, the incoming batsman Patsy Hendren said to him: 'They don't seem to like you very much over here, Mr Jardine.'

'The feeling's ****ing mutual,' he snarled in reply.

Jardine was not above a bit of tactical sledging himself out in the middle and he upped the ante when he returned to Australia as captain in 1932. When his demon fast bowler Harold Larwood bowled a ball that hit Aussie skipper Bill Woodfull over the heart at Adelaide during the infamous Bodyline series, Jardine responded with a cheery 'Well bowled, Harold!' as Woodfull writhed on the floor struggling to breathe.

Jardine then switched the field to Bodyline positions for the next Larwood over, and the crowd let Larwood have it as he came into bowl, chanting: 'One, two, three, four, five, six, seven, eight, nine, out. YOU BASTARD.'

Barracking from the crowd was the soundtrack to Jardine's match days in Oz, but he drew the line at opposition Australian players sledging him or his team-mates. The story goes that

Jardine went to the Aussie dressing room during the Third Test to complain that a fielder had called Larwood a 'Pommie bastard'. Their vice-captain Vic Richardson, future grandparent of Ian Chappell, apparently took Jardine's complaint very seriously and launched an immediate investigation, saying: 'Alright, which of you bastards called Larwood a bastard instead of this bastard?'

A spectator on the Hill at Sydney for the final Test neatly summed up Jardine's popularity in Australia. Spotting the England captain swatting a fly away from his face, he shouted: 'Leave our flies alone, Jardine! They're the only flamin' friends you've got here!'

MITCHELL BAITING, PORK SLEDGINGS AND 'CRICKETER' MIKE

Imagine coming out to bat with your team on their way to an Ashes series defeat and 25,000 fans swaying to the left and right, belting out a piss-taking song about you, as Aussie Mitchell Johnson had to at Sydney in 2011: 'He bowls to the left, he bowls to the right, that Mitchell Johnson, his bowling is shite . . .'

Unless you've got the brass neck of Jardine, it has to affect your concentration. And on that occasion it did, as Chris Tremlett bowled Johnson for a golden duck and he had to walk straight back to the pavilion listening to more gleeful choruses of 'his' song.

Maybe Johnson should have followed the examples of the notoriously crabby Sydney Barnes or Keith Miller. Once, when he was booed by the crowd at Melbourne, Barnes threw down the ball, folded his arms and refused to continue bowling until it stopped. Keith Miller simply sat down in response to jeers for supposedly bowling too many bouncers during the 1948 Trent Bridge Test. Mind you, I think if Johnson had chucked his bat down in a huff and sat down, he would have been waiting a long time for the England fans to shut up.

The Mitchell Johnson song was borrowed from the football terraces, but credit for one of the most original incidents of Ashes crowd sledging goes to a group of students at the Gabba in 1982, who came up with a way of saying 'You fat bastard' without actually saying it. Somehow they smuggled a little pig into the stadium, painted the names 'Botham' and 'Eddie' (as in Hemmings, England's other generously proportioned player) on its sides then released it onto the outfield. The whole ground was in hysterics and news got back to the English dressing room where they were troughing down their lunch. 'It was very funny, except for two people in our side,' recalled Geoff Miller later. My only criticism of the stunt is that if you're going to put Beefy's surname on the side of an animal, surely it should be a cow?

Smuggling a live cow into a Test cricket ground – now that would be a challenge.

The Beefy-Eddie pig was an extreme case, but the seasoned cricket heckler will pick up on anything. Big Bob Willis was barracked during the 1970/71 series for the crime of being tall ('I didn't know they stacked crap that high'). Even your cooking ability can come under attack, as Matthew Hayden found out at the SCG after publishing his own cookbook ('Hayden, your casserole tastes like shit').

In the face of such, er, wit, a lot of the time all you can do as a player is stand there and take it with a smile, but sometimes you've got to give something back in return. Matthew Hoggard tells a great story about an English fielder having the last word.

'Oi, Pommie, Pommie,' shouted a spectator. 'There's only one good thing about you and that's your wife.' Fairly bog-standard crowd abuse, but the England player wrongfooted his tormentor with his response:

'You reckon? You ought to try living with her.'

Naturally, the player who said that remains anonymous.

And don't think the players can escape the abuse once the match is over. The late Mike Denness, who captained England for five of six Tests during their 4–1 defeat in the 1974/75 Ashes, discovered that, sometimes, a fan's sledge is a dish best served cold. And in writing. Mike once received a letter from an Australian. It was addressed simply to 'Mike Denness, Cricketer'. Inside the note read: 'Should this reach you, the Post Office thinks more of your ability than I do.'

Ouch.

POETRY EMOTION

At Melbourne in 1986, England's spin king Phil Edmonds and young Aussie wicketkeeper Tim Zoehrer got involved in a spot of verbals on the pitch. Phil got hit on the pad and the ball was pouched by silly mid-off. Zoehrer and the slips appealed loudly. Phil had been wrongly given out playing (and missing) the same shot in the previous match at Adelaide, and he responded to the shouts with a smile, saying, 'Don't be silly. You're not going to cheat me out again this time, are you?'

Zoehrer went mental, calling Phil every name under the sun. Even Phil, who had played against the likes of Rod Marsh, Dennis Lillee and the Chappell brothers in their sledging prime, said he'd never heard anything like it in his life. Luckily, the television viewers didn't hear it this time because the microphone placed by the wicket to pick up the sound of leather on willow had a time-delay switch which some bloke in the Channel 9 control box kept his finger on for the duration of Zoehrer's outburst.

At one point, Phil asked who Zoehrer was, to which he replied: 'At least I have an identity. You're just Frances Edmonds' husband.'

Phil's journalist/author wife was in Oz covering the tour, and when he told his missus what had happened that night, she was inspired to write a couple of limericks:

> *There was a young glove man named Zoehrer,*
> *Whose keeping got poorer and poorer,*
> *Said AB from first slip,*
> *'Please stop giving me lip,*
> *And with extras, stop troubling the scorer!'*

The second one referred to the MCG's mostly Victorian crowd's dislike of Western Australian Zoehrer. The fans in

Bay 13 wanted their man Michael Dimattina to have the gloves, or even New South Welshman Greg Dyer, which showed how little they thought of Zoehrer.

> Bay 13, they shout 'Dimattina,
> This Zoehrer keeps like a cretina.
> And we'd rather,' they choir,
> 'Have that other clown, Dyer,
> Than Zoehrer, who is a has-beener.'

The next day, in probably the most cultured act of sledging in Ashes history, Phil went into the Australia dressing room and recited the poems to much laughter. And credit to Zoehrer, by lunchtime, he'd penned his own limerick in response:

> There was a balding old man called Philippe,
> Who stands in the gully too deep.
> When his turn came to bat,
> He opened his trap,
> And his innings just fell in a heap.

GET BY WITH A LITTLE SLEDGE FROM MY FRIENDS . . .

When there's so much stick flying around from opposition players and fans, at least you can always rely on your team-mates to back you all the way. Well, that's the theory.

Freddie Trueman was always good for a putdown whether

you were with him or against him. In one game, after the Revd David Sheppard dropped a catch, Freddie turned to him and said: 'Kid yourself it's a Sunday, Rev, and put your hands together.'

Later in the same match, Colin Cowdrey not only missed a catch but the ball went through his legs for four runs.

'Sorry, Fred, I should have crossed my legs,' said Cowdrey.

'No, but your mother should have,' Fred replied.

W. G. Grace didn't bother offering such pleasantries to his wicketkeeper Dick Lilley during the Old Trafford Test in 1896. He brought Lilley on to bowl only to send him back behind the stumps after one dodgy over, telling him, 'You must have been bowling with the wrong arm.'

Captain of the 1920/21 side, J. W. H. T. Douglas was equally encouraging to all-rounder Percy Fender, saying: 'You know, Fender, there is no man in England whose bowling I would rather face than yours; and there is no batsman in England I would rather bowl against either.'

With motivational chats like that, it's not surprising England got whitewashed five–zip.

In the Third Test of the 1936/37 series at the MCG, England captain Gubby Allen came out with a beauty. England were two-up going into the match, but a first-innings collapse to 76 all out meant Australia were 120-odd runs ahead going into their second innings. However, by the time the great Don Bradman came in down the order at seven, Australia had been reduced to 97 for 5 and England were back in business. Not only that, but Gubby had a cunning plan to get The Don out. He instructed fielder Walter Robins to rush back from square leg to deep square whenever Bill Voce bowled a short ball in the hope that The Don would take on the hook shot.

Bradman took the bait, hooking the ball in the air straight to Robins. Just one problem – Robins dropped a fairly straightforward catch. When Robins apologised to his captain, Allen deadpanned: 'Oh, don't give it another thought. You've just cost us the Ashes, that's all.'

He was right, too. Bradman went on to score 270, ably assisted by Jack Fingleton who also notched a ton in a triple-century partnership, to set up the win and Australia went on to record a famous 3–2 series victory.

Team-mate-sledging history repeated itself at Headingley in 1997. With the series poised at 1–1 after three Tests, Graham Thorpe dropped a simple catch off Australian opener Matthew Elliott early in his innings. Thorpe got the Gubby treatment from Athers – 'Don't worry, Thorpey, you've only cost us the Ashes' – Elliott went on to score 199 and Australia took the match by an innings, adding the next one to clinch the series.

I also borrowed the line in my retirement. I was at an awards ceremony in 2006 and couldn't resist reminding Shane Warne about him dropping Kevin Pietersen at The Oval the previous year, when KP went on to blitz the Aussie bowlers and save the match: 'Do you wake up in the middle of the night thinking you might have dropped the Ashes, Warney?'

MERV & SHANE

The shy, retiring Shane Warne and pantomime villain Merv Hughes were two of the most enthusiastic sledgers I came across during Ashes matches.

There was nothing too imaginative about Merv's insults, which usually focused on telling you what a 'Pommie bastard'/'arsewipe' you were, but you had to admire the relentless consistency of his abuse throughout a day's cricket.

Frankly, having a six-foot-four mustachioed brute of a man flinging down bouncers past my nose and then running down the pitch to scream insults in my face was not my idea of fun. But other English players gave as good as they got.

For instance, during the Australians' 1989 tour, Merv told Robin Smith: 'You can't ****ing bat.' Not exactly subtle and probably not his wisest choice of victim as Robin loved facing fast bowling and he really could bat. Judge responded by ripping a square cut for four and returning fire: 'Hey Merv, we make a fine pair, don't we? I can't ****ing bat and you can't ****ing bowl.'

I have to give Merv credit for another sledge aimed at Judgey, though. 'Mate, if you turn the bat over, you'll find the instructions on the back,' he told him.

At Lord's the same summer, Merv was giving Jack Russell the full treatment while he stood at the non-striker's end. Merv might have thought that he could intimidate Jack, who was five-foot-eight and weighed about ten stone wet through. But Jack, who was only playing his third Test and fighting to establish himself in the side, decided that he wasn't having anyone trying to put him off. This led to the comical sight of little Jack going face to face – well, face to chest – with Merv while umpire Dickie Bird danced about panicking that there was going to be a fight. It might have been a physical mismatch, but Jack went on to score a battling 64 not out and neither Merv nor any of the other Aussies sledged him for the rest of the series.

Although he was a big lad who liked his food and booze, Merv had the heart and stamina to bowl long spells for his team. The England fans might have chanted 'Sumo' when he ran in during his second Ashes series in England in 1993, but he bowled near enough 300 overs and took 31 wickets even though his old knees were buggered by then. He just loaded up on the painkillers and icepacks between sessions and kept going.

His constant sledging also did the trick of unsettling Ashes new boy Graeme Hick, but, as in 1989, he found other England players' nuts tougher to crack.

After one hard day in the field at Old Trafford, bowling well but without much luck as Graham Gooch powered towards a century, Merv arrived in the press conference covered in dust, dirt and sweat. He was asked what he'd learnt from the day.

'Is it that you've got a big heart and playing for the baggy green spurs you on?' suggested the journalist.

'No, mate,' replied Merv. 'What I've learnt today is that the more you sledge Graham Gooch, the better he plays.'

And it is true that it can be very dangerous to pick on a top player. Even more so if they are also a thoroughbred sledger. Shane Warne said as much during his innings of 71 at Sydney in 2007. 'You, mate, are making me concentrate,' he told Paul Collingwood who was unsuccessfully trying to sledge him.

But that never stopped Warney himself, who had a putdown ready for anyone and everyone whenever he had a ball in his hand. He was in typically fine sledging form in his farewell Ashes of 2006/07, calling Ian Bell 'the Sherminator' (after the ginger-haired geek in the *American Pie* movie), Geraint Jones 'the club pro' (for not being good enough, in his opinion), Kevin Pietersen 'Figjam' (as in '**** I'm Good, Just Ask Me') and ripping into Paul Collingwood for the Queen's honour he received despite playing in just one Test of England's 2005 Ashes triumph ('How can you get an MBE for getting just 17 runs', etc.).

Matthew Hoggard has said that when he first batted against Warney, he was surprised just how much he chirped. No matter how innocuous the delivery was, and how comfortably Hoggy played the ball, Shane would act like he was so close to getting him out, letting out a cry of 'Aw, ****, jeez.' Every ball. As Hoggy puts it, 'I thought he might have some sort of cricketing tourettes.'

A tweet from Hoggy's former Ashes captain, Michael Vaughan, on that subject made me laugh after Warney got banned for one match from the Big Bash T20 tournament at the start of 2013:

Michael Vaughan @MichaelVaughan
Just heard @warne888 has been banned for swearing????

If that's the case he should never have played an Ashes
test . . .

As a spinner it does help to have a sledge or two in your
armoury when nothing else is happening for you, though. In
an Ashes Test, sometimes you find yourself bowling slow
deliveries on wickets where there's little or no turn, against
the best batsmen in the world, so you have to try and make
them believe that it's harder than it actually is. Obviously, it
helped if you were Shane Warne in his prime and could get
the occasional ball to turn sharply on the featheriest of
featherbed pitches. And for the many England batsmen made
to look foolish by a Warney special, there was always his mate,
Ian Healy, behind the stumps to send them on their way back
to the pavilion: 'Back to the nets, dickhead.'

CHAPTER 13

THE BATTLE

SUPERSTARS AND SCARS

If I wanted anyone alongside me in the trenches, it would be an Aussie. Even nowadays with the Australian Test side going through relatively lean times, they keep battling, don't take a backward step. They don't mentally get any weaker. It's just that we've had better players than them in recent times.

I went into Test matches wanting to beat them, but never with any real confidence that we were going to. And with the scars of repeated defeat, it got worse. I knew that they were going to have to play badly and we were going to have to play really well, because the simple fact was they had better players.

We still thought we could fight hard and try to win, but they always seemed to stay a step ahead. We'd have them 150 for 5 and they'd end up 320 all out. Or we'd be 180 for 1 and end up 270 all out. We never quite got enough runs.

At vital points in Test matches, they always seemed to find a way to get the upper hand. We won Test matches against them occasionally, but it was often more them losing, than us dominating . . . and we knew that.

Our individuals had great moments, but as a team we weren't a match for them. It's like in a boxing match – if you keep getting jabbed and hit to the body, you will eventually go down. If your opponent knows that he can beat you to the punch, and you know it too, it's a no-win. When we played Australia in the nineties, even if we hit them with a century or a few quick wickets, more often than not they still found a way to win by their high-level consistency.

Ultimately, it's about personnel; who has got the better players.

On my first tour in 1990/91, I didn't think about that so much because we had the likes of Botham, Lamb and Gower on our side, but they were coming to the end of their careers. Then Shane Warne and Glenn McGrath came along and changed everything. Two superstars, legends-to-be, bursting on the scene at the same time, both capable of bowling any team out. You might get the odd 50 or 100 against them, but the rest of the batters would often fail.

Mark Taylor used to like to start every session with Warne and McGrath. So a batting pair might have fought their way through to an interval, only to return and have those two sharks waiting for them.

There was rarely a passage of play where you got on top.

THE BATTLE

You had to fight for every run. We had one or two world-class players, but Australia had Warne and McGrath plus five or six other potential match-winners and the sheer weight of talent would crush you eventually.

They were just as dangerous with the bat too, especially with the emergence of Adam Gilchrist right at the end of my Test career. That top seven of Matthew Hayden, Michael Slater, Ricky Ponting, Mark Waugh, Steve Waugh, Damien Martyn and Adam Gilchrist was ridiculously good (and their tailenders weren't bad either). They scored at such a fast rate because they knew they could afford to go for their shots as at least a couple of them would make a big score. And in going for their shots, our bowlers would get demoralised and the next men in could fill their boots. It was just relentless. They could take the game away from you in half a day. But if our batters tried to attack McGrath and Warne in the same way, they got out.

We were a bit scarred by them and they knew that. So on the occasions when we did get the upper hand, they were sitting in their dressing room believing they could turn things around, whereas we were questioning whether we could finish them off.

I always went into an Ashes match thinking I could get a wicket every ball, but as the game went on there was always that niggling feeling that whatever we did, something would go wrong. That's why when we did win a match it was such a big deal.

My best-ever personal Ashes performance was when we beat them in the final Test of the 1997 series at The Oval.

People thought I acted a bit strangely after that game because I sat in the corner of the dressing room with a towel over my head, not getting involved in the celebrations. But the truth is I was just totally mentally and physically exhausted. I'd taken a seven-fer in the first innings and then Andy Caddick and I bowled them out in the last innings when they only needed 124 to win. It was such a tight game, every ball I bowled seemed like it was win or lose; the intensity was something else. And that was a dead rubber with the Ashes already lost! It shows just how hard it was to win a game against that Australian team.

I was pleased to find out that a great Aussie player of the past had a similar experience to mine – in 1972, when Australia were struggling to get back up after a period in the doldrums. England had retained the Ashes already, but Australia squared the series in the final Test at The Oval. Rod Marsh, who smashed the winning runs that day, collapsed in a heap when he returned to the dressing room as all the tension caught up with him.

Graham Gooch, the England skipper on the 1990/91 tour, felt that a lack of mental toughness in the squad was our problem, and he later said I was one of the supposedly mentally weak players. I don't accept that. I was mentally tough, but it was my first-ever Test series so, while I wasn't overawed, I was nervous. Goochy was a bit of a freak in that he never suffered from nerves at all so maybe he found that hard to understand, and in the England set-up as it was then, there wasn't much support for players or a sense of teamwork.

I didn't get a wicket in my first Ashes match and came

back to the dressing room, thinking, 'How did I do? Well, I think I bowled all right . . .' But no one said a word to me.

So I'd just go to a mate like Phil DeFreitas and ask him how I did and of course Daffy would start off by taking the mickey out of me for not taking a wicket before telling me I'd done okay. But no one properly appraised my performance, no one encouraged, told me where I'd gone wrong or what I'd done well. The senior players and coach were all packing their bags, so I followed them and just got on the coach none the wiser.

Nowadays, as soon as you walk off there's analysts, specialist coaches, sports psychologists and the like to give the players feedback. And you need that because self-analysis can drive you nuts. We'd lost and I'm sure I'd learnt something from the experience, but it was down to me to work out what that was.

When I walked out to bowl for the next Test at Sydney it was, like, here we go again because I'd had no advice. Goochy did come up to me and said, 'Tuffers, listen, mate. You're a good bowler,' and then walked off. To be fair, I took some heart from that, but in four months that was just about the only thing he said to me to boost my self-esteem. Occasionally, my other team-mates would give encouragement to me and vice versa, but they had their own demons to fight. It was a rather selfish atmosphere. You had to find your own way, your own inner strength. No one gave you it.

You could see the difference with the Aussies in the field. When they got a wicket, they all ran up, celebrated together and egged each other on. Allan Border would run in from mid-wicket, fists clenched, patting the bowler on the back, getting them hyped up for more. Goochy would just walk in from mid-off and say, 'Well bowled, Phil.' It wasn't like, 'C'mon Tuffers, you've ****ing got 'em here, keep going, you're on a roll, keep going, son.'

Against those brilliant Aussie sides, you did have the feeling that when they got a wicket, they'd get another one. And when they hit a four, they'd hit another one. If something went wrong you had to be able to move forward and put it behind you.

So, yes, it's true that you need mentally tough players, but when you are up against better players, you also need to work as a team and feel supported. If not, the scars of defeat stay with you and it gets more and more difficult to win.

When Michael Vaughan led the team to the Ashes in 2005, I think that was down to three main factors. Number one, we finally had the players to match the Aussies again.

Second, they brought in fresh, fearless young players. Vaughanie himself had a brilliant batting record against the Aussies, so he had positive memories to draw on, and selecting players unscarred by past Ashes defeats paid off at crucial points in the series where previous England teams had cracked.

Third, they showed confidence in the players chosen, got them to play to their strengths. In my time, we were always trying to copy the Aussies rather than doing it our way. The dumbest example was the constant search for a so-called 'mystery bowler' to match Shane Warne. Which was a total impossibility.

When I was playing, all I heard was, 'You're not Shane Warne.' Well, what could I do with that advice? Nothing. It was all about 'We haven't got this', not 'What have we got? Let's make the best of it.'

In 2005, with 'Wheelie Bin' Ashley Giles, they didn't try to make him into something he wasn't. He was just encouraged to do his job as well as he could and he made a valuable contribution to the success of the team.

DO FIRST IMPRESSIONS COUNT?

In the Twenty20 international and three one-day internationals before the 2005 series, while the Aussies were just easing their way into the tour, England were hungrier for wins to give their younger team some confidence. An old-stager, Darren Gough, who'd retired from Tests, did his bit, getting himself on a hat-trick at the Rose Bowl. Then, rather than bowl a fast swinging full-length ball, Dazzler surprised everyone, including batsman Andrew Symonds who got straight onto the front foot, by bowling a quick bouncer. The ball hit Symonds and Goughie followed down the pitch and gave him the stare. He hadn't got the hat-trick, but the message was clear – England were not going to be intimidated, they were planning to be the intimidators. That continued from ball one of the Ashes, with Steve Harmison fizzing a bouncer past Justin Langer and nine England fielders all crowding in on Langer, chirping at him.

'During that first hour, Matty Hayden got hit on the helmet – first time I'd seen him get hit on the helmet,' recalled Langer.

'Ricky Ponting had his cheek split. Not one of them came up to see if he was okay.

'At drinks, I went up to them and said, "We're not in a war here. Show Ricky Ponting some respect." They were like, "Oh yeah, righto", almost like they were in a trance. They were so fired up and that's what they were like for the whole series.'

A year-and-a-half later, Langer was again facing the first ball of the Ashes from Harmison, this time at the Gabba. Harmy then went and bowled probably the biggest – and definitely the most infamous – wide in Ashes history, arrowed straight at second slip. It was a shocker – as commentator David Lloyd deadpanned, 'When the ball goes to second slip, it is usually followed by an appeal.' Ex-Australian wicketkeeper Ian Healy started referring to big wides as 'Harmies'.

The difference in atmosphere couldn't have been more marked.

'I was fired up, looking for a fight – we'd been to boot camp, we'd won every Test and we were so prepared,' said Langer. 'We had fire in our eyes . . . Harmison was giggling like a nervous schoolboy. I said in a press conference at the end of the first day – I can't help but wonder whether the first ball of this series will be as significant as the first of the last series.'

But how significant can one delivery actually be? England did actually lose the First Test in 2005, but from what Langer says it clearly had a psychological effect on the Aussies. That fiery start had to be backed up, though, and even after losing that match, Vaughanie was determined to remain positive even though the media coverage was very negative about England's defeat.

If anything he wanted them to attack more in the Second Test. He encouraged the players to get after Shane Warne, and make sure he went for at least four or five an over. They'd already singled out Jason Gillespie, who was bowling way below his best, for brutal treatment. And after Ponting bizarrely put them in to bat at Edgbaston, the England batters went ballistic on all the Australian bowlers, scoring at a run a ball to make over 400 in a day.

Matthew Hoggard, who played in both 2005 and 2006/07, reckons first impressions aren't that significant at all. Hoggy bowled the first ball of the 2002/03 Ashes tour in a one-dayer against the Australian Cricket Board Chairman's XI at Lilac Hill in Perth. Captain Nasser Hussain told him to bowl a bouncer first ball and then go and stare down the opener. He did as he was told. England lost that match and the Ashes series 4–1.

At the start of the 1997 series, Goughie steamed in and bowled a pearler, just beating Mark Taylor's outside edge. England stormed to a nine-wicket win and the crowd were singing, 'Ashes comin' home'. They weren't though – we lost the third, fourth and fifth Tests.

At Brisbane in 1994, Phil DeFreitas kicked off the series with a rank long hop that Michael Slater dispatched to the boundary, and people said that set the tone for the series. But if you look at the quality of the two teams, Daffy could have ripped out Slats's middle stump and it's still odds-on we would have got well beaten.

Again, ultimately, it comes back to who has the best players. No matter how positive or aggressive your tactics are or how well you start, you still have to outplay the other guys across the hundreds of overs that follow.

DAVO'S RING OF FIRE AND PUNTER PRATTLED

When you look back on Ashes matches, however, you can often identify a moment when the game tipped in favour of one side or the other. Some are more obvious than others though. For instance, the outcome of the 1961 Lord's Test was highly influenced by what happened in the Australian dressing room before the match had even begun. Australia's brilliant all-rounder (and notorious hypochondriac) Alan Davidson was nursing a sore back and had rubbed a Deep Heat-type cream into it to ease the pain before going out to bowl.

On that first day a big ridge was discovered on the pitch and Davidson took full advantage, generating startling lift from just short of a length. And as he sweated, the cream trickled down his back and beyond causing an, ahem, 'ring of fire'. Bringing a whole new meaning to the phrase 'in the heat of battle', Davo's burning orifice only made him run in harder and bowl faster on the way to a five-fer as Australia bowled England out within a day. Asked afterwards about how aggressively he'd bowled, Davo replied: 'Well, if your backside was on fire, you'd have done the same.'

Davidson's discomfort helped Australia to win that game, but sometimes a single incident on the pitch can prove pivotal to the outcome of the whole series.

In the closely fought 1953 Ashes, that moment came at Headingley. With the score still 0–0 after three Tests, Australia had a chance of victory, needing 177 runs in just under two hours.

Through dashing cameos by Arthur Morris, and then Neil Harvey in partnership with Graeme Hole, the target had been reduced to 66 in 45 minutes when Davidson joined Hole at the wicket. It was looking ominous for England until Hole swept a ball from Trevor Bailey and Tom Graveney held a magnificent catch above his head on the boundary. It was six or out, and thanks to Graveney, Hole holed out.

Australia finished 30 runs short and England capitalised on Graveney's great catch to win the final Test and regain the Ashes.

In my lifetime, probably the most amusing turning point in an Ashes series – well, for England fans anyway – was the run out of Ricky Ponting by supersub fielder Gary Pratt at Trent Bridge in 2005. With Australia following on, Ponting was on 48 and dragging the Aussies back into contention. Then his partner Damien Martyn pushed a ball from Andrew Flintoff into the covers and they went for a quick single. Pratt shot to his left, picked up and threw with his right hand in one movement and hit the stumps with a deadeye throw. The third-umpire replay showed Punter was well out of his ground.

Furious at what he believed was England's abuse of the rules to give their bowlers a regular rest and bring on dynamite sub fielders, Ponting cursed at smiling England coach Duncan Fletcher on the England balcony as he was walking off. That outburst cost him 75 per cent of his match fee, delighted

England fans, who always love to see Punter upset, and geed up the England players to gain the decisive victory in the series. The unlikely hero Pratt recalled: 'It was the Australian captain being rattled and showing it. I think that's when the lads thought, "We've got them here, we've got to hammer it home." It was a massive psychological blow.'

Even Australians who weren't playing were affected. Mike Hussey, captain of Pratt's county Durham, rang him at the end of play to tell him he wanted him to play in a one-dayer the next day. Pratt had to drive all the way back up north, only for Hussey to then leave him out.

In fairness to Ponting, at the end of The Oval Test, he had a few beers with Pratt, congratulated him and gave him a pair of his boots as a souvenir. 'He was a pretty nice, genuine guy, pretty magnanimous,' said Pratt. Ponting didn't mention the run-out at all. It's probably best that Pratt didn't tell Punter his strike-rate at the time, although he admitted later that he hadn't hit the stumps with any of his run-out attempts all season in the build-up to that moment, 'and I reckon I missed with my next 25 attempts too!'

He slipped out of county cricket when Durham cancelled his contract just a year later. But for what must be one of the shortest and greatest cameos in the history of sport, the name Pratt will always be remembered by Ashes watchers.

NERVOUS ENDINGS

Okay, you can have your psychologically important first balls or game-turning points, but there's nothing that can quite match a nerve-shreddingly, heart-poundingly, buttock-clenchingly tight finish to an Ashes match. After days of battle it can come down to a few runs either way, and it is one of the curiosities of cricket that often a team is dependent upon the people least equipped to score those vital runs, that is, tailenders. Luckily for England, as my batting average was even worse than normal against Australia (2.72 compared to my overall Test average of 5.1), I was never in a position to score a heroic 30 to get us over the winning line or stick around for 20 overs to save an Ashes game, but there have been some sterling efforts by nine, ten, Jack since the earliest series.

In the Second Test at The Oval in 1890, no one was expecting a close game as the Aussie 'Colonials' had generally been getting a hammering in recent times. But on a rapidly deteriorating wicket, England nearly blew it.

Needing just 95 to win in the final innings, England creaked their way to 32 for 4, before Maurice Read steadied the ship. He scored 35, but when he was caught at long-on with just 12 to win, panic set in. Three more wickets fell quickly leaving England two runs short of victory when number ten John Sharpe joined the brilliantly named Gregor MacGregor at the wicket.

Australian swing bowler J. J. Ferris, who finished with 5 for 49, had his tail up by now and Sharpe was a total rabbit. He played and missed and Ferris's off-cutters kept just missing the stumps. Five maidens in a row followed his arrival. Finally, Sharpe managed to hack the ball to cover and the England pair chanced a run. Under pressure, cover point threw, missed and overthrows saw England stagger over the line.

In 1902 there was another nailbiter at The Oval. This time England needed 263 to win in the last innings and after a crash-bang-wallop century from Gilbert Jessop, it came down to the last-wicket pair of Yorkshiremen George Hirst and Wilfred Rhodes to score 15 to win. Ultimately, amid unbearable tension, it was Rhodes who pushed the ball past mid-on for the winning runs.

The victory was only a consolation as England lost that series 2–1, and six years later, England only managed a solitary win Down Under as they went down 4–1 against a mighty Australian side featuring Warwick Armstrong, Victor Trumper, Monty Noble and co. At least their win in the New Year's Test was a thriller, courtesy of a decisive 39-run stand between number nine Sydney Barnes and last man Arthur Fielder.

Among heroic last-wicket stands in Ashes matches, the great effort of Allan Border and Jeff Thomson in the Melbourne Test of 1982 stands out. Needing 292 to win, Thomson came to the wicket with the score at a very unpromising 218 for 9.

They managed to see out the end of the fourth day and get the score up to 255, though, and the next morning 18,000-odd people turned up sensing a famous victory. The new ball was taken early on, but neither Thomson nor Border seemed troubled at all and kept chiselling away at the deficit.

With Australia needing just four runs to win, England captain Bob Willis, in his words, 'turned to "Golden Balls"' – Ian Botham. Sure enough, bowling the 18th over of the morning, Beefy got Thomson to edge the ball straight at Chris Tavaré standing at second slip.

Previously, wicketkeeper Bob Taylor had said to Tav and first slip Geoff Miller that they should both move a bit closer to make sure any edges carried. But whereas Miller had edged up half a yard, Tav had moved forward about two. So when the newish ball flew off the edge he couldn't react in time and it ricocheted off his hands over his head. Luckily for Tav, Geoff Miller at first slip was alive to the situation and quickly stepped to his right to grab the ball and clinch the win. At the non-striker's end, Border, who had first thought the ball had gone through Tav's hands for four, watched in horror as Miller sprinted off in celebration.

It was typical Botham to get the vital wicket and in such dramatic style. It was his 100th in Anglo-Australian Tests, and made him only the second Englishman to perform the double of 100 wickets and 1,000 runs in the Ashes (61 years after Wilfred Rhodes had done it).

Of course, 2005 was the ultimate Ashes series for tense finishes and Aussie quick bowler Brett Lee had a bat in his hand to the bitter end of the closest two. In the second at Old Trafford, he and Glenn McGrath survived the last 24 balls against the hostile Flintoff/Harmison combo to salvage a draw. And that really was against the odds. Ricky Ponting, who'd ground out an almost-but-not-quite-match-saving innings of 156 in seven hours before being dismissed with just four overs to go, summed up the expectations of the Aussie dressing room later, admitting: 'I didn't have much faith in them.'

The Aussies' belief had probably been shaken by the climax of the previous match at Edgbaston, another classic. With eight wickets down and still needing over a 100 to win, Warne and Lee, and then Lee and number 11 Michael Kasprowicz, fought their way to within one hit of victory.

Simon Jones had dropped Lee on the third-man boundary, but dropped catches don't always lose matches. With just three runs needed to win, Steve Harmison bowled a beauty which Kasprowicz gloved and stumper Geraint Jones took a great diving catch down the legside.

It was only after watching countless replays that someone spotted that actually Kasprowicz's hand was off the bat at the moment of impact, so he should have been given not out. There was no way umpire Billy Bowden could have been expected to see this and the Aussies didn't complain, but that decision could have changed everything.

If Kasprowicz had survived and got those last three runs with Lee, Australia would have been 2–0 up in the series and perhaps there would have been no Ashes win for the first time in 17 years, no open-top bus parade and no MBEs for the England boys.

MIXING WITH THE ENEMY

Within a few days of that Edgbaston thriller there was a DVD on sale called *The Greatest Test* and with good reason. It wasn't just the brilliant cricket played and dramatic climax that had made it special, but also the sportsmanship on display when the game was over.

THE BATTLE

As the England players went doolally all around him, poor Brett Lee, who'd been left stranded on 43 not out, crouched down on his haunches, absolutely gutted.

'Moments later, I felt this big hand on my shoulder,' wrote Lee in his autobiography. 'It was Freddie [Flintoff]. I still don't know exactly what he said, but it was something like: "Awesome game, bad luck, I thoroughly enjoyed it."'

This moment between Flintoff and Lee was captured by the photographers and has become an iconic image. And that spirit continued behind the scenes after the game. When Lee got back to the pavilion, he spent 20 minutes sitting in the shower block, with all his gear still on, numbed by the defeat having played possibly the best innings of his life.

Flintoff was the first English player to go into the Australian dressing room, and he poured Lee a beer and put his arm around him.

'Half an hour or so earlier, he'd been on the field trying to pin me,' recalled Lee. 'Both the "before" and "after" were sport at its best. It was a really, really special moment which cemented a great bond between us.'

It was after that Edgbaston match that the Australians and England players in general restarted the trend of having a drink together after the game. Once the series was over, Ricky Ponting was accused by ex-Aussie players of being too matey with the England team, implying that had cost them defeat. Punter said that wasn't the case and that the cricket was as intense as he'd ever played. Matthew Hoggard reckoned that all the players in that series just felt that they 'were part of something special and it was good to share that feeling with the opposition'. And, remember, less than two years later during the 2006/07 series Down Under, the two teams continued to socialise after the game and that time Australia smashed us out of sight.

The spirit in those series was great, but I have to admit that when I was playing I didn't like to mix with opponents. Although I loved going out and spending time with Aussie people in general, I kept my distance from their players. I didn't want them to get to know me, because I wanted to be unpredictable to them. On the pitch I always felt that they thought they could get inside my head. Like Goochy, they reckoned I was a bit mentally fragile, that I was a frontrunner and not so good when the pressure was on. Their batters used to try and get after me early to try and break my confidence. Luckily, I usually did all right.

Perhaps their low opinion of me might have dated from the first time I bumped into the Waugh brothers in a pub in Perth one Sunday afternoon. I was a bit pissed and they looked at me as if to say, 'If this is the competition, it'll be a piece of cake!'

Whether or not Ashes teams socialise together does seem to go in phases, depending on the characters in each team. Ex-England batsman and coach Keith Fletcher recalled very little socialising between the English boys and the brash Australian side captained by Ian Chappell in the early seventies.

'I could not bring myself to open a bottle and take part in the banter with chippy, chirpy people who had just been trying to knock my head off,' he wrote.

Later he worked with Allan Border and Mark Waugh at

Essex and found he liked them, but he wasn't sure about the rest: 'From a distance, one or two other Aussies such as Doug Walters appeared likeable, but others including Ian Chappell, I found aggressive and unpleasant.'

Mind you, Dennis Lillee wasn't too keen on Fletch either after an incident in the Sydney Test of 1975. Tony Greig bounced Lillee first ball and Fletch, who was fielding at gully shouted: 'Well done, Greigy, give 'im another.'

Lillee turned round shooting daggers.

'Who said that?'

'I did,' said Fletch.

At the end of the day, Lillee was interviewed and asked how he got on with the England blokes.

'The Poms are good sorts, I get on with them all,' he replied, before adding, 'Except that little weasel, Fletcher. I know you are watching and I will sort you out tomorrow.'

The next day, Fletch came out to bat to a hostile welcome from the spectators. He was wearing his MCC cap, with the emblem of St George on a horse, and Lillee proceeded to try and knock it and Fletch's head off his shoulders. Fletch was doing great until a bouncer didn't get up as much as expected, he took his eye off the ball and it hit him straight on the bonce. Ouch.

Back in the dressing room, Geoff Arnold, the ex-Surrey and England bowler, jumped up and shouted: 'Blimey, he's just knocked St George off his 'orse!'

While Lillee and Fletch were never going to be drinking buddies, Lillee and Ian Botham have always been best mates. Beefy got on with most of the Aussie players and he'd always be up for having a beer with them after the game, which the Aussie boys appreciated as much as his cricketing genius.

Geoff Lawson, who was unfortunate enough to have had to bowl to Beefy in the 1981 series, said about him: 'He didn't play like an Englishman. He didn't worry about the risks, he attacked with the ball and the bat. He was a great opponent no matter how he was playing, always giving it 100 per cent and giving it to the opposition. But what made him a great and respected opponent was that as soon as the umpires called stumps he was there having drinks with you, being a human being rather than an opponent on the cricket field.'

Allan Border put a stop to that in 1989 and when Steve Waugh became captain, he also took a dim view of socialising too much with the opposition. Waugh's logic was similar to mine, in that he didn't want England players to get to know them in case we saw their human weaknesses. He wanted us to see them as 'an invincible machine'. Okay, I didn't think the Aussies ever thought of me as an invincible machine, but you know what I mean. Preserving a bit of mystery can help your cause.

In an ideal world, though, it would be great if all Ashes series could have the same camaraderie between the teams as there was in 2005. The Ashes is a sporting battle, but as I've said before, it's not an actual war. Two men who understood that better than most were Keith Miller and his fellow Brylcreem endorser Denis Compton. While they were drinking mates, on the pitch Miller took great delight in trying to ruffle the immaculately turned-out Compton with a bumper or three whenever he bowled at him.

THE BATTLE

In Ashes games you would often see them have a joke with each other, including a private running gag that dated back to Compton's army days, serving in India. Compton had been sent out there during the Second World War and was deployed to Delhi when the war was over to boost troop morale by setting up a football team and also playing in a couple of cricket matches. In one of the cricket games, Denis represented an East Zone against an 'Australian Forces XI' who were on their way back from the Victory Tests in England, coming up against his mate Miller.

Compton was moving stylishly towards his century when some disturbances occurred in the crowd. By the time he was facing on 96, this disturbance was developing into a full-blown riot. He had a tickle outside off stump, the ball caught the edge of his bat and flew straight to first slip, but luckily for Denis first slip was busy watching the fight and the ball flew straight past him and to the boundary.

Unusual way to reach your hundred, but there was no time to celebrate because by now the 'unruly mob', as Compton called them, were spilling onto the pitch and heading towards the wicket.

Most of the players ran for it, but Denis and Keith stood their ground. Even though he had a bat handy, Denis was still a bit nervous as the man at the front of the rioting hordes came towards him. The bloke meant him no harm though, instead saying politely: 'Mr Compton, you very good player but the game must stop.'

After that, on and off the pitch, Miller would often repeat the line in his best Indian accent by way of greeting his old pal.

Hopefully, many players in Ashes series to come will have great battles on the cricket pitch and form great friendships just as Miller and Compton did.

TUFFERS' TEN ASHES WARRIORS

Many brave men have put their bodies on the line in search of Ashes victory. Meet ten of the pluckiest fellas who didn't mind taking a few for the team . . .

Tony Greig

In the 1974/75 series, few England players relished batting against Jeff Thomson and Dennis Lillee on lively Australian wickets, but the late, great Tony Greig was an exception to the rule. The South African-born all-rounder showed his lion heart in the First Test at Brisbane as the only England bowler mad enough to bowl bouncers at Lillee when he came out to bat. Infuriated, Lillee was fired up to give him the same treatment when it was his turn to bowl. But Greig relished the challenge, bobbing and weaving like a boxer under bouncers and shouting 'Fetch that!' as he struck boundaries on his way to a century.

All very macho, but speaking as a tailender, I would not

particularly have appreciated Greigy winding up their temperamental fast bowler before I came in to bat.

Archie Jackson

Don Bradman burst on the Ashes scene during the 1928/29 series, becoming the youngest batsman to make a Test century at that time. Bradman was just 20 years old when he made a ton in only his second Test match at the MCG. But his record lasted just one match, as 19-year-old Archie Jackson scored 164 on his Test debut for Australia at Adelaide. Those who witnessed the innings talked of his brilliant footwork, timing and his bravery, and many considered him to have greater potential than Bradman.

Indeed, when he headed to England in 1930, the *Sydney Morning Herald* described him as 'the greatest of present-day batsmen'. However, while Bradman flourished, Archie struggled with his form and health on that tour. He did show why many considered him a braver batsman than Bradman in the final Test at The Oval, though. This was the match where the England players first realised that Bradman might be vulnerable to aggressive bowling. In one session where the pitch was at its most treacherous and Harold Larwood peppered both Bradman and Jackson, it was Jackson who looked the more willing to step into line and he took numerous painful body blows as the pair put together a match-winning double-century partnership.

Sadly, Archie's health continued to decline and he died of

tuberculosis just four years after his stunning debut. It was a tragic loss of a great talent which left cricket lovers wondering what might have been.

Hon. Lionel Tennyson

Hon. Lionel Tennyson was an aristocrat and an army officer, and nothing that happened on the cricket field could scare him. Nicknamed 'The Brave Basher', he once said he enjoyed facing fast bowling because 'it came on to the bat so damned sweet'. Each to their own, Basher.

He played in just one Ashes series, when Australia romped to a 3–0 win in 1921, but Basher was one of the few English batsmen to have the cojones to take the attack to Australia's fearsome fast-bowling combo of Jack Gregory and Ted McDonald. He scored 74 not out on his first Ashes appearance in the Second Test, and so impressed he was given the captaincy for the remaining three matches.

In the next game at Headingley, he hurt his hand so badly fielding that he had to wear a basket guard when he batted. Despite the injury causing him pain every time he got bat on ball, he somehow managed to score 63 and 36.

In the final match of the series (and Basher's Test career), he was struck over the heart by a ball from McDonald at The Oval and the doctor told him he would have been killed if he hadn't been so 'well-padded' (he was a powerfully built chap).

Because of his experience, Basher had no time for Australians' complaints about Bodyline bowling a decade later.

'Every member of that England side was left black and blue from his knees up to his chin,' he said of the 1921 series. 'There were no squeals of protest to Australia at that time about leg theory or bodyline bowling. But now we have the fast bowlers who are making a success of the tactics adopted by Gregory and McDonald in 1921.'

Stan McCabe

Stan was arguably the best Aussie batsman of the Bodyline series, taking on England's fast bowlers with relish. A short, stocky fella, his lightning-quick footwork enabled him to get into perfect position to deal with leg-theory bowling in a way that even Bradman struggled to match.

His courageous innings of 187, including 25 fours, in the First Test at the SCG, when he repeatedly hooked the ball to the picket fence in front of and behind square, has gone down in Australian cricket history.

Luckily, for Larwood, Voce and co., brave Stan made sure his mum didn't attack them with the same fury. On his way out to bat, he'd told his dad: 'If I happen to get hit out there, keep mum from jumping the fence and laying into those Pommie bowlers!'

David Steele

A prematurely grey-haired, 33-year-old from Stoke with steel-rimmed glasses who'd been a journeyman county pro for 12 years, David Steele was the unlikeliest of Ashes heroes.

He got picked for the 1975 series after England captain Tony Greig rang round a few of the top county bowlers to ask who they found the hardest batsmen to get out in this country: the top two answers were Geoff Boycott (who was unavailable) and David Steele.

After England collapsed to an innings defeat against the fearsome pace of 'Lillian Thomson' in the opening Test, Steele was thrown in to bat at number three in the second match at Lord's. 'Who's this then? Father ****ing Christmas?' asked Jeff Thomson on his arrival at the wicket.

As it turned out, Santa had a perfect temperament for Test match cricket. Brave and technically correct, Steele played forward calmly when the ball was pitched up and hooked brilliantly when Lillian Thomson dug it in short. Greig later recalled how Steele hooked the Aussie bowlers off the front foot and pulled off the back foot: 'They seemed convinced that they would kill him [because of his middle-aged appearance] and he kept hitting the thing for four.'

While others melted against Australia's fiery attack, Steele was as good as his word to Australian wicketkeeper, Rod Marsh. 'Take a good look at this arse of mine. You'll be seeing a lot of it this summer,' he told Marsh, and proceeded to occupy the crease for over 19 hours in the remaining three

Tests of the four-match series, scoring 365 runs in six innings, his lowest score being 39.

England drew all three matches he played and ultimately lost the series, but it was a creditable improvement after the First Test shambles. And Steele charmed the British public to such an extent that he became only the second cricketer ever to win BBC Sports Personality of the Year.

Steele also tucked into some meaty meals off the back of his fine performances in the Ashes as his local butcher in Northampton rewarded him with a lamb chop for every run scored, plus a steak for every run over fifty. Luckily for the pigs of Northamptonshire, pork sausages weren't part of the deal.

Freddie Brown

The eccentric choice to captain England's weak touring side in the 1950/51 series, 40-year-old Freddie Brown showed plenty of courage against a powerful Australian team. A leg-spinning all-rounder, Freddie damaged tendons in his shoulder in a car accident during the Fourth Test at Adelaide.

With England 4–0 down, he had still not fully recovered by the next game at Melbourne and was hoping not to have to bowl. But when Trevor Bailey twisted his ankle, he was forced into action. Despite his discomfort, in his second spell he took the key wickets of Arthur Morris, Neil Harvey and Keith Miller in 17 balls for no runs.

By the end of the first day, Freddie was limping as well as

prodding his injured shoulder, but came back to take Miller's wicket again in the second innings helping England to victory by eight wickets.

He restored some pride to the English team which had been in the doldrums since the war and the Aussies loved Freddie for his wholehearted approach. Famously, a street seller down on Sydney quay shouted: 'Lovely lettuces, only a shilling and 'earts as big as Freddie Brown's.'

Simon Katich

A determined batsman, Katich didn't mind putting himself in the line of fire in the field either. Standing at short leg at The Oval in 2005, he copped a few nasty blows. One time, Paul Collingwood pulled a ball which hit him on the ribs, but he took it like a boxer and just carried on. It was only a few minutes later that he thought he might be in trouble when he realised he was spitting blood so he told skipper Ricky Ponting. Ponting was worried he might have broken a rib so told him to see the physio immediately.

He was back a couple of overs later though. 'False alarm,' he told Punter. 'Turns out I bit my tongue as I ducked for cover and that's what caused the blood.'

Denis Compton

A dashing batsman, Compton didn't lack for bravery either as he demonstrated in a lost cause during the 1948 series against Bradman's team of 'Invincibles'.

Compton scored 184 in the First Test at Trent Bridge despite being peppered by bouncers from Ray Lindwall and Keith Miller, who benefited from the MCC's decision to bring in a rule allowing a new ball every 55 overs.

But he showed even more courage at Old Trafford a month later after top-edging a massive no-ball from Lindwall onto his forehead. A lesser man might have crumbled, but after having his wound stitched up in the dressing room, a couple of thimbles of brandy and a quick net to check he was still only seeing one ball, Denis returned to the fray to hit 145 not out.

Steve Waugh

Australian captain Steve Waugh was sitting in a wheelchair in hospital when he heard that his team had retained the Ashes by winning the Third Test at Trent Bridge in 2001. Batting earlier that day, he'd stumbled to the ground in agony completing his first run and had to retire hurt. An MRI scan revealed he'd severe tears to his calf muscle and he was told that he would need at least three months to recover.

Naturally, Waugh thought that his tour was over and he should go back to Oz and get his leg right for the new season.

But a call home to his missus changed his mind. She told him that as this was likely to be his last Ashes tour, he should stay on, enjoy it and try and get back in time for the final Test so he could hold the replica Ashes urn aloft.

Never lacking for courage on the field, Waugh showed his mettle off it by putting himself through ten hours of physiotherapy per day – five hours of exercises in the pool, five hours of massage – in a bid to play the final rubber. His work paid off and, remarkably, just 20 days after he sustained the injury, he declared himself fit to play at The Oval. I really wish he hadn't as I had to bowl to him as he hobbled to 157 not out in what proved to be my final Test match and they won by an innings.

John Edrich

Norfolk boy Edrich was never scared to put his body in harm's way for the cause. Playing Test cricket in an era before helmets, he got knocked out cold by a bouncer from South African pace bowler Peter Pollock in 1965. You'd think that might have made him a little more nervous against the quicks but he never compromised his approach as he showed a decade later at Sydney when he had to go to hospital after being hit in the body by his first ball from Dennis Lillee. X-rays showed two broken ribs, but he returned to the crease and stayed there for over two and a half hours making 33 not out and stepping into line just as he had before. A good man to have on your side in a battle.

CHAPTER 14

FANS

BARMY MOMENTS

The spectators play such an important part in making an Ashes Test a special occasion. For me, the crowds in Australia were the biggest, most vocal and colourful I ever played in front of. I loved playing there and although I got plenty of stick, and some of it was below the belt – having a pop at you and your family – I never felt threatened. The nearest they got to physical violence was when a fella asked me for an autograph and when I went over to sign he slapped a mince beef and onion pie on my head, which was a bit uncalled for. And if you were offered a beer, it was always worth checking whether it was cold in case they'd filled it with their own personal amber nectar. Generally, though, in my experience, it was a friendly bitter rivalry.

And if an England player is fielding on the boundary in Oz and finds being called a 'wanker' repeatedly a bit of a chore, he can always look to the Barmy Army for support.

The name 'Barmy Army' was coined by the Aussie media during the 1994/95 tour which I played in, basically because they couldn't believe that they kept on singing and supporting us despite us getting beaten all the time. England had always had a strong travelling support but on that tour the fans seemed to mob up under one banner. At Sydney, I remember seeing a huge clump of people together with Union Jack flags on the old Hill. Since then the Barmy Army has just grown and grown, becoming a proper organisation with tens of thousands of members, organising tours, priority access to match tickets and selling their own range of merchandise.

Early on, though, while the Australian journalists immediately loved the Barmies, the older members of the English press establishment were not so impressed. Some didn't think the football-style chanting and trumpet-honking atmosphere the Barmies brought to games was in keeping with the more genteel traditions of English cricket spectators, but over time they've become more accepted.

Certainly, when I was a player, they often helped to keep my spirits up when things were going badly on the pitch (which was often in the 1994/95 series). Rather than waiting to be entertained like an audience at the theatre, they got involved and tried to give the players a lift.

When we were in the field on a blazing hot afternoon, the Australian batters were cruising along at a few hundred for one and we weren't looking like getting a wicket, they kept us

going. You'd hear the Barmies sing and shouting encouragement and it would give you that kick to keep going and try to
grab a wicket or two before the close of play. The Australian
supporters and players must have wondered how on earth
they could shut these blokes up – it didn't matter how much
the Aussies beat us, the Barmies kept coming back for more.

We did reward them with one Test win on that 1994/95
tour, though, at Adelaide in the Fourth Test when Devon
Malcolm and Chris Lewis blasted them out for 156 in their
second innings. That included a great moment for me
personally when I took one of the best catches of my career to
dismiss Michael Slater. Slats had miscued a hook and I took
the ball over my shoulder down at fine leg. I'd been so ill I'd
been on a drip (no, not a vodka drip . . .) and I'd got off my
sickbed to play, so I was very pleased with that one. I went
running over to the Barmies congregated on the Adelaide Hill
and pumped my fist as they all came rushing down to celebrate.
It was like a bundle on the old football terraces as they spilled
over the advertising boards onto the pitch. A great buzz for
me, and it was great to share that match win with the people
who had always been there for us through some pretty lean
times.

Michael Vaughan, captain of England's triumphant 2005
team, called the Barmy Army the side's 'twelfth man' and
that's what it felt like to me, even back then. I'm just delighted
that after sticking with us through the bad times in the nineties
and early noughties, they've had more success to celebrate in
recent years.

EGG-AND-BACON GANGSTA POSSE

However, over the long history of the Ashes there have only been a few occasions when spectators' passions have got the better of them. In the early days, when cricket in England was played to polite applause, the behaviour of more rough-and-ready fans that came to watch the Tests in Australia took some getting used to for touring English players.

In 1903/04, the First and Fourth Tests were played at Sydney and the atmosphere got decidedly nasty both times. First time around, a run-out decision by umpire Bob Crockett against Aussie hero Clem Hill almost caused a riot. Spectators booed and made death threats and totally unfounded accusations that the umps had accepted bribes from the England skipper Plum Warner.

Crockett wasn't much more popular when he returned to officiate at the Fourth Test and he and his co-umpire decided to keep the teams off the pitch due to light drizzle on the second day. This time he was pelted with bottles and fruit.

There is nothing like bad weather stopping play to get spectators' hackles up. The Centenary Test at Lord's in 1980 was staged to mark 100 years since the first Test played in England. It was a one-off match, and without the Ashes at stake, but it was attended by many Ashes heroes of the past from both countries. The match itself was a bit of a non-event, apart from some argy-bargy caused by the most unlikely people – MCC members.

Rain had caused hours of play to be lost on the first couple of days, and by day three the umpires were shipping dog's abuse as if the crap weather was all their fault. In mid-afternoon, as umpire David Constant walked off after a fifth pitch inspection, a couple of angry members of the egg-and-bacon crew lost it and went totally gangsta on his ass. They jostled Constant and the two captains Ian Botham and Greg Chappell had to step in to fend off the MCC hooligans. During the fracas even Beefy allegedly took a blow to the back of the head from these loons, who were no doubt tanked up on Pimms and canapés.

Constant's fellow umpire Dickie Bird was out on the pitch while all this was happening and when he got back to the dressing room he was shocked to find his colleague looking dishevelled and upset. 'We both sat there with tears in our eyes,' wrote Dickie later, 'I have never experienced anything like that anywhere in the world. Not even at Headingley.'

When play finally did get underway later that afternoon, the umpires got a police escort through the Long Room and onto the field.

'It tarnished the whole event,' said England batsman Bill Athey, who was making his Test debut that day.

At least there was a happy ending for Dickie Bird, when Dennis Lillee came up to him at the conclusion of the match with a present, telling him not to open it until he got home. Back at his cottage in Barnsley, Dickie opened it and found Lillee's official touring tie and a message: 'Going back to Australia with an open-neck shirt. You can have my tie because you are a great guy and we all think you are a fair umpire.'

Nice touch.

A year later, at the Headingley Test, it was bad weather and the umpires' misunderstanding of the rules which made the fans see red. That game is best remembered for Botham smashing balls around the park, but the crowd weren't shy of launching a few missiles of their own at the end of day three.

Bad light had stopped play, and the umpires Barrie Meyer and David Evans came out to inspect the pitch at five to six. The light meters showed the light was still inadequate and the umps called off play for the day. But no sooner had they walked off and the covers been put on, than the sun peeked through the clouds.

The fans naturally wanted their extra hour of play, but the umps thought that was only possible if play was in progress at the scheduled time of finish. They were wrong, because the rules stated that the conditions just had to be fit for play.

The spectators vented their fury by chucking cushions and abuse at the umps and the incident led to a rule-change so that when stoppages affected play, play could restart at any time.

HEALS'S HOOTER

When I encountered Aussie fans away from the matches Down Under, I never really had any hassle. The natives were usually very friendly, and as long as you took the attitude that someone saying, 'All right Tuffers, you Pommie bastard' was meant affectionately, you could all get along fine.

Sometimes fans go over the top though, as the great former Australian wicketkeeper, Ian Healy, found out to his cost.

Healy admitted that he couldn't resist biting back at supporters who gave him stick, and he chose the wrong people to confront after the final Test of the 1994/95 series in Perth. The Aussie boys met up with us to toast Graham Gooch and Mike Gatting who were playing their last Tests and then went off to a sponsor's function and drank some more.

By the time Healy arrived back at the team hotel he'd had a few and he ran into a couple of England fans at the entrance who started giving him grief. Mark Waugh had arrived back before him and just ignored them, but Heals made the mistake of getting involved. At first, he just asked them what their problem was and told them to calm down, but one of the blokes kept going at him and Healy snapped.

'What kind of loser are you, following this bunch of no-hopers round the country?' said the Australian vice-captain. (Incidentally, thanks for that, Heals!)

This did not go down well, and the fella who was standing on the step below him jumped up and headbutted him on the nose then ran off before Healy could grab him.

Hotel security told him that the two men had just been thrown out of the hotel for causing trouble. Healy asked them not to call the police but they did anyway and came to his hotel room.

'The first thing the officer said was, "Is your nose always bent?"' he recalled. 'I looked in the mirror, it didn't look much worse than usual.'

He had to go to hospital to get it checked out, and news leaked out to the media that a player had been involved in a scuffle. Healy managed to keep the truth from his manager and the Australian Cricket Board for a while, before eventually admitting what happened, telling journalists, 'You don't have to be a great shot to hit my hooter.'

GEORGE DAVIS IS INNOCENT . . . SORT OF

You don't see it happen nowadays, because the fines for doing it are so great, but there have been some spectacular pitch invasions by spectators during Ashes matches over the years. When Geoff Boycott scored his 100th first-class century, the first player ever to do so in a Test, at Headingley in 1977, he was mobbed by his adoring Yorkshire fans. In the commotion, someone nicked Boycs's cap before thinking better of it and giving it back.

Ian Chappell was not so lucky when he reached three figures in the Melbourne Test in 1971, though. His century triggered a mass pitch invasion with an estimated two thousand people hitting the turf. When the decks were finally cleared there were three items on the missing list – Chappell's cap, England fielder Colin Cowdrey's hat and a stump – and this time, none was returned.

That 1970/71 series, when England regained the Ashes, became notorious for the hostility of the Australians towards Ray Illingworth's team and an ugly incident in the Seventh Test at the SCG.

Near the end of Australia's first innings, tailender Terry Jenner ducked into a ball from England fast bowler John Snow and got hit on the head. Umpire Lou Rowan warned Snow against excessive use of bouncers and while he and Illingworth protested, saying it was the first bouncer he'd bowled at Jenner, beer cans were thrown onto the pitch.

At the end of the over, Snow walked down to his fielding position on the boundary, gesturing to seething spectators on the Hill as if to say 'come and have a go, if you think you're hard enough'. One bloke who was drunk (and stoned, according to Snow) grabbed him by the shirt. Snow pushed him away and more bottles and cans rained down. Illingworth led his team off the pitch and only agreed to return when the umpires warned that if they didn't the match would be awarded to Australia.

When Snow returned to Oz to do some commentary on the 1974/75 series, he discovered that some Aussies have long memories too. At Perth, the commentary position was high up on some scaffolding which the locals tried to dismantle to get at him, shouting, 'Come down, ya Pommie bastard!'

Perth was the scene of probably the worst crowd violence in the history of the Ashes in November 1982 on the second day of the First Test. England captain Bob Willis edging a Terry Alderman delivery to the third-man boundary to bring up England's 400 was the trigger for 15 or so fans to run on the pitch and one of them sneaked up behind Alderman and cuffed him on the side of the head.

The big Western Australian saw red, gave chase and rugby-tackled the uncouth youth a few yards from the boundary rope in front of the ground's main scoreboard. As he brought his man down, though, he fell awkwardly and dislocated his shoulder.

With Alderman in agony, his team-mates Allan Border

and Dennis Lillee hung on to the guy who assaulted him in the first place until police arrived to handcuff him. Eventually, Alderman was stretchered off – earning the dubious honour of being the first player to be seriously injured in a field invasion during an Ashes match (or a Test match in general for that matter). Aussie skipper Greg Chappell had to lead his team off the pitch as various other brawls broke out around the ground and it was a quarter of an hour before play could restart as 26 spectators were arrested and two policemen were hospitalised.

At least the game could continue this time – the Headingley Test in 1975 had to be called off following a different kind of pitch invasion which ruined it for players and fans alike.

The match was in the balance at the end of the fourth day, Australia needing 224 more runs to win with seven wickets remaining, but when the covers were taken off the next morning, the groundsman found that lumps had been dug out of the pitch at the Rugby Ground End and motor oil poured on a good length, which could have brought a whole new meaning to the phrase 'that ball skidded on . . .'.

There was no way to repair the wicket quickly, so captains Tony Greig and Ian Chappell examined other unused pitches on the square, but none was up to the job and the game had to be declared a draw. As it turned out, heavy rain from lunchtime would have washed out play anyway, but still.

Schoolboy Geoff Lawson was one of thousands of cricket fans left disappointed when that game was abandoned. At home in Wagga-Wagga, New South Wales, he'd studied hard all day so he would be allowed to watch the last day which was being screened live at 8 p.m. their time. It was rare to have the matches televised live in those days, and he was all geared up to watch Dougie Walters and co. chase down the target before the unusual pitch report came through. Fast forward ten years and Lawson himself was representing his country against England at Headingley. This time it was England batting last, and they made a bit of a meal of a 123 target, stumbling over the line with five wickets down and a few overs to spare. Lawson's luck was out again too, because as Allan Lamb hit the winning runs he had the chance to catch him but was put off by hordes of prematurely celebrating England fans running onto the pitch around him.

Back at Headingley in 1975, the graffiti daubed on walls around the ground saying, 'GEORGE DAVIS IS INNOCENT' and 'SORRY IT HAD TO BE DONE' revealed the motive for what had happened. It later emerged that Peter Chappell, mate of a rob . . ., er, minicab driver called George Davis, did it to protest Davis's innocence of an armed robbery for which he was doing 17 years in the clink. Chappell had breached security around Headingley overnight – although one police-man on duty was hardly a ring of steel – and then used a knife and fork to dig up the wicket before adding a sprinkle of oil to serve.

The vandalism stunt did the trick because it grabbed international headlines, and nine months later Davis was released having served just two years of his sentence. Davis was so delighted to have his conviction quashed that a year later he went out and robbed a bank and earned himself another 11-year stretch!

#tuffersashes

I put a shout out on Twitter (it's @philtufnell if you're not already following, folks . . .) asking for fans' perspectives on the Ashes. Within minutes, there were hundreds of tweets on the #tuffersashes hashtag from young and old, men and women, Poms and a few Aussies, each sharing their greatest, funniest, oddest and most emotional Ashes memories. I was blown away by the response which only reinforced in my mind just how much the Ashes means to so many people, and for very different reasons. Here's just a small selection, starting with some fantastic tales from probably the greatest Ashes series ever:

[*Editor's note: the original spelling and grammar of the tweets has been maintained, except where edits were essential for clarity.*]

2005 and all that . . .

Ben Callaghan @slapshot6032
2005 – the year I began playing cricket. What first made me pick up a cricket bat and head down to the nets. #memorable

Sean A @seanayling
Ashes 2005. Got made redundant the day before series started. New job started the Monday after the Oval test finished.

FANS

Ian Walton @BigSpeekaz
Being laid up with a back injury for the entire 2005 series!
Off work but what fantastic viewing!

Nicky Chadwick @nickychad
2005 in a pub on 10th anniversary & overhear a girl say
to b/f "Andrew Flintoff – is that Freddy's brother?"

Joanne Vickers @joannevickers
Walking up the aisle during my wedding in August 2005,
noticing my mate in one of the pews watching the test
on a hand held tv!

Nick Woodward @nickwoody89
Sat in class August '05, hand on head looking bored.
Headphone lead threaded down my sleeve and top
listening to Ashes on radio

Murpho @Murphisinoz
At Edgbaston '05 – seeing look on Dizzy Gillespie's
parents faces when Jones took THAT catch! #priceless

David Lyall @saynothingbut
Edgbaston 2005. Turned TV off in disgust as Aus got
within 10 runs. 9yr old daughter put it back on with
'don't give up dad!'

Nicky @somersetbagpuss
Edgbaston 05, Oz need 3 runs. Do only useful thing I could think of. It worked. Heard cheer from the loos behind Hollies Stand!

Johno Fairclough @JohnoDeRhino
Got to be the sporting character of @flintoff11 to Brett Lee after Edgbaston test and they won by 2 runs. #truesportsmanship

Dave Moist @Bingamin
Edgbaston 2005. Atherton interviewing Ponting. Entire crowd singing "you should've batted first". MA asks "should you have?"

Inglewood iom @inglewoodliom
Bought our hotel in 2005 and used to put every TV on in every room so as we cleaned we didn't miss a ball

bruce wilkinson @bwilky23
queuing from 6am 5th day Old Trafford 2005 the look on the English players faces as they arrived having seen the crowds

Jimmers Thomas @JimmersThomas
On beach during 05 Old Trafford Test with about a dozen strangers gathered round my radio and batteries ran out!

FANS

Benny Kets @benkettle
Day 5 Old Trafford 2005 getting thrown out after 1 ball for trying to pass my ticket out to a friend #onlybeingamate

Danny Crockford @Danny Crockford
Gary Pratt #enoughsaid

andy slee @aps280265
Warne bowling Strauss behind his legs in 2005 live is the best thing I've seen live in 40 years watching sport

Paul Thorburn @fruity1968
Singing "Are you standing in a ditch?" to Justin Langer in 05 at The Oval on the last day.

Sam Turner @STurnerTipster
Aussie fans all putting on sunglasses when bad light stopped play at Oval in 2005

Adam Ryman @adzrymano
My maths teacher giving us questions based on how many 6s KP had hit at the Oval. 19 x how many 6s KP hit (7) answer was 133

stuart white @bigstu73dxb
Flying to San Fran last day 5th Test 05 asking Dutch stewardess score captain saying KP had 150 then asking for a bottle of bubbly

Paul Bradbourn @Coseleylamb
Bottle of JD bought for my 18th (1998), vowed not to open until we'd won the ashes, remained untouched until 2005! #willpower

Missed out

Colin @colman6305
Going to MCG 94 waiting for prices to come down for after tea session and missing Warne hat trick.

Simon Robinson @Robo10_Stoke
Me and my mate won tickets for the Edgbaston test (09) which was the ONLY washout day of the summer

Twelfth man

mat dowman @ridrod267
I remember as 12th man getting bollocked by mr gooch in the huddle at Trent Bridge after Marty McCague got Mark Taylor lbw with a fully. Wrong water bottles!!!

School's out

nirmal singh @nirmski
missed an economics test watching bob willis headingley '81. All teacher wanted to know was who won.

FANS

Mark @PhilipHodgson6marksixtynine
My primary school teacher stopping lessons for the day so we (he) could watch the '81 Headingley Test

Rob Morris @lodgemeister
[Tweet 1] In my first teaching job skived off work to see Lord's Test of 1981 series. Headmaster spotted me in crowd watching on TV
[Tweet 2] Got almighty bollocking and threatened with the sack the next day

Liz D @muffinnuffin
Oval 2005 – My maths teacher telling my class to leave if they weren't interested in cricket. I stayed!

Kevin Garrett @kelvinJayrard
Sent out of class for being disruptive, secretly watched Aus bowled out for 118 on a tv with the sound off #result #edgbaston97

Ouch!

Jamie Allan @jamieauk
Knocked unconscious on the boundary as a ball boy at Trent Bridge when Stewart missed a ball in the warm ups

Goings on Down Under

Russell Chapman @reyhoopchip
Waugh twins pummelling us at Sydney in 99, decide 2 beat the rush & sneak out . . . 5 mins later @dgoughie hat trick

Sticky jones @Stickyjones1
Sydney Test, sister insisted we leave early & missed Gough hat trick & that's from an Aussie

Steve Rigelsford @steverigelsford
First day Brisbane '06. 2hr bus queues. Bus going other way took us anyway as mate was wearing an Arsenal top.

Jonathan Kay @jonnykickingkuh
Beating the Aussies at carpark cricket after day 2 at the MCG 2009 but having victory beers grabbed by police

Simon scuba Thomson @scubathomson
What about the bloke who er befriended a few girls on his way around Aussie on 90s tour pretending to be Graham Thorpe

Nikki Holmes @nikkstercricket
SCG refused me 2 beers as no proof of age (age 36!). Bloke behind offers to buy – nearly thrown out!

FANS

Richard Upton @richardupton1970
I never saw this verified but heard that a woman bought her ironing to day 5 of Adelaide in 1986

Graham Ekins @ekinsgj
Beefy & Lamby competing in a Horse Trotting event versus DK Lillee – Adelaide 1983 – wouldn't be allowed today

marc carrington @mcarro80
Talking to two frustrated Aussies in Oz who've watched their team spank England but can't stop their kids singing "Barmy Army!"

Spag Bol Buh @TooBadYourself
Boxing Day Test 2006 I missed @Warne888 700th test wicket to get my friend a hot dog . . . turned out kiosk was shut. Sour.

Ian bryan @IanBryan77
Oddest memory 1995 sat in hospital waiting room in Perth when you ran past closely followed by nurses #unpaidbill?

Family tales

Mark Evans @ev123uk
Last Boxing Day test, dad in law really suffering with cancer, pain turned to smiles as we had Oz 5 down at lunch

Nick Rose @nickrose0711
Well not a mem, but my 1st ashes was 83/84 in aus, I was 2 months old + dad watched with me as I wud never sleep.

Rob Edwards @thewritevoice
Listening to my mum who 'doesn't do cricket' tell me about Ricky Ponting getting out. Just hilarious!

John Varga @johnsvarga
'81 Holiday in France, Dad pulled over in lay-by, me with radio tuned into ashes with baited breath.

Gaz @gazmoncc
Tales from my dad of being the only Pom on the bank at Sydney when John Snow was being peppered with cans 1970/71

Robert Kingdom @robertjkingdom
1981 climbing over neighbour's fence to collect many lost tennis balls. Brothers Lillee & Alderman, me Beefy

Little Smudger @LittleSmudger
Watching the Test as a kid with my dad in 81 and saying "why don't I have to wear a box when I play netball?"...

russ nicholas @rucky70
Asking my old man 'what the **** is that' on Merv Hughes' upper lip

kevin whittred @whittyzz30
Taking the wife to her first ever Test match at SCG 2003.
Only Test we won that series. Still her only Test!!

Tom G @Beerandsk1ttles
My Dad and the removal men watching the '81
Headingley Test. New owners arrived . . . and sat and
watched too.

James Somerset @jamosomerset
Wanted a train set for my 10th b'day. Dad bought me a
Duncan Fearnley and the VHS of Botham's Ashes '81.
Been hooked ever since

Inspired

Simon Forsyth @fozzy73
Watching 89 ashes on tv in garden after GCSEs, Alderman
destroying us then pretending to be him getting Gooch
lbw again!!

Rob Sewell @fade2blackuk
@BeefyBotham . . . Headingley . . . . . . 10 year old boy
from Somerset . . . . . . Believed in miracles

Test Match Specials

Nick Taylor @NickTaylor30
Listening to Aggers describe Harmy's slower ball dismissal of Clarke on the car radio. Wonderful!!!

Simon Mills @Millsy1973
Listening to 1983 series from MCG on TMS. Miller catching Thommo with the Aussies 3 short #shame #wokehouseupwithwhoops

Simon Weeks @SimonWeeks1973
Celebrating in our car in the south of France after listening to the finale of the 2005 Edgbaston test on TMS!

Kate-Zillah Sharpe @KateZillah
2005 - me and 3 other cars pulled into a layby just before we won cos we were 2 excited to drive listening 2 TMS!

Alan Hughes @RhythmNHughes
Had a paper round during 06-07 Ashes. Would get up at 3am every morning and listen to TMS. Horrible series but great memories!

Lev Parikian @LevParikian
Trying to get reception on car radio to listen to Dennis Amiss 200 as we drove further south in France during Oval Test 1976.

FANS

Jacqueline Burrows @GreenPetticoat
Summer 1981: basking on a beautiful Welsh beach while Botham blasts the Aussies to bits. Blacksmith cricket. Radio. Suncream

PETER RICHARDSON @RICHARDSONPM
On a Devon beach 1981 listening to Willis steaming in on a tiny tranny – By the end I was surrounded by 300 ecstatic people.

Oops

Andrew Downes @devicesadesires
Shouting out to Warne at Lord's "get on with it fat boy" to find Mrs Warne sitting two rows in front of me . . .

Vintage tales

Marcia Malia @Golfing_grannie
Rushing home from school to watch Jim Laker v the Aussies at OT 1956 on a 9" screen black & white TV

Andy @Moody_Chops
Watching David Steele defy Lillee & Thomson in 75. Specs, grey hair & Duncan Fearnley bat

Kevin Chalklin @KevinKlonker
Will never forget Colin Cowdrey answering SOS to face Lillee & Thomson in 1974/75. Amazing courage.

Mike Thompson @mjt1966
Earning a few quid selling car parking spaces on a council estate to punters near the Oval in the 70s.

andy slee @aps280265
my brother's first ever two days test cricket – Bothams 149 at Headingley then his 118 at Old Trafford in 1981

Ian Parker @uncleteffs
Standing in Woolworths watching Botham's 100 at Old Trafford in 1981 on TV with MANY others

Mark Williams @mic_williams
As a 13 yr old playing cricket in Headingley car park Aug 75 after the George Davis protest

Andrew Jackson @andyinoz15
Staying up one Xmas night to 'watch' the Boxing Day Test on Ceefax. Our Aussie guest thought I was insane!

Peter Dawson @heedpeter
Got tkts for 81 test at Headingley on the Mon from an Aussie player and was sitting next to Chappell's parents. Their faces a picture.

Jonathan Hutchins @Sagitprop
Boss got me tickets for Headingley 1972, but only the first three days ;-) Cherished Ross Edwards' pair...

FANS

Christine Pampling @Mardyoldgit
Dennis Lillee didn't agree with going off for bad light so stayed at long leg signing autographs. Trent Bridge 1981.

Sally M @proverbial_one
1987, age 10. Class watches cricket. Man chases ball to rope. "He's not going to get that," I say, not having a clue. Ashes win.

dominic adam @EJ02DOM
seeing @BumbleCricket being carried off after getting one in the plums from Thommo. Classic. #WALLOP

Ian Jackson @Biscuitfrog
Watching Tavare score 6 in 2.1/2 hours at OT in 81, zzzzz, Botham then came out and smashed, sublime!

Stephen Callaghan @scally28
Getting on roof of changing rooms at OT in 1981 the Sunday after Botham's ton and chatting to Aussies. PA soon in action!

ian chesworth @ianchez
first ever test OT '89. I was only 14 took binoculars and just put em down when streaker came on! #gutted #matesmumthere

christine savill @christinesavil1
Hearing my 75 yr old Grandmother swearing at Thommo while watching him on her first colour TV. She only bought it to watch cricket.

Star encounters

Adrian Bennion @Adrian Bennion
Lord's test in 05, getting Gilchrist to sign my program while in the museum stood next to the actual Ashes!

Tom Watson @tommy_wat50n
Working on burger van, Trent Bridge in 2005, Nasser Hussain ordered 2 sandwiches had one look at the bacon and walked off #diva

Ray Hobrow @Bluehobba
In 81 at Edgbaston I ran on the pitch at the end of days play and Kim Hughes told me to "rack off"! I was 13 yrs old

Little Smudger @Little Smudger
Meeting Ian Botham at school and telling him "I love cricket but I ain't eating Shredded Wheat for anyone!"

Paddy Gregan @paddygregan
1977 me 16 and bro 12 late to sold out Trent Bridge but ITV reporter Trevor McDonald asks gateman to let us in – sat on field

FANS

Steven Smith @sasbfccc
Got told to F off by Mitchell Johnson after singing his song at him and Siddle in central Melbourne the day we retained.

Mike Cooke @mikeydenton2207
Catching @stephenfry trying to get his leg over! He climbed over some seats and fell backwards at the Oval 05

Crowd fun

Michael Chesterman @mdchesterman
Listening to a hearty rendition of "God Save Your Queen" at the Oval in 2001 when Australia was about to win.

Michael Massey @topklobber
TB 05 pouring jugs of beer from hospitality box to the thirsty Aussies below!! Flintoff 100 and Aus 90/5 at close!

Nikki Holmes @nikkstercricket
Matthew Hayden joining in with Barmy Army singing '5 haemorrhoids' to the tune of 12 Days of Christmas

Sam Tait @SamTait
1st day of the Ashes @ Cardiff, sitting near Jim Rosenthal. Landed him with the beer snake when the stewards came

Sam Crichard @SamCrich
2009. Watching the great escape at Cardiff. Monty got the loudest ever cheer for a forward defence in history.

Cameron Charles Paul @Cam_Paul
Wearing my Oz jumper to Day 4 of the 2009 5th Test to find my seat is 1 row behind the Barmy Army. Long day.

Nige.M @leginjohn
Early 80s Trent Bridge, bring ur own chair, sit @ rope days. Surrounded by Aussies sat on coolie boxes full of 4x, shared/drunk

Well, I don't like to boast, but . . .

John Scott @John7Scott
Your catch in the 94/95 Ashes series in the 3rd Test at Sydney to dismiss Michael Slater. #unbelievable

James Dry @Jimmyd1166
Watching PCR Tufnell hit Glenn McGrath back over his head for a four at the Oval 2001 – or was it a dream . . .

CHAPTER 15

THE VIEW FROM THE COMMENTARY BOX

BALL-BY-BALL ACHES

I was absolutely amazed to discover how the first Test radio broadcasts which covered the 1934 and 1938 Ashes series in England from an Australian studio were done. Alan McGilvray, who went on to become the voice of Australian cricket for half a century, would sit with other commentators in front of a studio microphone and receive written messages cabled from England describing each ball, how the batsman had played it, the number of runs scored. Sound effects of crowd cheers, 'oohs' and 'ahhs' were played in the background. They called it 'synthetic commentary'.

Of course, sometimes there would be a technical hitch and the cable would be delayed. Then the commentators would have to use their imagination to fill time by pretending the players were having a drinks break or whatever. It must have been so difficult. Mind you, I think Blowers would have been great in those situations, as he could always talk about an imaginary pigeon flying past or a nice-looking bus driving past the ground.

Hats off to McGilvray and his co-commentators who told Aussie cricket fans the story of those series without even being able to see what was going on. And even more credit to a chap called Alan Fairfax, a former Australia Test all-rounder, who was the first commentator to use this system in 1932/33 for the Bodyline tour. He gave ball-by-ball commentary on the series on his own without any assistance. If you think that the *Test Match Special* commentators are rotated throughout each day, it's incredible that he managed that.

The BBC started experimenting with ball-by-ball radio commentary on the Australian model in the 1930s, but it wasn't until 1948 that they introduced it for an Ashes series. McGilvray, John Arlott and Rex Alston formed the main team, with former Sussex and England captain Arthur Gilligan as summariser and E. W. Swanton joining in on Saturday when coverage extended up and down the country. A bigger commentary box than ever before at Trent Bridge was installed allowing three people to sit side-by-side at the front.

Alston decided the 'batting order' and time which each commentator would spend at the microphone and he changed it each day so those that tuned in at set times would not always get the same voice.

The commentators' job was complicated by the need to

greet new listeners. The first day, the BBC Light Programme joined the commentary for the opening overs, left after fifteen minutes, and came back for half an hour before lunch.

A producer sat at the back of the box wearing earphones and listening for an announcer to say 'Over to Trent Bridge . . .' He'd then quickly drop a 'Greet Light' card in front of the commentator on duty who would give the score and state of the game as soon as possible.

Later, a minute before the Light Programme listeners had to be returned to the studio, the producer selected the 'End Light' card, started a stopwatch and placed it with a card in front of the commentator. This was the cue for him to read through the scorecard, but there could be problems if a wicket fell. The biggest audience for the ball-by-ball commentary was in Australia, so the commentator had the dilemma of whether to continue reading out the scorecard for the English listeners about to be cut off or tell his main audience in Oz about the action taking place in front of his eyes.

For that First Test, the decision was taken to start talking to Australia 15 minutes before play was due to start. Typically, the great British weather upset their plans and as the rain fell that morning, Arlott and Alston had to fill time talking about the wicket, the teams and whatever came to mind.

These random chats in rain breaks have become an entertaining part of the *Test Match Special* listening experience, but Alston wasn't so sure at the time, saying: ' . . . the listeners must have been sickened to death . . . In the end we gave up the struggle and went back to the studio until definite news was forthcoming.'

When the game did finally get underway, Alston said the poor batting of the England team added to his problems, as he struggled to maintain a balance between making too many excuses for the team and giving the Australian team proper credit for their achievements.

On day two, Rex did admit losing the plot at one point after sitting through a mind-numbing passage of play in which Don Bradman and Lindsay Hassett batted out maiden after maiden. 'I might as well go out of the box during the over and come back at the end to report another maiden over,' he told listeners.

Things livened up in the box on the third afternoon, however, as England went in for their second innings needing 344 to avoid an innings defeat. Keith Miller started bowling quick bouncers at Len Hutton, and with memories fresh in their mind of how Aussie fans had treated Harold Larwood, the Trent Bridge crowd booed and shouted angrily, much to Miller's amusement. Summariser Arthur Gilligan was shaking with anger – not at Miller for bowling bouncers, but at the Nottingham crowd for their rudeness. On Monday morning, the Nottingham secretary addressed the crowd over the PA system and requested them not to behave like that again.

When bad light stopped play on that fourth day, rather than have the commentators rattle on, gramophone records were played for listeners.

Come the final day, Denis Compton seemed to be saving the game for England, between breaks for bad light and rain. Then disaster struck. Trying to hook a fast bouncer from Miller, he lost his footing on the slippery turf and fell on his wicket. He was out for 184 and with his exit went England's chance of salvaging a draw. Unfortunately, people in England didn't actually hear the commentary on this crucial moment – the message that play was about to restart following the most recent break for bad weather apparently hadn't reached the man on duty in the Light Programme studio, so home listeners remained in blissful ignorance until they were belatedly handed back to the action.

Bit of a nightmare finish, and although the first BBC ball-by-ball commentary had shown great potential and generally been enthusiastically received by listeners, there was the odd moan.

Alston received letters complaining about him giving his opinions, saying his job was purely to describe play and nothing else. When you listen to *TMS* commentaries today, they are full of strong views – I mean, imagine if you tried to stop Geoff Boycott giving his opinion? – so you can understand Alston's response.

'*You* try to describe a cricket match without offering comment,' he said, 'particularly when the play lacks incident or in the intervals between the fall of wickets!'

Another listener wrote to complain about Australian commentators' way of giving the score – wickets down first, then the batting total. He'd turned on his wireless during Australia's first innings and nearly had a heart attack (well, so he claimed) when he heard McGilvray say 'Australia are six four three for three'. He'd actually said, '6 for 343'. After that the commentators often gave the score both ways to keep both the Aussie and English listeners happy.

Reports from Australia commended the BBC on their coverage, although there was criticism that they hadn't said the score often enough for Aussie listeners' tastes.

Alston noted disdainfully: 'Those who have been to Australia tell me that the average Australian prefers statistics to colour. The enormous scoreboards, which supply all the details, and in fact act as a kind of dumb commentator, have doubtless inculcated this frame of mind.'

They also requested more frequent explanations of field placements and alterations, and Alston wasn't having that either: 'The English listener has not been brought up in this way, and correspondence indicated that, in the opinion of many, we were overdoing it.'

When Alston was commentating in Oz some years later, though, he discovered how easy it was to make yourself misunderstood when he didn't realise that the Australian slang for 'trousers' is 'strides'.

'Lindwall has now finished his over,' he said, 'goes to the umpire, takes his sweater and strides off.'

ARLO v McGILLERS

The different styles desired by listeners was sometimes reflected with a bit of Anglo-Australian tension in the commentary box in those early days, most notably between John Arlott and Alan McGilvray (or 'Arlo' and 'McGillers' as Brian 'Johnners' Johnston, who joined them on *TMS* in the sixties, tagged them). Both became commentating legends in their own countries, but they were the distance between

England and Australia apart in their approach to their craft.

McGilvray had opened the bowling for New South Wales and was a great commentator in his own right, but he was all about the facts rather than colour. For instance, McGilvray believed you should give the score three times in a six-ball over. When he mentioned this to Arlott, he just replied, 'Who wants the score? I'm not interested in the score.'

'He didn't care about the Aussies not listening – a lot of what he said was way above their heads,' said McGilvray.

On one Ashes matchday though, it wasn't Arlott's poetic style which was bothering McGilvray so much as his choice of lunch. McGilvray was known as 'the whispering commentator' for his habit of speaking very quietly close to the microphone so that others in the box could barely hear him. On this occasion, Arlott had eaten a lunch which included plenty of shallots and when 'Whispering Al' took over commentary he couldn't bear the lingering oniony odour on the shared microphone. He had to ask for another one and also for John not to eat such smelly food in future. Arlott apologised and said that he would do so.

McGilvray was highly respected for his ability to give totally unbiased commentaries and woe betide anyone who didn't meet his standards. Many years later, he gave former England captain Tony Lewis a frosty welcome at a champagne reception for Ashes teams soon after Lewis joined the *TMS* team.

'How dare you call England "we" on the air?' McGilvray scolded him. 'You're supposed to be impartial. I don't want to work with people like you. I never say "we" when talking about Australia.'

'Did you ever play for Australia?' Lewis shot back at the uncapped Aussie, before they agreed to have another glass of champers and forget it, and over time they became good friends.

Cricket was a serious business to McGilvray. 'He winced whenever Johnners talked about "turning the arm over" or standing "behind the timbers",' recalled Lewis. 'To McGillers, the players were going about "their work" and performances were measured in those terms.'

I don't think Mr McGilvray would have approved if he'd been in the box when I started singing 'Ashes comin' home' following Andrew Flintoff's run-out of Ricky Ponting at The Oval in 2009.

But working in the *TMS* box all those years with people like Johnners there was no way even McGilvray was going to get away without having a practical joke played on him.

Ever since Johnners thanked someone on air for sending him a birthday cake back in the seventies, people have been sending them in by the dozen. And one time at Lord's Johnners put the huge quantities of cake at his disposal to good use by playing a trick on McGilvray. He had cut up some slices of cake and put them on the desk next to him. While he was commentating, McGilvray walked in and sat down beside him ready to start his shift. Johnners continued talking and gestured for him to help himself to a slice of cake.

Just as McGilvray took a big bite, the ball caught the edge of the bat and looked to have fallen just short of slip. Seeing

McGilvray had his mouth full of cake, quick as a flash, Johnners said: 'We'll ask Alan McGilvray if he thought it was a catch.'

Crumbs sprayed everywhere as a shocked McGilvray tried desperately to splutter a reply.

After that, apparently, McGillers never so much as accepted a biscuit when he was in the box.

John Arlott brought a totally different, unique flavour to his commentary. Unlike McGilvray, he'd never played first-class cricket apart from as an emergency substitute fielder for Hampshire at Worcester in 1938, and even then the local paper report got his name wrong, tagging him 'Harlott'. But Arlott, as well as being a writer, poet and connoisseur of fine wine, had a thirst for cricket knowledge, as the Australian 'Invincibles' discovered. During their dominant 1948 Ashes tour, Arlott hung around in the lobby of the Charing Cross Hotel where the tourists were staying to try and speak to the players. The great former Aussie spinner Bill O'Reilly, who was in England covering the series for the Australian media, recalled: 'Whenever you went out into the foyer, you'd run across Arlott . . . He went to Ray Lindwall and asked questions about types of bowling he wanted to know more about. And then he'd switch to someone else for another skill.'

Arlott became very popular with the Aussie boys who liked to have a drink and a chat with him, especially the great Keith Miller, whom he'd met during the war, and he even had them over to his house for drinks during the tour.

So he knew his stuff. Then there was his wonderful, inimitable voice, once described as 'the voice of an English summer'. It was sort of a Hampshire burr with a bronchial edge, due to Arlott smoking too much in his youth.

Hard to believe that when he did his audition to be a cricket commentator at a county game at Lord's back in 1946, one of the BBC bods sitting in, Robert Hudson, was unimpressed: 'I thought to myself, "My God, no one with an accent like that will ever get anywhere."' By 1969, though, when Hudson became Head of Outside Broadcasts, he'd realised that Arlott was a genius. He later described him as 'the Denis Compton of the microphone. Nobody could copy someone like Compton, and you couldn't copy Arlott, although one or two people have tried.'

Still only in his thirties and only a couple of years into his commentary career, Arlott was fortunate enough to take the microphone just as Don Bradman began his last innings at The Oval. And who better to describe this iconic moment.

His colleague Rex Alston was commentating as Bradman walked to the wicket to a great ovation, with England skipper Norman Yardley calling for three cheers for The Don. Then he asked Arlott to take over the microphone. This is how he relayed the story of Bradman's surprisingly brief final innings:

. . . it's rather good to be here when Don Bradman comes in to bat in his last Test. And now, here's Hollies to bowl to him from the Vauxhall End. He bowls, Bradman goes back across his wicket and pushes the ball gently in the direction of the Houses of Parliament which are out beyond mid-off. It doesn't go that far, it merely goes to Watkins at silly mid-off. No run, still 177 for one. Two slips, a silly mid-off and a forward short-leg, close to him, as Hollies pitches the ball up slowly [*voice rises*] and [*sudden applause*] – he's bowled.

[*Once applause has died down, Arlott speaks again*] Bradman, bowled Hollies, nought. And – what do you say under those circumstances? I wonder if you see the ball very clearly in your last Test in England on a ground where you played some of the biggest cricket of your life, and where the opposing team have just stood round you and given you three cheers and the crowd has clapped you all the way to the wicket. I wonder if you really see the ball at all.

Brilliant – painting a picture of the scene for the listeners but also the emotion of the occasion.

On a totally different subject, one of my favourite bits of commentary by Arlott was his brilliant off-the-cuff description of a streaker invading the pitch during the Second Test at Lord's in 1975:

... And a freaker! We've got a freaker down the wicket now! Not very shapely and it's masculine. And I think it's seen the last of its cricket for the day ... He's being embraced by a blond policeman and this may be his last public appearance, but what a splendid one ... He's now being marched down in a final exhibition past at least eight thousand people in the Mound Stand, some of whom, perhaps, have never seen anything quite like this before. And he's getting a very good reception

which is acknowledged in extremely gracious fashion
... Fine performance, but what will they do about
finding his swimming trunks?

Wonderful stuff, but apparently John was gutted that he
didn't think of the perfect pay-off line at the time. When he
had a little more time to think, he came up with this gem:
'Perhaps his greatest disappointment is not to be deprived of
further cricket, but that he managed to straddle the stumps
without even dislodging a bail.'

The respect everyone had for him was shown when he
completed his last *TMS* broadcast during the Centenary Test
between England and Australia at Lord's in 1980. At ten to
three, he concluded by saying, 'Thank you for all for the years
you've listened to me.' And at the end of the over he handed
over to Trevor Bailey and CMJ and walked out into the
pavilion.

The PA announcer wasn't going to let him go quietly
though and announced that Arlott had just completed
his last-ever Test commentary. As Johnners recalled: 'The
Australians were fielding and they all applauded; the crowd
stood up and applauded; and Geoff Boycott who was batting,
took off his gloves and clapped!'

And if you could distract Boycs's attention from batting,
you had to be good.

'IT'S THE ASHES!'

One of the greatest thrills for a commentator is to be describing the action at the moment when the Ashes are finally won and lost. Brian Johnston was doing the honours for TV when England won the Ashes in 1953 for the first time in 19 years, and his cry of, 'Oh, is it the Ashes? . . . Yes, England have won the Ashes!' became famous.

Denis Compton struck the winning runs towards the gas-holders at The Oval that day off the bowling of Arthur Morris. A wonderful batsman, Morris was only an occasional bowler of left-arm Chinamen and only got put on by Australian captain Lindsay Hassett when it was clear that England were going to win. Later, Johnners noted that, bizarrely, Morris became the most televised bowler ever because footage of the five balls he bowled were used as a demonstration sequence in every television and radio shop in Britain and were played on a loop hour after hour, day in, day out.

WHEN AGGERS MET LILY BERGKAMP

Working for the BBC on home Ashes tours we get the best seat in the house, looking directly down the line of the pitch, but sometimes even from our prime position we can miss something. Jonathan Agnew had that problem when Shane Warne bowled his first ball in a Test match in England – and arguably the best delivery in the history of the Ashes – at Old Trafford in 1993. Sitting in the box at the Stretford End, Aggers was positioned directly behind batsman Mike Gatting and the combination of wicketkeeper Ian Healy standing up to the wicket and the sheer width of Gatt meant Aggers could hardly see anything.

He described Warne coming in to bowl and the ball pitching way outside leg stump, but was bemused to see Warne and Healy celebrating wildly a split second later. What he couldn't have accounted for at the time was the massive rip Warne had given the ball, the indecent late drift before pitching and the way the ball zipped across the face of Gatt's bat and clipped the top of off stump. Like Gatt who stood there motionless for a second, Aggers had no idea what had happened.

As Aggers wrote later: 'It really was the ultimate delivery: unplayable for batsman and commentator alike.'

It's rare for anything to get past Aggers though. He's the main guy, leading the BBC's Ashes commentary team, and aside from describing what's happening on the pitch, he's also responsible for interviewing special guest visitors to the box on the popular 'View from the Boundary' lunchtime feature. During the 2009 Ashes, listeners were treated to an unlikely conversation between Aggers and pop star Lily Allen.

It all started when Lily tweeted that she had lost her *Test Match Special* reception as she was driving and asked Aggers for help. Not being down with the kids – or even having a telly at home – Aggers had absolutely no idea who Lily was, so our producer Adam Mountford filled him in.

Other Twitter users instructed Lily how to retune her car radio so she could hear the commentary again, and at the end of the day Aggers tweeted her to ask if she fancied coming on *TMS* to be interviewed sometime. She replied immediately saying she'd love to and she was duly scheduled in for the Saturday lunchtime slot at the final Test at The Oval.

Aggers prepared with typical thoroughness, reading up on Lily's career and listening to her music. Songs such as '**** You' did make him wonder whether she might turn the air blue on air, so when she arrived on Saturday morning he asked her if she wouldn't mind not swearing on air. 'As if I would,' Lily told him.

And it was silly to think she would as she was clearly a huge fan of cricket and *TMS* and knew the form. Having attended the first day of the match, she'd had to go to do a gig in Holland on the Friday and had kept in touch by listening to *TMS* via a mobile phone rigged up to a set of speakers, before making an overnight bus journey back to The Oval.

Even though the world and its husband already knew she was coming on the show, during the morning's commentary we still pretended that she was a secret guest.

At one point, Aggers said to me: 'Our guest, Tuffers, has come by bus from Holland. Can you guess who it is?'

'Dennis Bergkamp?'

Well, he is Dutch and doesn't like flying!

As it turned out, Aggers and Lily got on like a house on fire. Lily talked knowledgeably about the game, her love of Test cricket and dislike of Twenty20. She also pleased Aggers no end by taking up one of his bugbears about modern cricket, arguing that players go back to wearing the old-fashioned cream kits for Test cricket rather than the ultra-white clobber they sport today.

Loads of listeners got in touch to say that they had been

cynical about Lily coming on the show but she'd won them over.

'THE LATE CMJ'

One person who will be sadly missed in the *Test Match Special* commentary box in forthcoming Ashes series is the late Christopher Martin-Jenkins. Long before he passed away, we all knew him as 'the late CMJ' anyway, due to his dodgy timekeeping. I will miss him bursting into the commentary box just a couple of minutes before he was due to go on air and then just sitting down and doing his job with such skill and ease.

CMJ was so knowledgeable and brilliant at painting the picture of what was going on for radio listeners. He was also a very warm and kind person. When I first worked as a summariser for *TMS* on the Ashes, I was a bit nervous. There was a realisation that 'Crikey, I'm commentating on the Ashes here', but working with CMJ, I always felt like I had a safe pair of hands to guide me. He was one of those chaps you could just chat away to and the time would fly past which made my job very easy.

However, the younger CMJ did once accidentally rub Aussie Alan McGilvray up the wrong way (who didn't?) when they were working together for ABC radio. When he politely asked the producer if he could juggle the rota to allow him to also do short reports for the BBC, McGilvray fumed that it was 'an Englishman ordering mere colonials around'!

CMJ was also a very humorous guy, a fantastic after-dinner

speaker and a great mimic – Tom Graveney called him the 'Mike Yarwood' of cricket dinners (for all you kids out there, Mike Yarwood was a famous TV impressionist in the seventies and eighties). Johnners reckoned CMJ was such a good impressionist that he could 'on his own, carry out a day's commentary so that listeners would think that we were all in the box taking our turn every twenty minutes . . . I really think he could get away with it.'

Johnners and he were close friends despite the great age difference. In his last year at school, CMJ had written to him asking how he could become a commentator. Johnners invited him to the Beeb, took him for lunch and advised him to practise commentating by himself with a tape recorder and to play and watch as much as possible. I doubt Johnners realised then that he was talking to someone who would become one of radio's finest-ever cricket commentators.

RIP CMJ.

CHAPTER 16

(PLEASE TELL ME) WHAT'S IT LIKE TO WIN THE ASHES?

ARKLE'S BALLS-UP AND FUNKY'S BAILS

What's it like to win the Ashes? I'm asking because I never did and it was the biggest disappointment of my career. Personally, I blame Shane Warne.

The only prize I ever won in Australia was the *I'm A Celebrity . . . Get Me Out Of Here!* crown of ferns, but I never came close to getting my hands on the replica wooden urn either Down Under or back home. Instead I can only imagine the thrill through the stories of the cricketers who've done it.

My old mate Phil DeFreitas won the Ashes in 1986/87 when he was just 20 years old and he said later that he didn't realise the significance of his achievement until he got back to

England and people kept asking him if he realised what he had done. Graeme Swann, who had to wait rather longer in his career to taste Ashes success, was not disappointed when it finally happened in 2009. 'Sometimes you look forward to something so much that it's a bit of a let-down,' he wrote. 'I feared it might be like that when we won the Ashes, but it felt better than I could possibly have imagined. It was like all your Christmases, birthdays, your first kiss, meeting your wife and your wedding day all rolled into one.'

When Andrew Strauss led England to glory in 2011, our first Ashes victory on Australian soil since Daffy and co. did it 24 years before, his thoughts drifted back to the horrible feeling of being whitewashed just four years before: 'We were constantly being made to pay for it off the pitch, with Aussies coming up and saying we were useless and English supporters saying that we were a disgrace and should be ashamed to be putting on those Three Lions . . . There were so many emotions – joy, relief, satisfaction – after all the hard work we'd put in.'

And just imagine what it's like to take the Ashes-winning catch. That wonderful fielder Derek 'Arkle' Randall (when he lapped them on a training run, Randall's Nottinghamshire team-mates had nicknamed him Arkle after the famous racehorse) made the catch that sealed England's series victory in 1977 and in his excitement Randall chucked the ball into the crowd and did a cartwheel of delight. Fast forward to 2009, and Alastair Cook was in the right place at the crucial moment to take a bat-pad catch off Mike Hussey to clinch the Ashes. While his team-mates were running towards bowler Graeme Swann to celebrate, Cooky was running in the other direction stuffing the ball in his pocket. Turns out Randall had been his teacher at school and Cooky had heard him say that throwing the ball away in '77 was his greatest regret.

Randall was fortunate enough to be part of another Ashes-winning team just a couple of years later, though, and this time he made his own keepsake. On the last day of the series, which England dominated, he decided to get the team to autograph his bat as a memento. The only problem was he'd forgotten he might have to go out and bat with it. Luckily he only had to face a couple of deliveries before England scored the winning runs so the felt-tipped signatures on the face of the bat survived.

After all that, the always unpredictable Randall didn't actually keep the keepsake for long though. He accepted a collector's offer of 75 dollars for it – not bad money then, but probably a better investment for the fan.

In 1997 at Trent Bridge, Mark Waugh chucked the ball in the air after making the series-winning catch for Australia and in his excitement forgot about it. Meanwhile, the crowd were charging onto the pitch and all making a beeline for the ball. An Aussie called John Sandy got there first and he proved to be a generous chap, seeking out Mark's brother Steve and presenting it to him.

Once the official presentations are over, the winning players can relax completely in the knowledge that it's a job well done. After the final Test in 2001, Aussies Jason Gillespie and Matthew Hayden performed a sort of ceremonial tribal dance which they called the 'Ashes Urn quest'. Later, Justin Langer attempted to burn the bails used in the day's play in a bid to recreate the original Ashes bail-burning. They taped up the smoke detectors in the dressing room and eventually set the bails ablaze using a lighter and some kerosene. They did manage to light their cigars off the flames, but sadly the bails never quite turned to ashes. Spinner Colin 'Funky' Miller, a man of many hair colours, kept the blackened remains anyway.

Back in 1997, a few hours after the Fifth Test at Trent Bridge, the proud trio of Michael Slater, Justin Langer and Steve Waugh made a drunken vow to all wear their Australian caps for the next four days. If you were a dejected England fan in Nottingham the next day, that would have been all you needed to bump into Justin Langer in the corner shop buying a bag of prawn cocktail crisps still wearing his baggy green cap.

At the conclusion of the 2010/11 series, once the crowd had dispersed, the England players all went out again and sat on the outfield at the SCG, drinking beers and smoking fat cigars. Fittingly, given the Sprinkler Dance craze which they'd started on the tour, they occasionally got soaked by the sprinklers as they reminisced about their highs and lows of the series.

Spare a thought for David Gower though. He played in all six Tests of England's winning 1978/79 series, but he was struck down with a fever before the final day's action at the SCG. He did try and join in the celebrations but, after one beer, had to return to his sickbed, poor chap.

THE EYES OF JARDINE, BILL EGG-RICH & DJ ELTON

When England sealed victory in the 1932/33 series, captain Douglas Jardine said he was just 'ready for a good night's sleep'. Aside from dealing with Australian outrage during the series, Jardine had a sleepless night before the sixth and final day of the Brisbane Test because he was worried that rain was going to scupper their chances of victory. As it was, Eddie Paynter, who'd been suffering with tonsillitis, finished things off in style, hitting the winning six just minutes before it started raining for two days solid.

Jardine was not a man for wild celebration, but one of his team-mates claimed he saw 'a most peculiar light in the Skipper's eyes' in the dressing room afterwards (that is not something I ever said to Goochy . . .). The player insisted on taking a photograph of Jardine straight away to capture the moment. 'The result, I am glad to say, was uninterestingly normal and generally voted a wasted negative,' wrote Jardine later.

The bad feeling between the teams did not stop the Aussies coming into the England dressing room after the match to offer congratulations. And never let it be said that Jardine had no friends in Australia, because a mate of his in Sydney sorted out drinks for the occasion.

Both teams attended a reception that evening hosted by the Governor of Queensland and Jardine turned out to be a gracious winner. In his speech, he said, 'I'm naturally delighted that we have regained the Ashes, but I hope I can say with

Kipling that cricketers can meet triumph and disaster and treat the two imposters in just the same way.'

When England won the Ashes in 1953/54, the first time we'd won a series in Australia since Bodyline, the team were less restrained than Jardine, meeting victory and treating that imposter to a massive party. They started with champagne in the dressing room at the Adelaide Oval before heading back to the Pier Hotel for a spot of 'mafficking' with England fans and a few more drinks.

Then it was on to a party at the mansion of a well-to-do local family, at which fast-bowling hero Frank Tyson was mostly asleep under a grand piano, while Bill Edrich attempted some tricks with eggs which failed messily. Not easily put off, when the boys returned to the hotel in the early hours, Bill shimmied to the top of a 20-foot-tall marble pillar to win a bet.

When their hotel bill was totted up the next day, it was discovered that the lads had demolished 56 bottles of champagne (and that's just at the hotel, remember), an impressive bottles-per-player strike rate by any standards.

In Sydney the victorious 2010/11 England squad splintered into happy little groups as the evening progressed. Hipsters like Stuart Broad and KP went off partying with rapper Tinie Tempah, while Graeme Swann, Alastair Cook and Tim Bresnan went to the pub with the Barmy Army.

Australia's celebration party after winning the 1989 Ashes was a very posh affair for players and their wives and girlfriends organised by Daphne Benaud, wife of Richie. They were picked up from their hotel in vintage and new Rolls Royces,

(PLEASE TELL ME) WHAT'S IT LIKE TO WIN THE ASHES?

Bentleys and Mercedes and taken to the Grovesnor Hotel on Park Lane. It was all pink and white champagne, Meursault white wine, Lynch-Bages red ... and, of course, cans of XXXX.

Later they decamped to Stocks nightclub on the King's Road, where Tom Moody grabbed captain Allan Border and hoisted him onto his shoulders. Tom is a tall fella, 6ft 8in, and as he bopped about Border's head smacked into the lighting rig above. Worried he might have brained his skipper, he lowered Border down, but moved a bit too fast and split his trousers. For the rest of the night, as AB fondly recalled, 'Tom had to dance around with his Reg Grundy's in full view.'

From what I've been told of the 1986/87 tour, the amazing success of Gatt's 'Team of Can'ts' was fuelled by some spectacular drinking escapades throughout. And when those 'Can'ts' wrapped up the Ashes in style in the Fourth Test match at the MCG, winning inside three days, their celebrations in the dressing room were given a touch of pop star glamour by Elton John (he wasn't Sir Elton yet). Elton, who was on tour in Oz himself, had been to watch every day of the match, so when Gatt belatedly arrived back in the dressing room after doing TV and press interviews, it was the Rocket Man who sprayed him with champagne and wrapped him in a Union Jack.

Later, Ian Botham hosted a victory party in his hotel room with Elton acting as DJ on the tape deck (note to younger readers: tapes are something people listened to music on in the olden days before they invented CDs ... CDs are something people used to listen to music on before MP3s).

This might sound like a once-in-a-lifetime experience, but the England players had got used to Elton spinning tunes for them.

Beefy, Lamby and Gower knew him well and it all started when the whole team went to see his concert in Sydney. He invited them backstage and after that became the team's unofficial mascot, throwing parties and DJing for the boys every time they won a match. As batsman Bill Athey recalled: 'It was like, "Elt, put on another one for us, please . . . oh no, not that one, that's one of yours . . ."'

THE HANGOVER

The morning after the massive night before, it's always nice to take it easy, pop a couple of Alka-Seltzer for the aching head, maybe risk a fry-up to stabilise the tummy and generally stay in a darkened room. Imagine then, instead, being paraded in front of thousands of people and going to meet the prime minister as Freddie Flintoff and co. did in 2005.

Most of the players had made it to bed for a couple of hours, but those that came down for a champagne breakfast found Freddie still propping up the bar with supersub fielder Gary Pratt.

The previous day, the players had been told that there would be an open-top bus parade through the streets of London in the morning, but no one had paid much attention. 'We thought, they'll be nobody there,' said Ashley Giles. 'A couple of old ladies and a dog and probably a couple of kids throwing abuse at us.'

So after pulling on their England blazers and staggering onto the bus they were shocked to see through bleary eyes that the streets were packed with fans.

'The sights we found were just phenomenal,' said Giles. 'Thankfully we hadn't realised at that point just how much the nation had been gripped by cricket. If we'd carried that pressure as well, I think it might have been too much.'

Most of the players decided that the hair of the dog would be the best way to deal with their monumental hangovers, although for sleepless Freddie it wasn't so much a case of the morning after as just carrying on. When they stopped off at Mansion House for a couple more drinks, they were greeted by the Lord Mayor who was dressed in all his traditional robes.

'What have you come as?' asked Freddie.

Next stop was Number 10 Downing Street for a reception with Tony and Cherie Blair, and the players were unimpressed with the drinks on offer – a choice of pineapple juice or water – so bottles of wine had to be rustled up.

On the way out a wall of photographers were waiting.

'Oh God, what do they want?' said Tony Blair.

'A photo, you knob,' replied Matthew Hoggard.

Well, ask a silly question . . .

An open-top bus ride, visit to Number 10, people jumping in the fountain at Trafalgar Square . . . compare that to when Len Hutton led England to regain the Ashes in 1953. It was a similar achievement, because it had been 19 years since England's last win, and the reception was held at the Albert Hall. No, not the Royal Albert Hall in Kensington.

The Albert Hall in Pudsey. The only big crowds seen on the streets of London that year were for the Queen's Coronation.

The 1989 Australian team that regained the Ashes were given a ticker-tape parade on their return to Sydney with tens of thousands lining the streets. Even their rock-hard leader Allan Border was moved to tears. Well, almost. He said later: 'There were no tears, but rather that burning feeling you sometimes get that makes you want to blink a little more than you normally would.'

Tough Aussies like AB obviously don't cry over winning at cricket. Or admit to it anyway.

Some people seemed to blame England's excessive celebrations in 2005 for their miserable performance in 2006/07. (Not sure about that, myself – I know it was a big night out, but a two-year hangover?) So when the boys regained the Ashes in 2009 there was no ticker-tape reception. Instead, in their wisdom, the ECB had arranged a one-day international in Belfast a couple of days later.

Captain Andrew Strauss managed to negotiate being rested for the match, but the rest of the lads had to play so off they went determined to have their own celebration even if the bosses weren't going to organise it for them. Belfast, of course, is not the worst place to go for a boozy night out, and Graeme Swann and Jimmy Anderson decided to have a Guinness drinking competition which ended with Swanny throwing up in a flower bed. I think that means he lost.

Of course, you don't have to get plastered to celebrate your success. The great Jack Hobbs was teetotal and he was happy to toast his four Ashes triumphs with a glass or two of ginger beer.

LOSING AND ALL THAT JAZZ

I never played in a close Ashes series so by the time the last ball was bowled we'd already had some time to come to terms with defeat. It's a bit different when it goes down to the last game and you finish on the losing side though. In 1982/83 Australia took a 2–1 lead into the Fifth Test at the SCG and secured a draw to ensure they regained the Ashes. England captain Bob Willis was given a glass of flat champagne while doing his post-match interviews and after that it was, he wrote later, 'A night of jazz in some of my favourite Sydney haunts. Thoughts of endless one-day matches to come. Wonder if we can get our game together. Wonder if I will now sleep better. Wonder why losing never comes any easier, even at 33.'

Whether it's been a close thing or a thrashing, the fans can help to lift the spirits once the last ball's been bowled. Alec Stewart said one of his great memories was the reception the Barmy Army gave his losing team at the SCG in 1999. England had been whopped in that series and yet as the players were waiting around for the post-match presentation the away fans at the Randwick End were still singing support, so Stewie led the boys over there to say thanks. The players also applauded the Australian fans who responded too, and the Barmies gave Mark Taylor's Australian team a well-deserved standing ovation when they did their lap of honour.

Back in the pavilion, it's time to have a drink with the

opposition and perhaps bury the hatchet with your fiercest rivals. After the 1997 series, the Aussies invited the England boys to have a drink with them and the first person to come up and shake Nasser Hussain's hand was Shane Warne, who'd been sledging him mercilessly throughout the series: 'He winked at me and basically said that we may have had a few clashes on the field and he may have called me a few things but he respected me and hoped I respected him.'

My pal Angus Fraser, who also never won the Ashes, recalled that his favourite moments were at the end of a series when there was an open invite from the Aussies to go into their dressing room: 'I had some wonderful afternoons spending four or five hours in the company of Steve Waugh, Shane Warne, Glenn McGrath, having a laugh and slowly getting drunk.'

All good, but I wonder if Gus would have fancied spending the next few weeks in the pockets of victorious opponents as the England touring side of 1901/02 did. They got thumped 4–1 Down Under and there was hardly a break before the return series so both squads caught the same ship back to Blighty. Not sure I'd have enjoyed coming down to breakfast every morning and seeing a load of blokes who'd smashed us, knowing we'd be doing it all over again when I got back home.

THE COMEDOWN

Once the victory toasts have been made or sorrows drowned (and perhaps a one-day series or two have been negotiated), thoughts of returning to reality bite. I remember it really hitting me a week or so before the end of an Ashes tour. I felt it and I could see other players did too. We'd been living in this bright, surreal parallel universe. Four adrenalin-fuelled months of soaring highs and crashing lows on and off the pitch. Playing intense cricket in the sunshine in front of huge, passionate crowds. People looking after everything for us, staying at some of the best hotels in the world, room service.

I remember stepping tentatively off the plane at Heathrow. 'Whoah, I'm back.' It was a huge comedown. I'd been tuned in to what we'd been doing, with all my mates. Suddenly it was back to normality. 'What, I've got to do my own laundry?'

I'd sleep for most of the following week, which of course would trigger arguments with the missus. 'What's the matter with you? You've been having all this fun. Am I no fun?' Well, actually . . .

Slowly, I'd get back into it, but it seemed so grey and dull in comparison. So I'd go to the pub or the bookies to try and recapture a buzz that can't possibly be replicated.

A couple of weeks later, it was pre-season training. And even though I was playing for a big club like Middlesex, it was hard to get motivated. The up-and-coming players, hungry to get in the team, would look at you and say, 'Who do you think you are? Are you giving it the big 'un?'

And I wasn't but it's a long way from the MCG to one man and his dog at Derby. That whole four months in Oz, I felt excited about life and this was not exciting any more.

That's why I always wanted to get on tour after my first Ashes. People said they didn't enjoy touring, and when I got a bit older I felt that, but as a boy the idea of touring Australia fully paid-up, playing cricket with my mates rather than being stuck in the English winter doing some cabbing to make ends meet . . . no contest.

I would punch the air when I got picked to go on tour. My dad would say, 'You lucky so-and-so. You're going to Australia while I'm going to be sitting here freezing, hammering pots and pans. It don't get any better than that, son.' I was living his and my dream.

It was decent money too and that all went straight into the bank because we got a *per diem*. When I came back from my first Ashes tour I had about sixteen grand in my account . . . mind you, I blew the lot straight away. Went out and bought myself a Porsche – then realised I couldn't afford to insure it.

Some people can't pinpoint the best time of their life, but I can – an Ashes tour. And that's from someone who never ended up on the winning side.

TUFFERS' ULTIMATE ASHES CRICKETERS

On my journey back through the history of the Ashes, I've encountered many great personalities who have represented England or Australia with distinction. It's been a delight to learn more about some fascinating characters from the past who've brought their own flavour to the biggest fixture in world cricket. What has become obvious is that there's no single way to win the Ashes, a team needs a combination of many qualities to succeed. So what if you were to combine the qualities (and quirks) of the legendary English and Australian players of the past into two ultimate players to represent each side? What would they look like? What special skills would they possess? How many tinnies could they drink after play without falling over?

I donned my white coat and goggles, went in the lab and these are the monsters of Ashes cricket I came up with. Be very afraid . . .

The Ultimate Aussie Player

With an Australian international cricketer, there's only one place to start and that's on top of the head – the baggy green cap. The only way to get one is to play for Australia; it can't be bought and its importance cannot be underestimated. As Steve Waugh once said, 'Everyone wearing the baggy green just seemed to send out a message that this team was really together and hard to break down.'

This baggy green has a couple of holes round the sides for the devil's horns of Fred 'Ain't I a Demon' Spofforth to poke through. Underneath is the luxurious hairstyle of Keith Miller and to add a bit of variety, the ever-changing hair colour of Colin 'Funky' Miller – during the final Test of 2001, Funky dyed his hair canary yellow on day one, changed to peacock green on day three and then burgundy red on the last day of series.

My ultimate Aussie has the gimlet eyes of Steve Waugh and the ginormous nose of Bill Lawry (although it was a toss-up between him and Fred Spofforth who was also blessed with a magnificent conk). There have been some wonderful moustaches sported by Australian cricketers over the years, but I plumped for the droopy 'tache of Merv Hughes, as I personally got to see it very close up, tangled with snot and dirt when he bounced me and then followed through down the pitch to call me a 'Pommie bastard'. And on his left cheek is the scar of Ricky 'Punter' Ponting (© Steve Harmison).

Of course, to be a top-class Aussie cricketer, you also need to be excellent at sledging . . . oops, sorry, Steve Waugh – I mean 'mental disintegration'. So many contenders to choose from here, but as we've got Merv's moustache he might as well provide the sledges too. But to give Merv's basic insults a bit more charm, my ultimate player will say them in the voice of Richie Benaud – how beautiful to be called a '****ing arsewipe' in Richie's rich tones . . .

Then there's the broad shoulders of Matthew Hayden (and as the Aussies love a barbie, Matty's cooking skills would come in very handy too on a long tour) and the chest hair, medallions and shirt open down to the navel of Dennis Lillee circa 1975. My man has the guts of Warwick Armstrong in his 22-stone prime, and the Big Ship also provides his proven gamesmanship skills.

As a multi-purpose bowler, he combines the wrist and spinning fingers of Shane Warne, the speed of Jeff Thomson, the relentless consistency of Glenn McGrath, and just to freak the batsman out a bit more, the mixed-up legs of Max 'Tangles' Walker.

With the willow in hand, he has the hand–eye coordination of Doug Walters, the anticipation and sheer run-gettingness of Don Bradman, the insane shotmaking of Adam Gilchrist and the bollocks of Stan McCabe – anyone who could stand up to the Bodyline bowlers without a helmet and score a century must have had balls of steel.

In the field, he has Ricky Ponting's all-round excellence, Andrew Symonds's speed and throwing arm and the hands of Mark Waugh (perhaps, wearing the 'iron gloves' of Rodney Marsh, which didn't seem to do Rodney any harm).

His personality mixes the permanent upbeatness of Mark Taylor with the nuggety attitude of Allan Border and the daredevil spirit of my old dad's hero, Keith Miller. Off the pitch, he'll have the dubious dress sense of Ian Chappell in the seventies, who turned up to a press conference back then wearing a purple shell suit, looking like one of The Scousers from *Harry Enfield & Chums*. And after a tough day's Ashes cricket, my ultimate Aussie cricketer is going to have worked up a hell of a thirst, so who better to drink for Australia than the record-breaking 'Keg on Legs' himself, David Boon.

The Ultimate England Player

To take on the bionic Aussie, I was tempted to create a cricketer purely in the image of 1986/87 Ashes-winning captain Mike Gatting, for his all-round British bulldogedness, and leave it at that. But there's too many other great players' attributes to call upon, so, starting from the top, I've gone for the cap of Geoff Boycott (he even wore it when he was bowling) and the manky old sunhat of Jack Russell which Jack'd insist on wearing underneath. The hair could only be that of Keith Miller's Brylcreem twin, Denis Compton, and as for our player's brain, I would have offered mine but I lent it to an Australian heckler, so we'll have to make do with that idiot Mike Brearley's grey matter instead.

When it comes to facial features, I've created a whole world of horror for our Aussie opponent. Behold the intense staring eyes of Bob Willis (Headingley '81), the ears of my old team-mate/wingnut, Andy Caddick, the nose of Nasser Hussain (to discourage the close fielders from fielding too close) and the beard, of course, of W. G. Grace (his gamesmanship will match up nicely to the Big Ship's too). You wouldn't want to run into that on a dark night in the Bourbon and Beefsteak, would you Ricky Ponting?

Rather than the cut-glass, Queen's English accent of David Gower, I've chosen the, ahem, classic English voice of Kevin Pietersen, just to get on the Australians' nerves.

My ultimate player to wear the Three Lions has personality traits for all occasions, from the brass-necked pomposity of Douglas Jardine to the huge heart of Freddie Brown, the macho combativeness of Tony Greig to the effortless nonchalance of Gower. He also has a strong, er, middle order with the gut/guts of Gatt, the knob of John Emburey (I'm saying no more . . .) and the 'golden balls' of match-winning all-rounder Ian Botham.

Alec Stewart's regimental neatness will ensure our player's coffin is kept nice and tidy. The immaculate dress sense of Colin Cowdrey and the ballroom dancing skills of *Strictly Come Dancing* champion Mark Ramprakash will mean he cuts a dash at social occasions.

In the field, he has the reflexes of a young Botham to stand ridiculously close at slip, the speed and agility of Derek Randall to patrol the covers and the arm of Jimmy Anderson to arrow in the throws. As a bowler with the silent feet of Harold Larwood, smooth action of Freddie Trueman, nasty streak of John Snow and shotgun speed of Frank 'Typhoon' Tyson, he's enough to test even the greatest players of fast bowling. And if he fancies bowling a bit of spin for variety, Jim Laker's fingers will allow him to give it a fearful tweak.

At the crease, he boasts the elegance and power of Frank Woolley, the strike rate of Gilbert Jessop and the ability to make score after big score of our own 'Don', Alastair Cook. And at the end of the chicken legs of Goochy, he's got the feet of Fred 'Mistletoe' Titmus, who lost a few toes in a boating accident. Ideal for when Jeff Thomson is bowling toe-crushers at you at 95 mph – less to aim at.

Bibliography

Agnew, Jonathan, *Over to You, Aggers*, Orion, 1997

Agnew, Jonathan, *Thanks, Johnners*, HarperCollins, 2010

Alston, Rex, *Taking the Air*, Stanley Paul, 1951

Arlott, Timothy, *John Arlott: A Memoir*, Andre Deutsch, 1994

Bailey, Jack, *Trevor Bailey: A Life in Cricket*, Methuen, 1993

Baldwin, Mark, *The Ashes' Strangest Moments*, Robson Books, 2005

Barnes, Justyn and Aubrey Ganguly, *The Reduced History of Cricket*, Andre Deutsch, 2005

Batty, Clive, *The Ashes Miscellany*, revised edn, Vision Sports Publishing, 2011

Bedser, Alec, *May's Men in Australia: The M.C.C. Tour 1958–59*, Stanley Paul, 1959

Benaud, Richie, *Anything But . . . An Autobiography*, Hodder & Stoughton, 1998

Benaud, Richie, *Spin Me a Spinner: Behind the Scenes in the 1962/63 Test Series*, Hodder & Stoughton, 1963

Benaud, Richie, *The Ashes 1982–83, Australia v England*, Lansdowne, 1983

Blofeld, Henry, *Cakes and Bails*, Simon & Schuster, 1998

Border, Allan, *Ashes Glory: Allan Border's Own Story*, Swan Publishing, 1989

Botham, Ian, *Botham: My Autobiography*, Collins Willow, 1994

Brearley, Mike and Dudley Doust, *The Return of the Ashes*, Pelham Books, 1978

Briggs, Simon, *Stiff Upper Lips and Baggy Green Caps: A Sledger's History of the Ashes*, Quercus, 2006

Broad, Stuart, *Bowled Over: An Ashes Celebration*, Hodder & Stoughton, 2009

Chappell, Ian, *Tigers Among the Lions*, Investigation Press, 1972

Colliver, Lawrie, *Dizzy: The Jason Gillespie Story*, HarperSport, 2007

Dirs, Ben, *Everywhere We Went: Top Tales from Cricket's Barmy Army*, Simon & Schuster, 2011

DeFreitas, Phil with Derek Clements, *Daffy: The Autobiography of Phil DeFreitas*, Apex Publishing, 2012

Derriman, Philip, *Bodyline*, William Collins Pty Ltd, 1984

Dexter, Ted, *Ted Dexter Declares: An Autobiography*, Stanley Paul, 1966

Edmonds, Frances, *Cricket XXXX Cricket*, Kingswood Press, 1987

Farnes, Kenneth, *Tours and Tests*, R.T.S.–Lutterworth Press, 1940

Fingleton, J. H., *Brown and Company: The Tour in Australia, 1951*, Collins, 1951

Fletcher, Keith, *Ashes to Ashes: The Rise, Fall and Rise of English Cricket*, Headline, 2005

Flintoff, Andrew, *Ashes to Ashes*, Hodder & Stoughton, 2009

Fraser, Angus, *Fraser's Tour Diaries*, Headline, 1998

Frindall, Bill, *Bearders: My Life in Cricket*, Orion Books, 2006

Fulton, David, *The Captains' Tales: Battle for the Ashes*, Mainstream, 2009

Gatting, Mike, *Triumph in Australia: Mike Gatting's 1986–87 Cricket Diary*, Macdonald Queen Anne Press, 1987

Gilchrist, Adam, *True Colours*, Macmillan, 2008

Gough, Darren, *Dazzler: The Autobiography*, Michael Joseph, 2001

Gower, David and Bob Taylor, *Anyone for Cricket? A Diary of an Australian Tour*, Pelham Books, 1979

Grace, Radcliffe, *Warwick Armstrong*, self-published, 1975

Graveney, Tom, *The Heart of Cricket*, Arthur Barker, 1983

Heald, Tim, *The Authorized Biography of the Incomparable Denis Compton*, Pavilion Books, 1994

Healy, Ian, *Hands & Heals*, HarperSport, 2000

Hill, Alan, *Les Ames*, Christopher Helm (Publishers) Ltd, 1990

Hobbs, Jack, *The Fight for The Ashes 1932/33*, Harrap, 1933

Hoggard, Matthew, *Hoggy: Welcome to My World*, Harper Collins, 2009

Hussain, Nasser and Waugh, Steve, *Ashes Summer: A Personal Diary of the 1997 England v Australia Test Series*, Collins Willow, 1997

Jardine, D. R., *In Quest of the Ashes*, Methuen, 2005

Johnston, Brian, *An Evening with Johnners*, Partridge Press, 1996

Johnston, Brian, *Another Slice of Johnners*, Virgin Books, 2001

Kidd, Patrick and Peter McGuinness, *The Best of Enemies: Whingeing Poms Versus Arrogant Aussies*, Know The Score!, 2009

Larwood, Harold, *Body-line?*, Elkin, Mathews & Marrot, 1933

Lee, Brett with James Knight, *My Life*, Ebury Press, 2011

Lewis, Tony, *Trevor Bailey*, Richard Walsh Books, 1998

Lewis, Tony, *Taking Fresh Guard*, Headline, 2003

Lloyd, David, *G'day ya Pommie B . . . . . . !*, Weidenfeld & Nicolson, 1992

BIBLIOGRAPHY

McCann, Liam, *The Revised & Expanded Sledger's Handbook*, Artists' and Photographers' Press Ltd, 2012

Mackay, Ken 'Slasher', *Quest for the Ashes*, Pelham Books, 1966

Malcolm, Devon, *You Guys Are History!*, Collins Willow, 1998

Mallett, Ashley, *One of a Kind: The Doug Walters Story*, Allen & Unwin, 2008

Martin-Jenkins, Christopher, *CMJ: A Cricketing Life*, Simon & Schuster, 2012

Miller, Keith and R. S. Whitington, *Cricket Typhoon*, Macdonald, 1955

Noble, M. A., *The Fight for the Ashes 1928–29*, Harrap, 1929

Ponting, Ricky, *Captain's Diary 2007*, HarperSport, 2007

Ponting, Ricky and Brian Murgatroyd, *Ashes Diary 2005*, HarperSport, 2005

Ranjitsinhji, Prince, *With Stoddart's Team in Australia*, James Bowden, 1898

Rayvern Allen, David, *Arlott: The Authorised Biography*, HarperCollins, 1994

Rosewater, Irving, *Sir Donald Bradman: A Biography*, Batsford, 1978

Searle, Andrew, *S. F. Barnes: His Life and Times*, Empire Publications, 1987

Smith, Rick, and Ron Williams, *W.G. Down Under: Grace in Australia 1873/74 and 1891/92*, Apple Books, Tasmania, 1994

Stewart, Alec, *Alec Stewart: A Captain's Diary: The Battle for the 1998/99 Ashes*, Collins Willow, 1999

Strauss, Andrew, *Testing Times: In Pursuit of the Ashes*, Hodder & Stoughton, 2009

Strauss, Andrew, *Winning the Ashes Down Under: The Captain's Story*, Hodder & Stoughton, 2011

Swann, Graeme, *The Breaks Are Off*, Hodder & Stoughton, 2011

Tyson, Frank, *In The Eye of the Typhoon*, The Parrs Wood Press, 2004

Underwood, Derek, *Deadly Down Under: England in Australia 1979–80*, Arthur Barker, 1980

Vaughan, Michael, *Calling the Shots*, Hodder & Stoughton, 2005

Veysey, Wayne, *KP Cricket Genius? The Biography of Kevin Pietersen*, Know The Score!, 2009

Walker, Max with Neill Phillipson, *Tangles*, Garry Sparke & Associates, 1976

Warner, P. F., *How We Recovered the Ashes*, Centenary edn, Methuen, 2003

Waugh, Steve, *Ashes Diary 2001*, HarperSport, 2001

Wellings, E. M., *No Ashes for England: The Story of the Australian Tour 1950–1*, Evans Brothers Ltd, 1951

BIBLIOGRAPHY

Willis, Bob, *The Captain's Diary: England in Australia and New Zealand 1982–83*, Collins Willow, 1983

Wisden on The Ashes, ed. Steven Lynch, John Wisden & Co., 2009

Wolstenholme, Gerry, *Trumper Triumphant*, Red Rose Books, 2002

Cricketing Tales from the Dressing Room, BBC Audio Books, 2009